BOOKS BY DANIEL YANKELOVICH

Ego and Instinct: Psychoanalysis and The Science of Man,
with William Barrett
The Changing Values on Campus
The New Morality: A Profile of American Youth in the Seventies
New Rules: Searching for Self-Fulfillment in a World Turned Upside Down

NEW RULES

NEW RULES

Searching for
Self-Fulfillment in
a World
Turned Upside Down

Daniel Yankelovich

RANDOM HOUSE
NEW YORK

*Grateful acknowledgment is made to the following for
permission to reprint previously published material:*

Bantam Books, Inc.: Excerpts from *Even Cowgirls Get the
Blues* by Tom Robbins. Copyright © 1976 by Thomas Robbins.
Used by permission of Bantam Books, Inc. All rights reserved.

Industry Week: Excerpt from "Inflation" by Irving Friedman from
Industry Week. Reprinted by permission of Industry Week;
November 10, 1980.

The New York Times Co.: Excerpts from January 4, 1980
and May 14, 1980 articles which appeared in *The
New York Times.* © 1980 by The New York Times
Company. Reprinted by permission.

Library of Congress Cataloging in Publication Data

Yankelovich, Daniel.
New rules, searching for self-fulfillment in a
world turned upside down.

1. United States—Social conditions—1960-
2. United States—Moral conditions.   3. Self-
realization.   I. Title.
HN59.Y33   1981   973   80-6011
ISBN 0-394-50203-5   AACR1

Manufactured in the United States of America

24689753

FIRST EDITION

For Hassie and Nicole

"You really don't believe in political solutions, do you?"

"I believe in political solutions to political problems. But man's primary problems aren't political; they're philosophical. Until humans can solve their philosophical problems, they're condemned to solve their political problems over and over and over again. It's a cruel, repetitious bore."

—TOM ROBBINS, *Even Cowgirls Get the Blues*

Contents

·••———◉◀———••·

Preface

─────◆◉◆─────

The Giant Plates
of Culture

Throughout the nineteen-sixties, while the news media focused on the ferment in American life—civil rights marches, the assassinations of John and Robert Kennedy and Martin Luther King, protests against the war in Vietnam and other spectacular events—my work in studying cross sections of the public showed the vast majority of Americans going about their daily routines unruffled, their outlook on life hardly touched by these momentous happenings. In the past few years, however, as the media tell us that we have reverted to a nineteen-fifties-style normalcy—quiet campuses with well-dressed young people more concerned with finding jobs than bringing the Establishment to its knees, and much talk of a retreat from the liberal social attitudes of the post-World War II era toward more conservative values—our recent studies show evidence of startling cultural changes. These range from marginal changes (fewer V-8 engines, white wine instead of hard liquor before dinner) to changes that penetrate to the core of American life—into the private spaces of our inner lives, the semipublic space of our lives within the family, at work, in school, in church, in the neighborhood and into the public space of our lives as citizens.

Indeed, so far ranging are these changes that each time I encounter them a recurring image comes to mind, the image of the earth moving deep beneath the surface and so transforming the landscape that it loses its comfortable familiarity. According to the geological theory of plate tectonics, giant "plates" undergird the earth's surface and keep it stable and rigid. Sometimes these immense geologic formations, grinding against one another beneath the surface of the earth, shift their positions. Their movements may be slight, but the plates are so massive that along their fault lines even slight shifts cause volcanoes and earthquakes on the surface.

Increasingly in recent years, our studies of the public show the "giant plates" of American culture shifting relentlessly beneath us. The shifts create huge dislocations in our lives. Those living closest to society's fault lines are the first to be thrown into new predicaments. But even those living at a remote distance feel the tremors.

The shifts in culture manifest themselves in many different ways:

· Every year throughout the nineteen-seventies, a million or so Americans had themselves sterilized. In just one decade, ten million Americans made sure that they would not have children. This is only one cause of a declining birth rate in a society that seems to have set itself against biological imperatives that prevailed in the past. At an anticipated 1.7 children for each woman of childbearing age, we have fallen below the 2.2 zero population replacement rate needed to keep the population from shrinking, and dramatically below the 3.7 rate of the nineteen-fifties. Our studies show that, unlike most American women in the recent past, tens of millions of women no longer regard having babies as self-fulfilling. Large-scale and deliberate childlessness is a new experience for our society.

· Among the most startling changes are those in household composition. In the nineteen-fifties a typical American family consisting of a working father, a stay-at-home mother and one or more children constituted 70 percent of all households. This was the norm, the familiar American nuclear family.

It shocks most Americans to learn to what extent this norm has collapsed in a single generation. Far from being the dominant mode, the "typical American family" does not now constitute even a large minority of households. Rather, it accounts for only 15 percent of them. There are fewer "typical American families" today than households consisting of a single person—the fastest growing category of households counted by the U.S. census. Single households grew from 10.9 percent of all households in 1950 to 23 percent in

the late seventies. We have moved from a society dominated by one
type of arrangement, the husband-provider nuclear family, to a more
variegated society with many types of households, no one of which
predominates.

· A General Motors plant in Tennessee gives its union, the UAW,
first chance at fifty custodial jobs—janitoring, cleaning up, doing
routine maintenance work. They expect ten or twenty applications
from older workers who have not quite reached retirement age but
have worn themselves out and are seeking a resting place. To the
astonishment of both union and management, they receive not ten or
twenty inquiries, but an overwhelming two thousand applications
from men who hold higher-paying, higher-status jobs. Furthermore,
most of the applicants are young, vigorous and far from retirement.
The union doesn't know how to allocate the fifty jobs. Seniority
rights were originally conceived with upward mobility in mind, giving
the person with the longest service the right to higher-paying, not to
lower-paying, jobs. Who ever heard of bargaining for downward mobility rights?

· Vast shifts are taking place in the composition of the workplace. A
generation ago, the typical worker was a man working full-time to
provide complete support for his wife and children. Today, fewer
than one out of five people who work for pay conform to this
standard. By the late seventies a majority of women (51 percent)
were working outside the home. By 1980, more than two out of five
mothers of children age six or younger worked for pay. In families
earning more than $25,000 a year, the majority now depend on two
incomes: the husband's and the wife's. Ironically, while women have
been clamoring to get in, men have been slowly edging out of the
work force. Between 1947 and 1977, the number of men in the prime
working years (from ages 16 to 65) who dropped out of the work
force nearly doubled, from 13 percent to 22 percent.

Most jobs are still organized as if these changes had not taken
place: they continue to be full-time, five-day-a-week, regular-hour
jobs, with pay and fringe benefits based on the assumption that the
jobholder is the sole earner in the family. We can expect vast
changes in the future in how paid work and child care are organized.

· In 1978, for the first time in our history, more women than men were
admitted to U.S. institutions of higher learning. This trend reflects
women's determination to achieve parity with men in education,

training and job opportunities. But it also reflects a decline in the proportion of male high-school graduates going on to college—a reversal of the post–World War II pattern. For many American men, going to college is no longer the royal road to success as they define success.

In 1970, my firm's surveys of cultural trends identified almost two out of five Americans as having a "sour grapes" outlook on life. These people believed in the American dream of "bettering oneself" by acquiring education, money, possessions, recognition and status, but in their own lives the dream had failed. My associate, Florence Skelly, named these people "retreaters" because so many felt bitter, negative and withdrawn about their lives. Among the retreaters were many older Americans: their median age was fifty-three compared to twenty-eight for the population as a whole. Astonishingly, a decade later in 1980 the number of retreaters had been slashed in half—reduced from 38 percent to 18 percent, reflecting several changes in American life. One is that we are growing less fiercely competitive with each other: the average American no longer defines success as surpassing the Joneses. Far fewer Americans now than in 1970 judge their own fulfillment in life by the standards of competitive success. Therefore a failure to surpass others economically no longer stigmatizes a person in his own eyes.

A University of Michigan study discloses another change. It shows older Americans becoming less miserable, anxious and depressed than in the past. On the other hand, it reveals that younger Americans are growing ever more fretful, anxious, off balance and goalless.* Yankelovich, Skelly and White studies also show that as the retreater attitude of older Americans declines, a new restlessness is spreading among younger Americans. Each year for the past several years the number of young Americans who lack clearly defined goals and feel utterly aimless about their lives has increased.

Until a few years ago, I assumed that these various shifts signified no more than the normal accommodations our culture makes to new conditions. Change is the one constant we expect in our history, and yet, despite all the changes, certain themes in American culture persist generation after generation. In the nineteen-seventies, the National Science Foundation supported a team of social researchers who repli-

* *ISR Newsletter*, Vol. 7, No. 1, Institute for Social Research (Ann Arbor: University of Michigan, Winter 1979).

cated, after a fifty-year hiatus, the classic Middletown study that sociologists Robert and Helen Lynd carried out in Muncie, Indiana, in 1923. The Lynds had compared their nineteen-twenties' findings to life in Muncie in the 1880s and 1890s. Almost a full century of American life passed under review.

The Middletown III researchers found abundant evidence of cultural change in the Muncie of the seventies: more divorce, pot smoking, overt pornography, greater tolerance. But what struck them most forcefully was not change, but continuity. In the midst of social upheaval, they were astonished to find that Muncie high-school students gave the same answers to certain questions in 1977 that their grandparents had given to the Lynds in the 1920s: the same numbers reported disputes with parents over getting home late at night, and a majority said they still regard the Bible as a "sufficient guide to all the problems of modern life."*

The Muncie researchers are not wrong to stress the continuity of American life. In any culture there will usually be more continuity than change; ordinarily, cultural patterns persist for long periods of time. In my three decades as a student of changes in American mores, I too have grown accustomed to more continuity than change. Almost every survey measuring trends in American values and behavior exhibits extraordinary stability.

In American life, continuity and far-reaching change do coexist with each other. So variegated is American culture that an observer who wishes to highlight its continuity can easily do so; and conversely, an observer who wishes to document the changing nature of American life can also have his way. The subtle question of judgment is always: Have the important things remained the same, or have *they* changed? If important things have changed, as our findings seem to show, they will overflow the confines of culture and flood into our economic and political lives as well. And, if they are important enough, they will break the continuity of American experience in decisive ways, even when on the surface life follows its familiar path in Muncie and other typical American towns and cities.

The shifts in ways of life we will be examining in this study *are* important ones; they do mark a decisive break with the past, and they do affect our economic and political destiny as well as our cultural lifestyles.

* Howard M. Bahr, "Changes in Family Life in Middletown, 1924–77," *Public Opinion Quarterly*, Volume 44, No. 1 (Spring 1980), p. 24.

(ii)

The story I want to tell in this book concerns a particular expression of American culture—the search for "self-fulfillment" and the predicaments it creates for the individual and for the nation.

These predicaments are frustrating to those who live through them and often exasperating for the rest of us—involving as they do the breakup of families, a restless movement from job to job and place to place, and endless rumination about one's inner needs and unfilled potentials. The ethics of the search for self-fulfillment discard many of the traditional rules of personal conduct. They permit more sexual freedom, for example, and they put less emphasis on sacrifice "for its own sake." In their extreme form, the new rules simply turn the old ones on their head, and in place of the old self-denial ethic we find people who refuse to deny *anything* to themselves—not out of bottomless appetite, but on the strange moral principle that "I have a duty to myself."

But despite its exasperating characteristics, the search for self-fulfillment is not merely, as its critics claim, an outpouring of self-centeredness and self-indulgence—the excesses of a "me generation" made decadent by too much affluence. This is not to deny that many people *are* preoccupied with themselves. But the self-centeredness may yet prove to be an incidental feature of the search for fulfillment, a transition phase from slavish rejection of the old rules to a synthesis of old and new.

Emphatically, the search for self-fulfillment is not, as some observers have insisted, proof that the American character is changing for the worse. Social character does not change from year to year, or even decade to decade. The Middletown researchers are surely correct on this aspect of continuity. What does change within these short time spans are the symbols and meanings of culture. For a brief period in this century, from the mid-sixties to the early eighties, for reasons I will discuss later in this book, the search for self-fulfillment expressed itself in language borrowed from pop psychology: the need to "keep growing," the urge to express one's "potentials," to "keep-in-touch with one's own true feelings," to be recognized for "one's self" as a "real person," etc. But this psychological outlook grows out of a too-narrow conception of what a self is and how it should be fulfilled, a conception that now, as we shall see, shows signs of fading. As it does, we shall come to understand better why today's self-preoccupation neither reflects an enduring change in our culture nor is it what Americans are really looking for in their search for self-fulfillment. The preoccupation with self is a deflection, a false start in a journey toward a goal that is as important for our society as for the individual.

Since affluence helped to stimulate the search for self-fulfillment, some observers have also concluded that in today's troubled economy, economic pressures will force the culture to return to the outlook that prevailed in less affluent periods of American life. But evidence from surveys suggests that this is not happening. To be sure, people grow cautious in hard times. With jobs now scarcer than they used to be, employees refrain from pressing their demands for self-expression as aggressively as when jobs were more plentiful: our studies show that in the past few years money demands have risen more sharply than demands for "interesting work."

But the search for self-fulfillment is not a yo-yo riding up and down the string of the economy: it is a powerful force that once unleashed works its way irreversibly into the society. For example, many women joined the work force as much for their self-fulfillment and independence as for economic motives: they did not find the role of dependent housewife a satisfactory life choice. But in the strained economic conditions of the eighties these women are not now returning to the kitchen; quite the contrary, as women find that their contribution to the family budget is needed to make ends meet, their commitment to working outside the home has strengthened. At the same time, the political pressure for equal pay for equal work has also grown more intense. And simultaneously, blacks, other ethnic minorities, young people and older people who cannot afford to retire are competing ever more fiercely for available jobs, creating a vortex of new problems for the society. These cultural, economic and political cross pressures cannot conceivably lead us back to the tidy status quo and sharply compartmentalized lives of the past. The plates of culture do not shift backwards.

The self-fulfillment search is a more complex, fateful, and irreversible phenomenon than simply the by-product of affluence or a shift in the national character toward narcissism. It is nothing less than the search for a new American philosophy of life. And although the new outlook on life is often maddening, it may yet prove better adapted to the economic realities that lie ahead than were the consumer values that prevailed in the postwar years. A person who gauges his or her self-worth in terms of a bigger car, a better neighborhood and a steadily rising income does well in good times. These signs of success are satisfyingly tangible, visible to others as well as to one's self. When incomes fail to keep pace with inflation, however, the person who gauges self-worth in

terms of less tangible quality-of-life values may have a broader range
of life satisfactions to fall back on.

But the emerging philosophy of life is far more than a source of
consolation for bad economic times. It is a breeding ground for better
times. It generates new energies to revitalize the economy and it seeks
human goals broader than those measured solely by annual increments
of the gross national product. It is not that the new philosophy of life
rejects materialistic values: Americans are far too practical for that. But
it broadens them to embrace a wider spectrum of human experience.
Under its influence, Americans may become less self-absorbed and
better prepared to face the difficult choices that now confront our
civilization.

We are not accustomed to crediting changing social values with
shaping the country's economic and political fortunes. But we had better
learn to think in these terms, for many of our troubles—and also the
means to alleviate them—are now coming from this unaccustomed
source. Generally, we look to economics, or technology or political action
for *fortuna*—the turn of luck or fate that determines our destiny. I want
to show, however, that while a prognosis of our future based solely on
our political/economic prospects may leave us pessimistic, even desperate, one based on our cultural prospects—our shared social values—may,
rather unexpectedly, point the way toward a brighter future.

Focusing then on the search for self-fulfillment, we shall examine in
this book how this search expresses itself in the lives of Americans, how
inflation and other economic realities are shaping and being shaped by
it, how seekers of self-fulfillment pursued a self-defeating strategy in the
seventies, and how Americans in the eighties are learning to distinguish
false and destructive strategies from valid ones adaptive to a world that
is just beginning to emerge.

This is not a self-help book. It contains no prescriptions for formu-
lae, and it does not presume to tell people how to live their lives. And
yet, I shall be disappointed if those entangled in the predicaments and
contradictions of the quest for self-fulfillment do not find here some new
perspective within which to view their own future.

I believe the struggle for self-fulfillment in today's world is the leading edge of a genuine cultural revolution. It is moving our industrial
civilization toward a new phase of human experience.

Acknowledgments

There are many people I want to thank for their assistance in writing this book—those who helped indirectly by influencing my thinking as well as those directly involved in the research and editing. In the first category, I acknowledge a great debt to my colleagues, Florence Skelly, Arthur White and Ruth Clark, and to a number of seminal thinkers who have reflected on the contemporary scene: Hannah Arendt, William Barrett, Daniel Bell, Isaiah Berlin, Erik and Kai Erikson, John Gardner, Robert Heilbroner, Gerald Holton, Irving Howe, Clark Kerr, Irving Kristol, Robert Lifton, Robert Nisbet, David Reisman and Leon Shapiro.

More directly over the past three years, much of the burden of collecting and distilling research data related to the book fell on my associates, Deborah Barron and Larry Kaagan. Larry Kaagan tracked down elusive data, and helped me to clarify my thinking and draftsmanship. His contribution has been significant.

Thanks to Nancy Wexler, Barbara Lee and Paula Sepinuck, I grasped many of the subtleties in the life histories taken for this book. Everett Carll Ladd, Jr., helped supply some valuable data. Robert Moskin, T. George Harris, Jackie Farber and Hassie Yankelovich read the manuscript and guided me in important matters of style and tone. Jane Thompson made sure, as always, that the charts had the proper professional touch. My secretary and friend, Sona Beshar, showed endless patience with my constant redrafting, with the valuable assistance of Robert Szwed. And my editor, Jason Epstein, brought his unfailing critical acumen to bear, eliminating many (but not all) of the dangling abstractions that had crept into earlier drafts.

Above all, I want to thank the hundreds of people who, in sharing their lives, illuminated the many possibilities of the search for self-fulfillment. Gratefully acknowledging their help, I accept full responsibility for my use of what they offered.

NEW RULES

Chapter 1

...◆◉◆...

Introduction:
A Simple Question

Western literature and history are full of stories of individuals searching for self-fulfillment. They seek it in many ways—in great deeds, money, love, fame, revolution, epic fornication, the quest for inner peace, sustained bursts of creativity or by simply wandering about. As backdrop to their adventures, one takes for granted the muted presence of the great mass of people routinely living their daily lives: busy with family, scrambling to make a living, going to church. What is extraordinary about the search for self-fulfillment in contemporary America is that it is not confined to a few bold spirits or a privileged class. Cross-section studies of Americans show unmistakably that the search for self-fulfillment is instead an outpouring of popular sentiment and experimentation, an authentic grass-roots phenomenon involving, in one way or another, perhaps as many as 80 percent of all adult Americans. It is as if tens of millions of people had decided simultaneously to conduct risky experiments in living, using the only materials that lay at hand—their own lives.

And the experiments *are* risky. Acting boldly in the name of their self-fulfillment, many people are startled to wake up one day and find themselves with a broken marriage, a wrong-headed career change or simply a muddled state of mind about what life choices to make. But despite many failures the experiments persist. There is something about our times that stimulates Americans to take big risks in pursuit of new conceptions of the good life.

Spontaneous transformations of life style are rare events, or so it would appear from history. Ordinarily, new cultural ideas enter our consciousness in prepackaged form: by the time we encounter them in "great books," the confusion and excitement and false starts that may have accompanied their beginnings have been tidied up. The history of ideas usually registers the views of small elites—leading philosophers, religious thinkers, scientists, artists and world statesmen whose thoughts are formulated with precision or eloquence. But every now and then a new way of conceiving life and its meaning arises spontaneously from the great mass of the population.

When this occurs we had better pay attention, for this kind of un-organized social movement can transform America and the world. But it is not easy to know what to pay attention to, for the true nature of the transformation remains hidden from view, its sheer diversity of expressions making it difficult to find a coherent pattern.

In the 1960s the search for self-fulfillment was largely confined to young Americans on the nation's campuses, and was masked by the political protests against the war in Southeast Asia. When the war ended in the early seventies, the campuses quieted and the challenge to traditional mores spread beyond college life to find a variety of expressions in the larger society—in the women's movement; in the consumer, environmental and quality-of-life movements ("small is beautiful"); in the emphasis on self-help, localism and participation; in the hospice movement; in the flood of books on cultivating the self; in the questioning of the scientific-technological world view; in greater acceptance of sexuality (nudity, sex outside of marriage, homosexuality and open eroticism of varied sorts); in a new preoccupation with the body and physical fitness; in a revival of interest in nature and the natural; and above all, in a search for the "full, rich life," ripe with leisure, new experience and enjoyment as a substitute for the orderly, work-centered ways of earlier decades.

Our surveys showed that new questions had arisen. Instead of asking, "Will I be able to make a good living?" "Will I be successful?" "Will I raise happy, healthy, successful children?"—the typical questions asked by average Americans in the 1950s and 1960s—Americans in the 1970s came to ponder more introspective matters. We asked, "How can I find self-fulfillment?" "What does personal success really mean?" "What kinds of commitments should I be making?" "What is worth sacrificing for?" "How can I grow?" "How can I best realize the commitment I have to develop myself?" and, by the start of the 1980s: "How can I prevent inflation from taking away the gains I have won and my chance to live the good life?"

In the sixties cross-section surveys showed that the shifts in culture barely touched the lives of the majority of Americans (a fact those enmeshed in the sixties "revolution" found difficult to comprehend). By the seventies, however, most Americans were involved in projects to prove that life can be more than a grim economic chore. Americans from every walk of life were suddenly eager to give more meaning to their lives, to find fuller self-expression and to add a touch of adventure and grace to their lives and those of others. Where strict norms had prevailed in the fifties and sixties, now all was pluralism and freedom of choice: to marry or live together; to have children early or postpone them, perhaps forever; to come out of the closet or stay in; to keep the old job or return to school; to make commitments or hang loose; to change careers, spouses, houses, states of residence, states of mind.

In the nineteen-seventies all national surveys showed an increase in preoccupation with self. By the late seventies, my firm's studies showed more than seven out of ten Americans (72 percent) spending a great deal of time thinking about themselves and their inner lives—this in a nation once notorious for its impatience with inwardness. The rage for self-fulfillment, our surveys indicated, had now spread to virtually the entire U.S. population.

The search for self-fulfillment has developed into a prime source of energy in American culture, and like many vital things, it is sprawling, messy and unfinished; not good or bad, but good-and-bad. American society is probably freer, less fearful, less status-ridden, and more diverse and tolerant than ever before. But in our preoccupation with self-fulfillment we have also grown recklessly unrealistic in our demands on our institutions. And we are becoming less sensitive to the plight of the most vulnerable citizens in our economy, growing bored, for example, with the problems of race and unemployment that the nation had begun to address in earlier decades. At times our narrow self-concern threatens to get out of hand.

The life experiments of self-fulfillment seekers often collide violently with traditional rules, creating a national battle of moral norms. Millions of Americans are hungry to live their lives to the brim, determined to consume every dish on the smorgasbord of human experience. But their appetites have scandalized other millions, including groups such as the Moral Majority. It and other like-minded organizations have linked religious fundamentalism and political action to combat the moral evil of what they call "secular humanism," by which they mean social pluralism—that freedom to choose one's own life style within certain generous limits that identifies the dedicated seeker of self-fulfillment.

The Moral Majority strongly supports Senator Paul Laxalt's bill, the Family Protection Act. Among its thirty-eight proposals are: removing prayer in schools from the jurisdiction of the federal courts; giving parents the right to censor textbooks; giving local school boards the right to prevent boys and girls from participating in sports together; denying food stamps to college students who are "voluntarily unemployed"; excluding from child abuse laws all forms of corporal punishment; removing all tax advantages from cohabitation without marriage; and eliminating federal funds from any program that presents homosexuality as an "acceptable alternative life style."

When the values they cherish are challenged, people react passionately. Some Americans have come to hate the new morality associated with the search for self-fulfillment. Their reactions range from mere distaste for a self-indulgent generation to the judgment that the new life styles are morally evil and must be relentlessly crushed. The waves of emotion stirred by abortion, easier divorce, ERA, sex education, homosexuality and other developments the Moral Majority regards as anti-family, anti-American and anti-Christian show how deep-seated the issues are. For the rest of this century American culture will be a cockpit of conflict as political passions rise, single issue politics gain momentum, and new religious movements abound. The shifts in the plates of culture are creating deep fissures in our society.

(ii)

Only if we find a pattern that unifies the astonishing variety of self-fulfillment experiments can we hope to fathom the significance of a phenomenon so diverse, so socially divisive and so morally ambiguous.

In seeking a pattern I have examined a vast array of survey findings, census data, economic information and life histories. From this jumble of information, a pattern has gradually taken shape, emerging in response to a few fruitful questions. The one question that proved most productive was the simplest: "What are the people pursuing their self-fulfillment actually looking for, and how are they going about finding it?" A first approximation of an answer will introduce the various life experiments and research findings presented later in this book. A complete answer will not be clear until the end of the book.

Confirmed seekers of self-fulfillment, often surprisingly vague and inarticulate, voiced their goal as a poignant and inchoate yearning to elevate what might be called the "sacred/expressive" aspects of their lives, and simultaneously, to downgrade the impersonal, manipulative aspects.

"Sacred," in this context, is not used in its strictly religious meaning. Though most familiar in religious thought, the idea of the sacred is also a sociological concept, used here in opposition not to the secular or profane as in religious belief, but to the instrumental. The distinction is an important one. We adopt an instrumental philosophy whenever we ask about something: what is it good for? From this perspective a tree is good for lumber, or to give shade, or to enhance the appearance of the landscape. A forest that no one harvests or sees is not good for anything. It is not valued in itself. From an instrumental perspective, a person is valued because he or she is a good worker, or provider, or sex object, or is useful in meeting one's needs in some other fashion. Everyone knows someone about whom you can say, "Oh, he's only interested in you if you can do something for him, otherwise you don't exist." This is an instrumental outlook. People and objects are sacred in the sociological sense when, apart from what instrumental use they serve, they are valued for themselves.

Our studies suggest that seekers of self-fulfillment are reassessing what is sacred and what is instrumental in American life. Should people in the workplace be exploited exclusively for instrumental purposes, or do they have intrinsic value as well? Should we value certain aspects of nature and society—a wilderness, a vanishing species, a primitive culture, old automobiles, old buildings—for themselves, apart from their instrumental value?

Some joggers maintain a purely instrumental attitude toward their running—it is a way to stimulate the cardiovascular system; but others come to regard their sweaty exertions as a "sacred" ritual. The cult of organic gardening develops a deep attachment to what is grown. For many Americans nature is a sacred object; for others art and human artifacts are too; still others endow sexuality or science or a region of the country or an ethnic link to one's roots with such meanings.

The domain of the "expressive" is also opposed to the instrumental. While instrumental actions are always a means to an end, what is expressive has value in its own right. Myths, art, poetry, monuments, storytelling, song, dance, customs, architecture, ritual, the harmonics of nature—all make expressive claims over and above any instrumental purpose they may serve. The idea of "style"—a decorator's style, styles in clothing, life styles—clearly connotes expressive values. Our daily living is drenched in expressive style: recent American visitors to China, for example, report a "color hunger" that manfests itself when Chinese audiences in a theater or puppet show grow wild with excitement when scenery and colorful costumes are presented. Except for young children's clothing, the Chinese were virtually deprived of color throughout their cultural revolution and the first few years following it. They now seize upon displays of colors as if they were gasping for air.

Seekers of self-fulfillment invest the best of their creativity in inventing expressive styles of living. For, at the heart of the self-fulfillment search, is the moral intuition that the very meaning of life resides in its sacred/expressive aspects, and that one must, therefore, fight to give these the importance they deserve.

From an historic perspective, the effort to keep the sacred/expressive side of life from being overwhelmed by the instrumental addresses a problem that has haunted Western civilization for centuries. Our advanced industrial society, for all its strengths, has long harbored a fundamental weakness: it has prodigiously generated goods and services, but has been seriously deficient in creating some of the basic conditions of human community. In some profound sense, all self-fulfillment experiments are struggling to overcome this weakness.

But average fulfillment seekers are not concerned with abstract historic issues; the arena within which they struggle is their everyday life. Their life experiments engage what we might call the "giving/getting compact"—the unwritten rules governing what we give in marriage, work, community and sacrifice for others, and what we expect in return. This giving/getting compact is almost never explicit. We take it so much for granted that we rarely see how extensive and powerful it is—until it begins to change. Indeed, so vital to American life are these unwritten rules that if we are truly launched on a cultural revolution the upheavals we encounter in the giving/getting compact are among the principal signs of its arrival.

The following comments are taken from my interviews with people between fifty-five and seventy years of age. In recalling their experiences in the early post–World War II decades, they hint at the terms of the giving/getting compact as it then prevailed:

· "Even though we no longer had anything in common we stayed together. We didn't break up our marriage even when the children were grown."

· "We lived on his salary even though I was making good money at the time. He said he would not feel right if we spent the money I earned for food and rent."

· "I never felt I could do enough for my parents, especially my mother. She sacrificed a promising career as a singer to take care of us. I realize now that she must have been miserable most of the time. [Why?] Because she said so. She kept reminding us what she was giving up, but we didn't take her seriously."

· "It never occurred to me not to have children. Now I realize I'd have felt less put upon if I had freely chosen that destiny and not had it chosen for me."

· "I've worked hard all my life, and I've made a success out of it for myself and my family. We have a nice home. We have everything it takes to be comfortable. I've been able to send my kids to good schools, and my wife and I can afford to go anywhere we want. Yes, I have a real sense of accomplishment."

· "Sure it was a rotten job. But what the hell. I made a good living, I took care of my wife and kids. What more do you expect?"

The old giving/getting compact might be paraphrased this way: "I give hard work, loyalty and steadfastness. I swallow my frustrations and suppress my impulse to do what I would enjoy, and do what is expected of me instead. I do not put myself first; I put the needs of others ahead of my own. I give a lot, but what I get in return is worth it. I receive an ever-growing standard of living, and a family life with a devoted spouse and decent kids. Our children will take care of us in our old age if we really need it, which thank goodness we will not. I have a nice home, a good job, the respect of my friends and neighbors; a sense of accomplishment at having made something of my life. Last but not least, as an American I am proud to be a citizen of the finest country in the world."

It is difficult to exaggerate how important this implicit contract has been in supporting the goals of American society in the post–World War II period. It lies at the heart of what we mean by the American dream. All the symbols of success and respectability in American society—the material goods; the opportunities to get ahead or have your children do so; the churches, graduations, promotions, celebrations—fit comfortably together as links in this social bond.

But now tens of millions of Americans have grown wary of demands for further sacrifices they believe may no longer be warranted. They want to modify the giving/getting compact in every one of its dimensions —family life, career, leisure, the meaning of success, relationships with other people and relations with themselves.

On traditional demands for material well-being seekers of self-fulfillment now impose new demands for intangibles—creativity, leisure, autonomy, pleasure, participation, community, adventure, vitality, stimulation, tender loving care. To the efficiency of technological society they wish to add joy of living. They seek to satisfy both the body *and* the spirit, which is asking a great deal from the human condition.

To many it is worth the try. Why, they argue, should we accept as inevitable that resourceful, highly educated people have to choose between the efficiency of technological society and quality of life? Why can we not have both? Are we to serve the machine, they ask, or is the machine to serve us? Must we accept poverty of spirit for wealth of goods? What meaning in life shall we seek beyond insuring economic security and creature comfort?

The predicaments of self-fulfillment seekers arise from the defective strategies they deploy to achieve these ambitious goals. These strategies are defective, first, in their economic premises. The typical self-fulfillment strategy presupposes that economic well-being is a virtual citizen's right, automatically guaranteed by both government and economy. A strategy built on the presumption of ever-expanding affluence is bound to run into trouble even in a country as abundant as our own.

The most serious defect, however, is psychological. People unwittingly bring a set of flawed psychological premises to their search for self-fulfillment, in particular the premise that the self is a hierarchy of inner needs, and self-fulfillment an inner journey to discover these. This premise is rarely examined, even though it leads people to defeat their own goals—and to end up isolated and anxious instead of fulfilled.

For example, among the married people I interviewed for this book those most devoted to their own self-fulfillment are having trouble in their marriages, as one might have predicted. Invariably, the trouble starts when one or both spouses abruptly introduces a change in the giving/getting compact. One or the other decides, for example, to take greater sexual license, or to press for a different division of effort in relation to work, home and children, or simply to become more self-assertive. Many couples take these changes in stride, but truly committed fulfillment seekers focus so sharply on their own needs that instead of achieving a more intimate, giving relationship, they grow further apart from each other. In looking to their own needs for fulfillment, they are caught in a debilitating contradiction: their goal is to expand their lives by reaching beyond the self, but the strategy they employ results in constricting their lives, drawing them inward toward an ever-narrowing, closed-off "I." People want to enlarge their choices, but by seeking to keep "all options open," actually diminish them.

Sensing this contradiction between their goals and strategies, and being aware of a change for the worse in economic conditions, what Americans most fear today is ending up empty-handed. Many of us suspect that at the very moment in our history when we are psychologically ready to satisfy our hunger for the best of the material and spiritual worlds, we may in fact be confronted with the worst of each. Americans fear we may have to endure, in exacerbated form, all of the familiar ills of advanced technological society—from high blood pressure and urban decay to the absence of community—and also to put up with an unstable economy and a lower standard of living.

Given this disparity between goals and means, what justifies the sanguine view expressed in the Preface that the shifts in culture may help us cope with a turbulent world and thereby become part of the solution to our problems as well as part of their cause? Why should we not join those critics who dismiss the self-fulfillment phenomenon as narcissistic folly? What aspects of it are a source of strength rather than stress?

My relatively hopeful outlook grows from a conviction that out of the present disorder something vital and healthy is struggling to be born. From a multitude of life experiments Americans are learning bitter lessons. Many who started out with ill-conceived strategies are learning to correct them in the light of their experience. And, as Americans assimilate these lessons and adapt to new economic conditions, new rules are gradually starting to emerge. Along with self-absorbed strategies our surveys also show some fragmentary evidence of a growing concern with community and caring relationships (for example, over the past several years, the number of Americans engaged in activities to create closer bonds with neighbors, co-religionists, co-workers or others who form a community has grown by almost 50 percent). There is less talk than in earlier decades of status symbols (big homes, diamond rings, fur coats) and less comparing one's self to the neighbors. Young people speak more openly of their religious beliefs and their concern for the future. In my interviews, people express a longing for connectedness, commitment and creative expression.

From people's life experiments, a new social ethic is gradually starting to take shape. I call it an *ethic of commitment* to distinguish it from the traditional ethic of self-denial that underlies the old giving/getting compact, and also from the ethic of duty to self that grows out of a defective strategy of self-fulfillment. It will take several years before this new ethic (discussed in the last chapter) emerges clearly from the confusions of the present.

It is on these embryonic beginnings that our hopes must rest, for without a new social ethic there is no assurance that the adaptive side of the self-fulfillment search will triumph. In our demand for greater fulfillment in a time of economic turbulence we have set in motion forces that can lead either to a higher stage of civilization or to disaster. Will we achieve a synthesis between traditional commitments and new forms of fulfillment to create a new direction for our society? Or will we indeed end up with the worst of two worlds—our society fragmented and anomic, the family a shambles, the work ethic collapsed, the economy uncompetitive, our morality flabby and self-centered, and with even less personal freedom than under the old order? If so, we enter a period of bitter, polarizing social conflict that will tear us apart, wreck our society and crush our spirit.

Clearly, the stakes are high. The outcome is uncertain. The prospects for success or failure are evenly balanced; or perhaps the odds are against us. The outcome depends in no small measure on how we define, approach and solve the predicaments associated with the search for self-fulfillment described in this book, and how we nurture and develop the still embryonic ethic of commitment that may perhaps emerge.

Throughout this book, then, we shall want to examine the strategies of those who seek self-fulfillment in order to identify which approaches make sense in today's world and which are self-defeating. An old philosophical truth applies here: how one sees and interprets one's experience actually becomes a part of it. How each of us interprets our own search for fulfillment will shape its nature and partly determine its outcome.

My hope in this book is to stimulate a heightened sense of "doubleseeing," the ability to perceive our attempts at self-fulfillment as an historic process as well as personal drama. Doubleseeing is the gift of transcending the prison of one's ego to partake in the wider drama of the times. It means dwelling in the open spaces where social, economic, cultural and political realities merge with private desires. It means understanding that the resolution of our private predicaments will also shape the civilization in which we live, and conversely, that any new social ethic will decisively redefine the individual search for fulfillment.

(iii)

There are a handful of concepts I have found indispensable in analyzing self-fulfillment strategies. Two of these—the giving/getting compact and the relationship of the sacred to the instrumental—have already been introduced and others will be later. The concept of culture is one of these indispensable ideas, so I should state here what it means.

"Culture," as anthropologists use the term, is a concept that has been compared in scope and grandeur to Newton's law of gravity, Freud's exploration of the unconscious and Marx's theory of the organization of the means of production.* Anthropologists use the word culture to refer both to the physical and the intangible contents of the human habitat: the values, shared meanings, social norms, customs, rituals, symbols, arts and artifacts, ways of perceiving the world, life styles, behaviors and ideologies by which people participate in organized society.

But the idea of culture is too fertile and sprawling to belong to a single discipline. Sociologist Daniel Bell, for example, gives it a philosophical slant. "Culture for me," writes Bell, "is the effort to provide a coherent set of answers to the existentialist situations that confront all human beings in the passage of their lives."† The humanities, too, draw on the concept of culture, though in a different context. We are all familiar with "high culture," considered as the best of art, literature, music, architecture, philosophy and the other expressive symbolic modes of an era. And increasingly, we accord respect to "pop culture"—the rock music, films, popular art, fashions and other artifacts that vitalize our communal life.

The breadth of the term adds to its richness but limits its usefulness. When a word like culture means nearly everything, it comes dangerously close to meaning nothing. Anthropologists recognize this danger, and in recent years some of them have sought to narrow its scope so as to enhance its power. The gifted anthropologist, Clifford Geertz, offers a conception of culture congenial to our purposes here. Following the great German sociologist, Max Weber, Geertz emphasizes *shared mean-*

---

* Clifford Geertz, *The Interpretation of Cultures* (New York: Basic Books, 1973), p. 5.
† Daniel Bell, *The Cultural Contradictions of Capitalism* (New York: Basic Books, 1976), p. 12.

ings as the essence of culture. "Believing with Max Weber that man is an animal suspended in webs of significance he himself has spun," Geertz writes, "I take culture to be those webs."*

What does it mean in our culture to work hard, to be successful, to own a Mercedes, to be a housewife, to be a "real man," to fail, to be a homosexual, to have money, to attend Princeton, to be a cop, a Republican, to wear a girdle, to grow a beard, to be young, to be a Texan or a bureaucrat or an accountant? When you know a society's shared understanding of these phenomena you have insight into its culture; when you track the changes in these meanings, you are measuring shifts in culture.

Cultural meanings are always shared, in contrast to psychological meanings, which are private. One woman I interviewed for this study had a brother in jail. For her the term "convict" conveyed poignant connotations of pain, embarrassment and anger. She had added a private meaning to a shared cultural one. In the consciousness of any one person, cultural and private meanings are so interwoven that they cannot easily be separated, which is why a psychotherapist deliberately strips away the shared meanings of culture to concentrate on the idiosyncratic private ones.

In this book we will be engaged in the opposite process. We will be examining individual lives and the results of social surveys from a perspective that permits us to distill out purely private meanings so that what remains is the precipitate of culture—meanings shared in common by large groups of Americans.

To distinguish this conception of culture from so-called high culture, pop culture, culture as artifacts and other definitions, I shall use the term "psychoculture." Psychoculture is concerned with the webs of meanings Americans hold in common. Unlike other aspects of culture, psychoculture focuses exclusively on inner processes, on consciousness. It is in this respect psychological, hence the term psychoculture. The word may be awkward, but it avoids confusion.

In this book, then, I shall focus on one expression of contemporary psychoculture: the webs of significance Americans have spun around the shared meaning of self-fulfillment. The book is divided into four sections. The first part takes a brief look at the changed environment with which we now struggle, and from this perspective assesses the negative features of today's self-fulfillment strategies as well as the more resilient and productive responses that some Americans are making to a

* Op. cit., p. 5.

less yielding world. Part II examines some personal histories and survey research results to illustrate the wide range of life experiments Americans have launched in search of self-fulfillment, and it describes the characteristics of those people most directly involved in the search. Part III takes a closer look at the economic realities we must take into account in the self-fulfillment quest of the future. Part IV elaborates on the lessons Americans have learned from experimenting with their lives, and describes the emergence of a new social ethic of commitment in our society (new rules of living) on which many of our hopes for the future must rest.

Part I

***

Flaws and Strengths

Chapter 2

...━◉━...

The Threat of
the Great Reversal

Let us start with the most obvious flaw in people's self-fulfillment strategies: the desires of most Americans to move toward expanded choice, pluralism of life styles and greater freedom, while the economy, besieged by inflation and recession, moves relentlessly in the opposite direction—toward restriction of choice. This creates many dilemmas for Americans.

Consider, for example, one case from the several hundred life histories I gathered for this study, that of David and Cynthia Muller. David Muller,* a thirty-four-year-old photographer who is a lobster fisherman by avocation, explained his situation this way: "When my wife told me she was going back to work full-time, even though we have a three-year-old girl who needs a lot of care, I said, 'Sure. That's great.' What the hell, I get pleasure out of my work. Why should she be stuck in the house all day? She has a right to her own fulfillment. Well, it didn't work out as well as we thought it would. The first thing we did when she went back to work was to buy a more expensive

* Place names and people's names and occupations have been changed in order to safeguard the identity of the subjects who consented to be interviewed only under this condition.

house because we had two incomes to count on. But inflation gobbled up the extra money we had from her earnings. Now we're stuck with mortgage payments at 15 percent interest. The bloom is off the rose with her job—she likes it all right but not as much as at first. We take turns caring for our little girl, so we hardly see one another: when she's home, I'm working, and vice versa. Now she can't quit the damn job even if she wants to; we can't afford it. Both of us still think we did the right things, I'll tell you, but we're not as sure as we once were."

The Mullers' plight is typical of the predicaments that entangle people's lives as they break away from old patterns of behavior in search of self-fulfillment. In the interviews almost everyone concerned with self-fulfillment stressed how directly their plans hinged on their economic prospects. For many years Americans in the middle and upper income ranges had grown accustomed to steady increases in income and had taken for granted that in a flexible economy they could enjoy flexibility in their lives. In today's more stringent economy they find themselves saddled with the consequences of choices made in easier times.

My interview with Cynthia Muller, David's wife, confirmed her husband's story. She had had a job before they were married and kept it until she gave birth to their daughter. Then she quit to take care of the baby. At first she unreservedly enjoyed being a housewife and mother. But when the novelty wore off she began to worry about being "just a housewife." Her husband had shared in caring for the baby as an infant: he would get up at night to give the baby her bottle, and he even helped with the laundry. But gradually his help diminished without either of them talking about it much. It was understood that since she was home all day, and he worked, she would carry the main burden of child care.

Cynthia said she returned to her job "mainly for my self-fulfillment, but also because the money came in handy." She had assumed she could quit her job any time she wanted, especially if her daughter needed her. Now, she says, she feels she has been tricked. Her mother told Cynthia that because discrimination against women was so widespread in the past, when she was first married and also working her bank had refused to count her income in calculating how large a mortgage she and Cynthia's father could manage. Cynthia commented wistfully that she wished her bank had done the same; then she and David wouldn't both be working to support their house. But she quickly added she thought the house an excellent investment, and since they were not managing to save any money despite their two incomes, the house represented their future security.

The worst feature of their present life, she said, is that she and David seem almost to lead separate lives. "It's as if we have this business partnership in the house and in our child and in our jobs. It's all right, I guess. But somehow there's a difference between a business partnership and marriage. There's definitely something wrong with this arrangement but I can't put my finger on what it is."

(ii)

Economic growth helped to create an extraordinary cohesiveness in postwar America. From the late forties well into the sixties most Americans shared a vision of what they wanted for their lives, their families and their country. Under the impetus of the vision an entire nation devoted itself single-mindedly to the task of achieving a perpetual-motion machine of economic growth, and then used the machine to satisfy the national hunger for homes, cars, beefsteak and gadgets. The growth machine accomplished something the world had never seen before: the combination of human striving, technology, organization and cheap energy moved a mass population from want and scarcity into proud middle-class status.

For almost three decades the U.S. economy was marked by dynamism, rapid growth and expanding opportunities. A growing economy encouraged upward mobility: year after year, people improved their lot and came to take for granted ever-increasing levels of material well-being. Between 1950 and 1973 average family income doubled—from $5,600 to $12,000 in constant dollars—moving the mass of Americans from the edge of poverty to modest material comfort.

Americans quickly came to cherish the new freedom their affluence secured for them and to depend on the benefits of an expanding income. Middle-class Americans may find it hard to achieve psychological fulfillment, but in the sixties and seventies the practical aspect of the search was made easier than it had ever been before. If you didn't want the responsibility of caring for your aging parents, there were Social Security benefits, pensions, retirement villages, old-age homes and state-provided medical programs to do this for you. If you wished to supplement your income there were jobs. If you wanted training, there were training facilities. If you needed to acquire more education, schools and universities existed in abundance for doing so.

If you thought moving to the Sunbelt would make you happier, the Sunbelt welcomed you and offered you an affordable place to live, cheap gasoline to get to work, and rambling schools for your children.

Then, abruptly, came a stunning turnabout—a great reversal of the economy and the culture. Without warning or adequate preparation, in the late nineteen-seventies we suddenly found ourselves plunged into an unfamiliar world. Unaccountably, the culture and the economy seemed to have traded places with each other. As the culture has expanded, the economy has grown more restrictive. Economic opportunities have become less abundant. The tempo of growth has decelerated. Inflation is consuming our savings. The cost of living is outstripping disposable income; it is more difficult to save for the future, own a home, pay for college, and meet one's tax, food and medical bills. Inflation is forcing many people who planned to retire early to abandon their plans. Women like Cynthia Muller who originally chose to work outside the home for self-expressive reasons, are now obliged to continue working to pay the mortgage. People struggling to hold on to earlier gains find themselves working harder just to keep from falling behind. Suddenly, to the psychological difficulty of making the right choices is now added the haunting fear that the choices may be futile, and that new self-fulfillment goals may be unattainable because of economic reasons.

Starting in the seventies one economic trouble has followed another. Our annual rate of productivity increase began to falter; some of our key industries, such as steel, textiles and automobiles, grew less competitive with those of other industrialized nations, notably Japan. New floating exchange rates for the dollar saw the value of currency decline steadily as the price of gold moved ever upward, reflecting a world-wide inflation that has left in its wake severe structural problems.

In a matter of a few years we have moved from an uptight culture set in a dynamic economy to a dynamic culture set in an uptight economy. The search for self-fulfillment was conceived in the America of jet vacations to Europe because "your dollar goes so much further there." It has survived, somewhat battered, into the era of chronic stagflation, the dual-earner family that still cannot make ends meet, the decline of U.S. technological innovation, the rise of Soviet military power, the ninety-billion-dollar-a-year bill for OPEC oil and the influx of European tourists into New York City, some of whom come "because it is cheap to live there." The world we live in has been turned upside down.

Such a reversal in the relationship of culture to the economy is profoundly disorienting, especially when there are no warning signals.

Nowhere did we find signs telling us: CAUTION: CULTURAL EXPANSION AHEAD, or LOOK OUT FOR SLIDING ECONOMY.

The economic reverses of recent years have disoriented Americans because the shifts were so unanticipated and so seemingly arbitrary. People do not know what these bleak economic changes signify for their freedom to choose among life styles. What happens to choice when economic growth slows? What does the future hold for those who conceived their self-fulfillment in an economy of abundance and must now pursue their search under less promising economic conditions? How permanent are these new conditions? What does the future hold? These troubling questions are very much on people's minds, and for good reason.

It is useful to remember that the search for self-fulfillment began in the economic climate of the 1960s and among a group—college students from affluent families—not notorious for their economic realism. Perhaps it made sense at one time to assume our economy was so well-heeled that everything was possible at once—high growth in a clean, safe environment, with social justice for all and a life replete with leisure, jet travel, second homes, glowing health and other "simple things" of life. But it does not make sense now and will not for the foreseeable future. Sad to say, hard choices are what now make sense.

But in the seventies, swept up in the psychology of the me-firstism and more-of-everythingism, we were not ready, psychologically, for hard choices. We took a vacation from our traditional American let's-be-realistic orientation. Americans in the past have been able to tighten their belts without growing panicky or gloom-ridden. But our recent political leaders knew that Americans were in the mood to enjoy, not cut back. They made little effort to alert the nation to economic dangers and to keep it from getting hooked on that most vicious of reality-avoiding addictions, the inflation habit. Of course, our political leadership is itself a cross section of American life: it reflects the public psychology, it does not create it. It, too, was caught up in the disorienting effects of a world turned upside down.

The new vulnerability of the American economy cannot be blamed on a public preoccupied with the search for self-fulfillment. Musings about sex, mid-life career changes and fulfilling one's potentials did not create OPEC, or the Japanese auto industry, or Third World demands for a new economic order, or a Soviet military build-up. There are many geopolitical explanations for the relative decline of U.S. economic strength in our quarrelsome world, a decline that contributes directly to inflation.

But the main problem we are now obliged to face in the 1980s is that we are living far beyond our means. The inflation that has plagued the country since the war in Vietnam is a symptom of a national failure to adapt to this reality. Between the mid-sixties and the early eighties the gap between the nation's assets (the market value of all listed shares of companies) and what we owe grew almost tenfold—from 366 billion to 3 trillion dollars.* Henry Kaufman, the economist who made this calculation, interprets this trend as a dangerous erosion of the capital America needs to maintain economic growth. This massive build-up of debt reflects the demands Americans are making on the economy and government in their determination not to narrow their life choices. A society preoccupied with introspection is easily caught off-guard by an unanticipated shift in economic relationships. An era in which people are eager to enjoy the benefits of thirty years of unparalleled economic growth is a terrible time, psychologically speaking, to face disagreeable economic truths.

Americans are just beginning to realize that a change for the worse has taken place in the economy—and it disturbs them. We have an abundance of survey data to document public response to economic conditions. My review of this data, stretching back over the past three decades, suggests that in the past ten years, a significant shift in American attitudes has taken place—from an optimistic faith in an open-ended future to a fear of economic instability. We now find a nation hovering midway between an older postwar faith in expanding horizons and a newer sense of lowered expectations, apprehension about the future, mistrust of institutions and a growing sense of limits.

Consider two survey statements posed by my firm, Yankelovich, Skelly and White. One states, "Our current standard of living may be the highest we can hope for." A recent cross section of 62 percent of Americans agreed. To the other statement, "Americans should get used to the fact that our wealth is limited and most of us are not likely to become better off than we are now," 62 percent also agreed. Moreover, agreement on both questions cuts across all demographic groupings, with virtually no differences between men and women, black and white, or urban and country dwellers. The largest differences relate to age and education, with older and less-educated people being somewhat more pessimistic, and younger people, especially well-educated ones, being less so. But there is one statistic that our surveys turned up that power-

---

* Jason Epstein, "Is the Party Over?" *New York Review of Books,* Vol. XXVII, No. 16 (October 23, 1980), p. 10.

fully encapsulates how Americans are responding to the present economic climate. *Almost three out of four Americans (72 percent), shocked by the economic reverses the country has undergone since 1973, have concluded that, "We are fast coming to a turning point in our history. The land of plenty is becoming the land of want."*

Chapter 3

························●◉●·······

The Self-Fulfillment Contradiction

The great reversal in the relationship of culture to economy is a momentous event in American history, one we will be struggling with for years to come. It has rendered obsolete all self-fulfillment strategies based on the assumption that our standard of living will, of course, improve in the future as it has in the past.

Now let us look at another kind of flaw in the self-fulfillment strategy. It is true that a tighter economy has created difficulties for people who, like the Mullers, made their plans under one set of economic assumptions, only to find themselves saddled with burdensome commitments as conditions changed. But it would be a mistake to assume that all was well with people's self-fulfillment strategies when the economy functioned smoothly. A tighter economy has merely intensified strains and contradictions in the self-fulfillment search that have been present all along.

To illustrate, here are two more examples from life histories. The two people, one a man, the other a woman, are not "average Americans," but they are struggling with typical cross pressures arising from the search for self-fulfillment. The two people occupy roughly the same socioeconomic and age brackets. But one sees herself a winner in the self-fulfillment game, while the other sees himself a loser and a victim. Though their life styles are hardly typical, both share the epochal experience of our times: early conformity to traditional norms followed by a growing preoccupation with self-fulfillment projects that run counter to these norms.

Robert Agnoli, Ph.D., is Associate Professor of Political Science at one of those colleges in Boston that struggles for its identity under the shadow of Harvard and M.I.T.

In my interview with him, Professor Agnoli admitted that for the first time in his life he has come to think of himself as a loser, and he makes an impressive case to support his claim. In his early forties, he is married, with two children, ages twelve and fifteen. After some hesitation, he told me that his wife, Carole, whom he married when they were graduate students, had abandoned him and the children several months ago and had gone to live in Newport, Rhode Island, with a woman who they had met on a summer vacation a few years earlier.

He said he knew that his wife had grown discontented in recent years and that their sexual life had been perfunctory. He said that his wife had never previously indicated in action or in words that she was sexually attracted to other women. He was convinced that she was not really gay, and this seemed to agitate him. It was as if he could accept her decision to leave if she were truly a lesbian, but the same act was intolerable—and incomprehensible—to him if she were not.

I reconstructed the following sequence of events from the interview. Professor Agnoli's father, now dead, had owned a small grocery store in Boston's North End where he, two brothers and two sisters had grown up. He was the only one of the five who had persisted in his education (one brother and sister had gone to a local two-year community college; the others completed high school but did not go to college), and he was proud of his accomplishment. He said he realized as early as junior high school that teachers liked him: he always had an answer to the teachers' questions, though not always the correct one, he added wryly. Gradually, he came to see this talent as a way out of the grime and penny-pinching he associated with his upbringing. Academic achievement became his ladder for social mobility.

His parents wanted him to become a high school teacher, a prospect he angrily rejected. He thought of high school teaching as a low status calling, hardly better than tending a small grocery store. But he had assumed that becoming a college professor meant prestige, security, and even, at least from his youthful perspective as a student, an affluent way of life.

Before their marriage, Carole had completed a year of graduate work in history at N.Y.U. Once married, however, she dropped out to find a job to support them while he stayed in school to complete his Ph.D. Once Robert had his degree and a teaching position in Boston, she left the job, became pregnant and did not work outside the home again.

"Both of us have been unbearably restless these past few years," he said. "Before she left me, Carole had turned into a real pain-in-the-ass feminist. We'd have these unending arguments about how much I owed her for putting me through graduate school and how much I should be doing around the house. I come from an old-style Italian background where everyone waited on Papa, and it hasn't been easy for me to adjust to unisex housekeeping. And anyway, I always felt that our arguments about what I owed her were a cover for something else. They were not the real issue. Both of us had reached a crisis in our lives and we knew we were not being fulfilled. I just don't feel like a middle-aged professor with tenure, two kids and a house in Lexington with a big mortgage. And she didn't feel like a typical housewife. We were living a stereotyped life but we didn't fit the stereotype. When we weren't arguing about who should do the dishes or the shopping, we'd sometimes talk about making a drastic change in our life style."

Several months before Carole left, the Agnolis had a serious argument. For years he had been complaining about his colleagues, the college and teaching itself, and he and Carole talked often about moving to California. He admitted to her that for the past five or six years the teaching was no longer as satisfying as it used to be. "It just doesn't use all of my potentials," he said, "and if you don't use them, they dry up."

For both of them "California" had become a codeword for escape from frustration. He had some vague ideas about getting a job with a West Coast "think tank" and making more money. Carole had fastened onto the move to California as a way of starting a new life. She thought that once they moved she would find a part-time job, or perhaps go back to school to finish her degree: she was vague on what she might do then, but, Agnoli insisted, she was quite precise in her view that her present life was stifling her chances for fulfillment. Then—and this is what precipitated the argument—he told her he had begun to worry seriously about the state of the economy and that good jobs in government-supported "think tanks" like the Rand Corporation seemed to be drying up. He argued that even though his salary as a professor wasn't keeping up with inflation, he had the security of a tenured post at a time that his brightest Ph.D. students were finding it difficult to get any job at all. He had concluded, he said, that they must abandon the idea of moving and stay put at least until the economy looked more promising.

He said he knew she was disappointed. But he also described how surprised he was when, after the first explosion of anger and recrimination, she had quieted down and hardly ever returned to the subject. Several months later she left without warning.

"She is doing what *she* wants to do," he commented bitterly, "leaving me saddled with the kids, a career I no longer find meaningful and a house that was a burden even before she left. She says she loves the kids, and she phones them all the time. But it just doesn't make sense. I don't even know whether she is coming back when her girl friend gets tired of her. And I'm not sure that I want her back anyway . . ." His voice trails off as he struggles with this confusing prospect.

Unlike Robert Agnoli, Margaret Greenson considers herself one of life's winners, not a loser.

I interviewed her in her husband's office in the Indian Museum in Santa Fe where he is the curator. She was waiting for him to finish work so they could go home together; she works at the museum part-time.

Mrs. Greenson is a few years older than Agnoli, in her middle forties, and the mother of four grown children. (Only the youngest, a boy of fifteen, still lives at home.) She says somewhat ruefully that she and her husband married young and were so busy having babies they didn't notice until it was too late that the baby boom had ended. The museum job was everything her husband had always wanted, and they had moved to Santa Fe from Cincinnati even though it meant a cut in income at a time they could hardly afford it, just after the birth of their second child. Margaret Greenson, who had majored in math and anthropology in college (a "funny combination," she admits), found herself obliged to "take in bookkeeping the way women take in washing" to help set aside college tuition for their children.

Actually, she says, things worked out on the economic front reasonably well. The museum gave her husband small but steady raises each year, and her bookkeeping (for a number of local doctors) yielded enough that "we were able to do most of the things we wanted to."

Under the circumstances, she said she found it difficult to express openly—even to herself—her increasingly frequent flashes of resentment. She told herself that everything was going so well, just as both she and her husband had planned, and that she had fully accepted the role of the wife and mother—she-who-makes-sacrifices-for-the-family. But, to her surprise, she found herself "feeling angry almost all of the time at my children and my husband. It was as if everybody else was entitled to do what they wanted in life except Mother." When her feelings grew too oppressive to keep bottled up, she decided to talk about them with her husband. "At first his reaction was defensive," she says. "He felt I was criticizing him for decisions we had both made in good faith." But after a few tense months and "more misunderstanding than I thought was possible, he began to hear what I was trying to tell him."

Together, they sat up nights trying to devise a practical plan. Since they had successfully saved in the past for at least part of their children's college tuition, they decided they could do the same "for the fifth kid, me." For another year and a half Margaret Greenson continued to take in bookkeeping, but this time she did it for her "own account."

She discovered a program associated with the University of Maryland for which she could work toward a degree at home and at the same time take a part-time job at the museum. The museum paid less than the bookkeeping, but now she could begin "to learn the ropes" while earning her formal credentials.

She had come to hate bookkeeping, which had somehow grown into a symbol of a way of life she wanted to shed. "I have to work like a maniac now," she said, "but it's worth it. Twenty years ago I would have died at the prospect of getting a mail-order degree. But I think I have my priorities a little straighter now. My big fear, frankly, is that with life being so expensive, it will be back to the bookkeeping before I know it. I'm not sure I could take that. Somehow I feel I've used up my ability to compromise and always look on the bright side of things. But maybe it won't have to come to that."

Neither the Agnolis nor the Greensons are average Americans. Certainly, the Agnolis' response—the husband's as well as the wife's—remains exotic even in today's let-a-thousand-flowers-bloom culture. Also, the Agnolis' marital bond seemed to disintegrate faster than most under pressure, while the Greensons seemed to adapt with less apparent stress.

But the two families *are* typical in several respects. Both families gradually became aware that a greater range of life choices might be available to them than in earlier periods of their lives. Each of them strived to win greater freedom of movement and flexibility in their lives. And in each instance, the newer self-fulfillment values came in conflict with older, more traditional ones.

Under conditions of economic strain, the Agnoli marriage came apart. But it is clear that the economic constraints which discouraged Agnoli from moving to California did not wreck his marriage; they merely precipitated a crisis long in the making. For the Greensons, tighter economic conditions added to the pre-existing strain on a family struggling to take advantage of new life choices. Even under conditions in which both husband and wife seem genuinely responsive to each other, the new circumstances create stress.

As we shall see more clearly when we examine other life histories and surveys gathered for this study, the truly determined seekers of self-fulfillment are plunged into confusing predicaments even when they are affluent. In recent years, all of us have come to know of marriages that have broken up for reasons that would not have led to divorce a generation ago; of young people who have more choice than young people enjoyed in the past and yet cannot decide what to do with their lives; of men and women who, being discontent with themselves, transform their lives in the name of self-fulfillment, however disastrously this turns out for themselves and others. All around us we see signs of aimlessness and dissatisfaction with conventional choices. We see people unable to settle the basic questions of where to live, with whom, under what conditions and with what focus for one's time and life. Among people like the Agnolis who are involved in what I call "the strong form" of the self-fulfillment predicament, the search for self-fulfillment raises more fundamental questions than most people can take in stride without stumbling.

My interviews with Professor Agnoli and other middle-income people involved in self-fulfillment experiments remind me of types of adventures that used to be confined to the very wealthy. It is as if upper-crust life styles have been democratized and made part of the conventional psychoculture—but with an important difference between the life experiments of the wealthy and those of the rest of us. Leaving aside the emotional wear and tear that affects us all with relative equality, the wealthy can afford, from a practical point of view, to make more than one mistake. When they take a risk and it fails, they can afford to walk away from it: for the very rich, being obliged to maintain several households or failing in a new career are not terminal dilemmas. The middle class, however, suffers all the emotional trauma of failed risks, and devastating practical consequences as well. People on tight budgets are plunged into instant hardship when marriages break up and former partners are obliged to support two households, usually on the same income that had barely sufficed for one. In the life experiments of the average American, there are no safety nets woven of excess dollars.

Chapter 4

The Promise
Beneath the Guises

In the sixties the search for self-fulfillment was celebrated in some quarters as a "greening of America"—a benign transformation of consciousness that would enrich our lives as individuals, tame the corporate state and advance our civilization to a new peak of excellence. But as the economic climate changed the self-fulfillment movement began to get a bad press. Tom Wolfe labeled the seventies the "me decade." Daniel Bell criticized our infatuation with the "unrestrained self," and cultural historian Christopher Lasch angrily condemned our "culture of narcissism."

Clearly, the search for self-fulfillment has not proven to be the magical greening celebrated in the sixties. In retrospect, Charles Reich's best-seller, *Greening of America*, which came at the end of the decade, was blinded by a curious infatuation. Reich loved the trappings of the student counterculture—the bell-bottom trousers, long unkempt hair, pot smoking, granny glasses, belt making and the student fondness, which he shared, for "genuine, old-fashioned, unhomogenized peanut butter." He saw all these as totems, symbols endowed with a mystical purity. To preserve this purity from a corrupt culture he advised his students to serve American society by dropping out of it.

Reich pandered to the snobbery of his well-to-do Yale students.

Referring to blue collar workers, he wrote of ". . . their sullen boredom, their unchanging routines, their minds closed to new ideas and new feelings, their bodies slumped in front of television to watch the ball-game Sunday." And in his theory of the "liberation of the self" he contributed to the narcissistic tendencies that were to stand out so starkly in future years. As psychologist Nancy McWilliams observes, Reich writes ". . . as if the self is pre-existent, extracultural, independent; all one has to do to insure a world of people who feel whole and fulfilled is to open up all possible options for self expression."*

Like so many observers of the self-fulfillment phenomenon, Reich failed to distinguish between accident and essence, and instead indulged his own personal biases. Even the most disciplined observers find it difficult to retain their objectivity when writing about the youth of their own society; Reich was neither disciplined nor objective, and his work was innocent of data that might confirm or qualify his sweeping judgments.

Almost a decade later, Christopher Lasch, in *The Culture of Narcissism*, is the mirror opposite of Reich. Where Reich celebrates, Lasch denounces. Where Reich welcomes the change in consciousness as a blessing come to save our civilization, Lasch prophesies that disaster will come with the change. Lasch is a mighty hater, angry and gloom-ridden in his images of American life and the narcissism he associates with the search for self-fulfillment. He describes our social life as inevitably "becoming more warlike and barbaric." He deplores the "collapse of personal life." He writes: "Bourgeois society seems everywhere to have used up its store of constructive ideas. . . . It has lost the capacity and the will to confront the difficulties that threaten to overwhelm it."†

Lasch sees an international crisis in the capitalist world—decadence, exhaustion of will, inability to control events, failure even to understand them. Lasch writes:

> The concept of narcissism provides us . . . with a way of understanding the psychological impact of recent social changes . . . It yields a tolerably accurate portrait of the "liberated" personality of our time, with his charm, his pseudoawareness of his own condition, his promiscuous pansexuality, his fascination with oral sex,

* Philip Nobile, ed., *The Con III Controversy* (New York: Pocket Books, 1971), p. 219.
† Christopher Lasch, *The Culture of Narcissism: American Life in an Age of Diminishing Expectations* (New York: Norton, 1979), p. 30.

> his fear of the castrating mother (Mrs. Portnoy), his hypochon-
> dria, his protective shallowness, his avoidance of dependence, his
> inability to mourn, his dread of old age and death.*

This inventory of personality traits is colorful, but arbitrary. Nowhere is there the slightest tendency for these characteristics to form a
coherent pattern. Nor is there even in Lasch's work evidence that
Americans have developed these traits of personality as a response to
developments unleashed by late capitalism. Nor is there, theoretically,
any reason that they should.

I take Lasch seriously, for he is a learned observer of the American
scene. He is surely correct in noting a preoccupation with self as a sign
of the times, but he is wrong to reduce the American quest for self-
fulfillment to the pathology of narcissistic personality disorders. This is
like reducing an otherwise healthy hospital patient to his disease—the
"swollen glands in room 232."

The narcissism that Lasch sees everywhere is not the essence of the
recent American search for self-fulfillment. Indeed, far from being its
defining characteristic, narcissism is a betrayal of it. It defeats it. The
Agnolis, for example, are more narcissistic than the Greensons and their
quest for the self-fulfillment has worked out worse than the Greensons'.
In seeking to change the giving/getting compact in her relationship to
her family, Mrs. Greenson did not place her narcissistic concerns ahead
of the family's needs, nor did her husband react out of a narcissistic
preoccupation with his own needs. He was simply a little slow in his
response. Indeed, if Mrs. Greenson does fail in her self-fulfillment
goals, it will be for practical economic reasons; if she succeeds, it will
be because she has not broken every commitment that happens to interfere with her desires for her own fulfillment.

Had he looked at people's actual lives, Lasch might not have concluded that our changing culture breeds nothing but decadence. In
principle, he acknowledges the possibility that the shifts in American
culture may not be all bad. In his preface to *The Culture of Narcissism*,
he writes, "much could be written about the signs of new life in the
United States." But then he quickly adds that he is more interested in
describing "a way of life that is dying—the culture of competitive individualism carried to the extreme of the war of all against all, the pursuit of happiness to the dead end of a narcissistic preoccupation with

* Ibid., p. 50.

the self . . . a cultural revolution that reproduces the worst features of
the collapsing civilization it claims to criticize." For reasons of his own,
he seems preoccupied with the negative side of American culture.

(ii)

Unlike Lasch, I regard the Mullers, the Agnolis, the Greensons and the
others whose life experiments we shall examine as carrying out an
important and positive communal function. They are serving a social
purpose as well as a merely private one. Just as a scientist's discoveries
advance the state of knowledge for the society as a whole, or an entrepreneur's success swells the growth of the economy, so too the seeker
of self-fulfillment is, consciously or unconsciously, performing a vital
social role. He or she is confronting a set of crises that our industrial
civilization as a whole must face if it is to thrive in the future. Para-
doxically, those most caught in their private predicaments may be an
advance guard for the rest of us.

This proposition is far from self-evident, and may at first seem im-
probable. Most of the people I interviewed for this book assumed that
their search for self-fulfillment concerned only themselves and the few
persons intimately involved in their lives. Most of them also assumed
that each person harbors an inner being possessed of specific needs and
potentials that cry out for a matching "life style." What could be of less
social value than the private search to bring the two together—the
unique inner being and the custom-built life style?

The case of the Agnolis surely contains ingredients of farce: a professor is cuckolded by a lesbian and is irritated by the suspicion that his
wife may not even be a "real lesbian." The threat to his self-esteem
comes from his suspicion that she did not accord him the minimum
respect either of abandoning him for another man or for reasons of perverse sexuality. This is the stuff of comedy that playwrights, from
Aristophanes to Woody Allen, have exploited.

Woody Allen likes to emphasize the comic aspects of the search
for self-fulfillment. But most commentators sound a grim and earnest
note. One can imagine how the Agnolis might be interpreted from various perspectives. An angry radical might excoriate their behavior as
capitalist decadence. A life-cycle theorist might interpret Mrs. Agnoli's
actions as a phase of painful "growth" associated with moving through
the predictable stages of adult development. A women's movement ad-
vocate might see it as an act of liberation bravely taken to break out of
the rigid sex roles to which women have been relegated in a sexist,

male-dominated society. An economic determinist might judge it a form of behavior consumers can afford to indulge in only as long as after-tax discretionary income permits. And now I come along with the seemingly implausible theory that those engaged in their own search for fulfillment are at the same time doing society's necessary work, conducting experiments with their lives that will in the long run benefit society, even if the experimenters themselves make a mess of their own lives—and those of others—in the process.

I do not mean, of course, that every act of folly committed in the name of self-fulfillment automatically transmutes itself into a social good. Rather, I want only to emphasize that almost nothing of enduring cultural value is ever born without struggle, confusion, contradiction. Culture evolves in an indirect, dialectical fashion; some forms of social conflict are necessary to healthy adaptation to change.

Writing some years ago about how Western civilization came to abandon the view that slavery was morally justified and to believe instead that it was morally abhorrent, the philosopher Alfred North Whitehead reflected on the moral ambiguities of history, concluding that "great ideas often enter reality in strange guises and with disgusting alliances."

Even in the short thirty-year span of American culture that my own studies encompass, I have often seen this dialectic at work. A new idea emerges in our culture—for example, what it means to be a woman. At first this idea is urged by extremists, purists and ideologues and derided by people whose morality is offended or whose interests are threatened. Initially, the majority rejects the idea that women should have the same rights as men, partly because of the extreme, even shocking ways by which its enthusiasts support it. But once a new idea of this sort has been planted in prepared soil, it takes root and begins to sprout in many forms. Inevitably, it stimulates further resistance that breeds further conflict, but the new idea also advances its cause by forcing adjustments and compromises. Gradually the new meaning of womanhood changes as it works its way from the periphery into the center of society. By the time the new idea has triumphed, the advance guard—the extremists, purists and ideologues who first expressed it—may no longer recognize it as theirs. But victory does not change the fact of its origin. The women's movement did arrive on our cultural scene in many strange guises.

With the search for self-fulfillment, too, strange guises are clear for all to see: the putative insincerity of Agnoli's wife's lesbianism, Agnoli's own self-centeredness, his rejection of his own success in fulfilling his earlier ambition to escape from the grocery store. Of course, there is self-preoccupation too. But just as there is more than self-interest involved in the women's movement, so too the significance of the search for self-fulfillment, even in the case of the Agnolis, goes far beyond the merely private. In ways we can as yet barely discern, the Agnolis' and the Greensons' and the Mullers' personal choices, combined with those of many others like them, will change American life for better or worse.

Throughout this book I emphasize personal relationships in my examples of self-fulfillment strategies, for it is here that the most far-reaching life experiments are occurring. Eventually these do affect the economy. A generation ago, if a family was pressed for money a typical husband would moonlight or cut back on expenses before he would "send" his wife to work outside the home for the essentials of life. His pride, after all, was at stake. Today most of the time it is she who decides whether or not to work outside the home. The two-income family, not the moonlighting husband, has become the norm, and the economy is thereby deeply influenced.

But the seekers of self-fulfillment do not confine their life experiments to the domestic aspects of the giving/getting compact. They test every element of it, including some that are more directly economic in their implications, such as the relationship to working and consuming. An example of a change in the working-consuming aspects of our psychoculture will show how the new rules associated with the search for self-fulfillment can help America respond to its new economic challenge, and how these values may stimulate a new inventiveness and dynamism in our economy.

Each year between the mid-sixties and the mid-seventies my firm conducted cross-section studies of young adult attitudes toward the work ethic and other traditional American values.* One of the largest changes we discovered in the research was a sharp drop in the number of college students who believe that "hard work always pays off." In the mid-sixties, 72 percent of college students subscribed to this view. By the early seventies, its adherents had been almost cut in half—to 40 percent.

Knowing that the views of college students do not always mirror the

---

* Daniel Yankelovich, *The New Morality: A Profile of American Youth in the Seventies* (New York: McGraw-Hill Paperbacks, 1974).

national outlook, my firm started to include this inquiry in studies of the general public. These findings showed a change in the same direction, thought not as drastic. In the decade between the late sixties and the late seventies, the number of Americans who believe "hard work always pays off" fell from a 58 percent majority to a 43 percent minority.* This is a significant shift in a short period of time. What does this change mean?

Some Americans have grown disillusioned about their chances of sharing in the bountiful rewards of American life, however hard they work. But this is not the dominant response. College-educated people in particular reject this interpretation; most of them believe that if they are willing to work hard by the old rules they can win the traditional rewards—the car, the TV set, the house in the suburbs, respectability. What they question is not whether the old rules work, but whether they are worth the bother: they question both the kind of work the society demands and the "payoffs" it provides. In effect, the research shows that increasing numbers of Americans, particularly the young, are questioning the economic core of the giving/getting compact—the value of giving a particular kind of hard work in exchange for a particular set of economic benefits.

If this research finding really does signal an important shift in psychoculture—the shared meaning of hard work—we should expect it to show up in people's actions as well as in their attitudes. We should look at what people *do* as well as what they say, because people often grumble about changing the rules without actually doing so.

Probably the best place to look for changes in America's economic behavior, if such changes are occurring, is in relationship to automobiles. The automobile plays a central role in our culture and in our economy—as a major consumer purchase, as an industry, as a symbol of material success and as the precondition of suburban life styles. The automobile of one's choice has long served as a payoff for hard work, and the automotive assembly line is probably the most familiar symbol of hard work in industrial society. Any significant change on the economic side of the giving/getting compact should reveal itself in relation to making and buying automobiles.

For social critics, American automobiles of the fifties with their soaring tailfins and chrome-laden chassis were a favorite object of ridicule. Psychoanalysts speculated freely on what fantasies they symbolized:

* Daniel Yankelovich, "Work, Values and the New Breed," in *Work in America*, eds. Clark Kerr and Jerome Rosow (New York: Van Nostrand Reinhold, 1979).

mere transportation seemed the least of their purposes. And yet, pound for pound they gave the consumer extraordinary economic value. Detroit has always been cost conscious: in the fifties and sixties its favorite slogan was "more car per car." The industry's engineers and production designers were relentlessly driven to pack as much value in size, performance and power as they could into every model. To social critics the cars of the era may have seemed "insolent chariots," but they were chariots average Americans craved to own.

In that period, Detroit's vigor in expanding the car market became the leading edge of the nation's economic prosperity: American-made steel and low-price gasoline seemed inexhaustible, limited only by consumer demand. And the more chariots sold, the better the economy worked. This was the climate of thinking that prevailed when, in the late fifties, the Ford Motor Company commissioned its first "small car" study. Volkswagen Beetles and other small cars imported from Western Europe and Japan had begun to penetrate the American market, and Ford was eager to learn what American motorists thought of them.

Ford's study discovered a significant group of consumers with a keen interest in purchasing a small car, American or foreign. But the study also showed that when these car buyers were asked what they meant by a "small car," they described a car with a low purchase price and high operating efficiency. They were indifferent to its size: they didn't care if the car was small, medium or large. Mainly, they wanted a car to take them to their destination with the least trouble and the lowest cost. They wanted efficient low-cost transportation, and little else.

But the vast majority of car buyers of that era had different demands. This was the era of the baby boom, and families were large. They did not want to be squeezed into little cars. They wanted comfort, especially for long-distance driving. They wanted performance. They wanted weight and power which they associated with safety as well as with speed. And they wanted a car that would make a personal statement about themselves: it would signify their achievement in life and social standing, indicating how far they had come and where they were going—figuratively as well as literally.

The values of America in the nineteen-fifties were remarkably homogeneous—at least for the majority. Social status was clear, uniform and rigid. It was personified in the General Motors product line of the period, with its finely calibrated gradations in price, chrome and size: GM's customers celebrated each advance in earnings and social status by moving up the line from the Chevrolet to the Pontiac to the Buick to the Oldsmobile to the Cadillac. To move up the GM line was to send a message—not only to the Joneses next door but also to one's self. The message said: hard work and sacrifice had indeed paid off. General Motors' line of cars symbolized as nothing else could the value system of American society in the Eisenhower years of suburbs, gray flannel organization men and family togetherness.

Everywhere it looked, Detroit received confirmation of the prevailing consumer outlook, and it built both its economics and its "religion" around it. The automotive people of Detroit have always known how important their industry is to the nation's economy, but when American values began to shift in the sixties and seventies the auto makers were unprepared to accept the evidence that the role of the automobile was changing. They even ignored their own sales data: prior to the Arab oil embargo between 1968 and 1973 the sale of large American cars increased by only 10 percent, while sales of small foreign cars grew by 122 percent. Despite this provocative signal that the market had shifted, Detroit resisted the evidence. The automobile executives took it on faith that most Americans would always want more from their cars than mere transportation. To them a small car upended a cherished dictum. Detroit's word for the production of smaller fuel-efficient cars is "downsizing." In the minds of many of Detroit's automen to downsize the American car was to downsize the American dream.

There are many Americans who still hold that view. They still hunger for the big ones—those lovely, insolent chariots. But in general, Americans have found it relatively easy to accommodate to the idea of smaller fuel-efficient cars. Our culture changed faster than Detroit did. To be sure, in some ways the American love affair with the car goes on. When surveys ask Americans what they would find most difficult to give up in hard times, most people (94 percent) name the family car. Americans find it more difficult to give up their cars than, say, their own homes (84 percent), or the family TV set (62 percent), or having meat once a day (48 percent), or taking an annual vacation (42 percent).*

While Americans continue to cherish their cars, the psychocultural meaning of owning a car *is* changing. People feel that a car means freedom and independence and convenience—it takes you where you want to go when you want to. Our cars still make personal statements about us, but what they express is our taste, individuality and autonomy, not our social status. Also, to increasing numbers of Americans a car is

* Daniel Yankelovich, "The Impact of Scarcities" (Report prepared for the Ford Foundation, Common Problems Grant #740-0597).

"just a car," a necessity of life that should be comfortable and styled to "suit me," but need not symbolize one's achievement in life.

Therefore bigness, newness, excess power and the other elements of conspicuous consumption are not as important as they once were—not worth endless sacrifice. Ninety percent of the public say they are willing to do without annual model changes in automobiles.*

These changes are not universal. Millions of Americans still regard the big expensive car as a status symbol worth whatever sacrifice may be needed to acquire it. But the trend is unmistakable. OPEC and Iran's revolution may have forced us into smaller, more fuel-efficient cars, but even before their effects were felt, Americans searching for self-fulfillment were expressing via their purchasing behavior a preference for a different kind of automobile, one which connoted not the owner's status, but his life style and one which would, as it happened, anticipate the national requirement to depend less on foreign oil.

The shift to smaller cars reflects a change in the "payoff" side of the hard-work-pays-off compact. What about its other side—the willingness to do hard work? If the car itself symbolizes one kind of payoff for hard work, the assembly line symbolizes the kind of hard work an industrial society seems to require. It embodies the philosophy of "scientific management" as pioneered by Frederick Taylor, the industrial engineer armed with stopwatch and slide rule.

In the early years of this century, Taylorism burst on the scene with a host of "scientific" theories about eradicating inefficiency and applying technology to the industrial process. But accompanying some sound engineering principles, Taylorism also introduced a set of sociological assumptions that were arbitrary, naïve and offensive. These took for granted the sharpest possible split between management and labor. In Taylorism, the working man, often an immigrant, was assumed to be an ignorant, uneducated, unmotivated but physically strong creature who could, oxlike, be forced to do productive work once management, with its superior intelligence, succeeded in breaking work into its simplest components. The worker, then, had merely to be trained in mindless repetitive motions. It was Taylorism that Charlie Chaplin mocked in his classic film of the thirties, *Modern Times.*

The assembly-line managers never assumed that the men who worked the line needed to be motivated to do a good job, only that

---

* "The Impact of Scarcities," loc. cit.

adequate wages would induce workers to accept its discipline, and that economic insecurity would keep them "in line." Few assembly-line workers speak well of the hard, grimy and monotonous work. Nor are they expected to.

Nonetheless, for many years most hourly workers showed up most of the time (if less so on Mondays and Fridays than midweek), and they did produce cars. To improve productivity, management depended on capital investment, management systems and technology, not on the motivation of the worker on the line.

These systems did improve productivity, and with it the automobile worker's standard of living as negotiated by the unions. With this success, "scientific management" seemed vindicated. It had passed the hard test of pragmatism: it worked. In retrospect, however, it is likely that it worked *despite* and not because of the theories of scientific management. In the 1950s and 1960s, assembly-line workers, like the majority of the work force, were mostly married men, sole providers for their families. In keeping with the traditional work ethic, those men were expected to sacrifice for their families, and work on the assembly line permitted them to do so in full measure.

While such sacrifice was not always welcome, most men accepted the need for it with good grace, though sometimes the humiliation was hard to swallow: not only was line work difficult and monotonous, but the men were tied to time clocks, their toilet and smoking breaks were strictly monitored and, in contrast to salaried workers, they were discouraged from using the telephone or "schmoozing" on the job. Many Americans would be shocked by the rigidity of the social-class barriers separating hourly workers from salaried employees in the automobile industry.* But throughout most of the postwar period, the sacrifice was acceptable to most of the family men because it underscored the importance of the man's role as he-who-brings-home-the-one-and-only-paycheck.

But on the line, the symptoms of worker frustration were visible everywhere: in absenteeism, tardiness, carelessness, indifference, high turnover, numbers of union grievances, slowdowns in the periods preceding collective bargaining and even sabotage. Mostly, worker frustration showed in poor product quality. Management reacted by adding layer upon layer of costly supervisory and control systems in accordance with its view of labor relations as an adversary process. As recently as

---

* Robert Schrank, *Ten Thousand Working Days* (Cambridge, Mass.: M.I.T. Press, 1978).

the late seventies, the University of Michigan reported that 27 percent of all American workers, more than one out of four, felt so ashamed of the quality of the products they were producing that they would not want to buy them themselves.*

Clearly, nothing can be further from the values of self-fulfillment seekers than the class-conscious, hierarchical, authoritarian, adversarial attitudes that characterize the managerial outlook in many American industries. Balking at these attitudes, workers engaged in the search for self-fulfillment retaliate by holding back their commitment, if not their labor. They resent sharp social class distinctions between employee and employer. They do not automatically accept the authority of the boss. They want to participate in decisions that affect their work. They prefer variety to routine and informality to formalism. They want their work to be interesting as well as to pay well and to give them an outlet for creativity. They seek responsibility and they like to set their own goals. They enjoy working in small groups in a relationship of collegiality rather than in a rigid hierarchy. They desire constant feedback: a running commentary on how they are doing on the job.

In short, they are struggling to revise the giving/getting compact in the workplace: for them to give themselves unstintingly to the job, they demand in return important psychological incentives as well as economic ones. These demands make them troublesome to work with—as a condition of their commitment they are constantly demanding things for themselves. But there is increasing evidence that the work style they prefer may be far more productive in tomorrow's service/information/ high technology economy than the work relationships of the past.

To strengthen its competitive position in the world, the automobile industry, along with others, has now begun to experiment with new approaches to worker productivity. Its experiments take a new attitude toward the worker. General Motors, for example, has developed a new approach to the workers who make its cars in several plants that had previously suffered from low productivity and poor worker morale. In the experimental plants, the assumptions of Taylorism have been swept aside and replaced by precepts such as these:

· The people on the line who are assembling the cars may have good ideas about how to improve productivity that managers do not have.

* Robert P. Quinn and Graham L. Staines, *1977 Quality of Employment Survey*, Survey Research Center of the Institute for Social Research (Ann Arbor: University of Michigan, 1979).

· Workers should have a voice in decisions that affect their job, and if heeded, productivity and product quality should improve.

· At least some workers should have their work made as interesting and challenging as possible—and should share the rewards of success.

· Workers should be treated with dignity and class lines between management and labor should be blurred.

These experiments based on the value system of self-fulfillment seekers have now begun to pay off, and General Motors has vastly expanded them and promoted the executives who helped to make them work.

Buying smaller, more fuel-efficient cars and humanizing the workplace do not by themselves "prove" that the new rules will be more adaptive than the old ones to the economic environment of the future. But they do indicate that there is more to the search for self-fulfillment than self-concern. And they do suggest that Americans concerned with quality-of-life issues may be a potent source of new economic energy. For the economic changes the search for self-fulfillment stimulates do not stop with cars. For example, owning one's home has long been part of the American dream. But inflation is now making this dream impossible for millions of Americans. As the old status rules weaken further, Americans will no longer insist that a "home" be the traditional free-standing single-dwelling unit with lawn, picket fence and dog. In the coming years we can expect to see an explosion of new types of "homes": cooperatives, condominiums, multiple-dwelling units, houses built to be shared by singles or by other types of "timesharing" occupants. The search for self-fulfillment combined with limited economic means is derigidifying the housing market.

The values associated with the search for self-fulfillment are also transforming how we dress (more casually and in a more variegated fashion), how we eat (with greater consciousness of physical well-being), how we take care of ourselves (less dependency on the "expert," more self-care), how we spend our leisure time and in general how we live our lives. The economic consequences of these changes are difficult to exaggerate.

In the postwar era it was widely assumed that the problems of production were solved and that the national task was simply to consume as much as we could. Inevitably, the emphasis on consumption led to a heightened concern with self—the ultimate object of consumer values. For three decades we consumed mightily and we struggled to break the fetters of a restrictive culture. But now we confront a radically new condition: the economy is less productive than it needs to be, while the culture is exploding with vitality. And so, the national task changes. The objective is no longer to expand the frontiers of consumption; it is to build a more productive economy and at the same time a society in which the cravings of the spirit as well as material well-being can be satisfied. The life experiments of millions of Americans are breeding strategies to achieve these new goals.

Let us now turn to these experiments and the people who are conducting them—scanting neither their weaknesses nor their strengths.

Part II

Experiments in Self-Fulfillment

Chapter 5

⚫

The Strong Form of the Self-Fulfillment Predicament

Mark and Abby Williams are both in their early thirties. He is a lawyer; she is an assistant editor of a magazine published for stockholders by a large multinational chemical company. She makes $36,000 a year. He works in a public interest law firm and earns $24,000 a year. In my interview with him, Mark claims he is delighted that Abby makes more money than he does—adding quickly that he is doing what he wants to do: He is staying clear of the "corporate jungle" and using his skills to "humanize the system" from within.

The Williamses have been married for six years. For the first five years they delayed having children so that each could establish a firm base for future careers. They are still delaying. Abby, in her interview, said she would like to have a baby, and that one child would be enough. She added that she is reluctant to take a long five- or six-year break at this stage in her career just when she is beginning to edit entire issues of the magazine on her own. But if she has a child she would want to take at least a six-year leave. Unlike many of her women friends who returned to full-time jobs within months after their babies were born, she is convinced that it would be unfair to an infant to be cared for by strangers. She believes a child needs a full-time mother—at least until it is five or six years old, and she is struggling to find a balance that would acknowledge both her own goals and a child's needs. Also, tensions have begun to crop up in her marriage, and that too makes her reluctant to become pregnant.

She talks about these easily. Without ever having agreed explicitly to an "open" marriage, in fact having more than once argued with Mark that it would be too risky, she admits that though she doesn't want to appear possessive, she has been silently "going along" with a way of life that makes extramarital affairs all too easy to carry out. She and Mark both "work late" several nights a week, and it is understood that no questions will be asked. She is almost certain Mark is sleeping with one of his clients, a recent college graduate named Robin who got caught in a drug mess and is now in trouble with the law for selling cocaine.

Abby admits that she, too, experimented with brief affairs, but she did not pursue them. While seeing nothing morally wrong with them in principle, she says nonetheless she found herself flooded with guilt. If she and Mark drift away from each other, as she suspects they might, she does not want to have a child. In the past few years she observes that their relationship has seemed more like a strained friendship than a marriage.

In the interview she confides that she now often finds herself in a conflicted mood. She knows that she has more freedom to shape her own life than her mother had. (Her mother, in most respects a conventional woman, had a few years earlier abruptly divorced her husband of twenty-eight years and moved to San Jose where she now lives with a wealthy Volkswagen dealer.) Abby is determined to avoid her mother's long years of playing what she called "Mrs. Dutiful Wife-and-mother." She likes being married, even though she says her needs for sexual fulfillment and intimacy are not being fully met by her husband. Eventually she wants a child "to fulfill my maternal needs." She wants to travel more, spend more time with friends, read more, listen to music and relax and enjoy life more than she has been doing, savoring the fruits of her hard work "while I still have the vigor to appreciate those other values." She does not, she says, resent paying most of the rent and food expenses. She *does*, however, resent her husband's assumption that this is how it should be, because his job, at least as he sees it, has greater social value than hers.

She cherishes her job: both the good pay and the work that she finds constantly stimulating. But she is worried about whether the corporation will be willing to entrust the editor's job to a woman when the present editor, a sixty-three-year-old man, retires. Apart from a personnel manager and an outside woman director, added only recently, there are few women executives in the company. She has recently heard rumors that the increasing cost of paper and other inflationary pressures may cause the company to give up the magazine or cut it back severely. If this were to happen, she fears she would lose her job.

At least once a week for the past year she has experienced what she calls "mini-anxiety attacks." During these episodes her optimism is drained as if by vacuum, and she feels dry-mouthed and empty. At such moments her throat tightens and she begins to panic, fearing that she is going to lose everything she now has. A recurring fantasy of growing fat and slovenly frightens her. Abby finds herself identifying with "those shopping-bag ladies who dig around in wastebaskets and sleep outdoors on benches."

These episodes do not last long; she pushes them out of her mind. In explaining them, she says: "I guess it is guilt. My mother always warned me not to be too piggy and self-centered. Sometimes I feel I really am part of the 'me generation,' too preoccupied with my own needs and wishes. I really don't think this is true though. I don't think I'm a narcissist; I care too much about other people. But sometimes I'm afraid of ending up with nothing just because I crave so much out of life." Later she adds, "I know you can't have everything. But I'm not sure what to give up and what to hang on to. Sometimes I feel like all the doors in the world are open to me and yet at other times I feel as if they are all closing."

Her husband Mark is also caught in conflict. He complains that Abby is pushing him too hard. He says that sometimes he wonders whether she makes so many demands on him because she is earning more money than he at her "chemical factory." He has also begun to wonder whether it makes as much sense as he once thought to give so much time and emotional involvement to his legal-aid service. "It's futile," he comments. "You help people one day and they are in trouble the next."

Mark comments bitterly that the budget for his legal-aid group gets shaved every year. "The government," he says, "is slowly choking us to death because we take on some of the other government agencies. They don't like to have their feathers ruffled." Some of the lawyers get steady annual raises despite the budget cuts, enabling them to keep up with inflation. Others do not, and he is one of the others. Mark wonders whether he is being discriminated against because he is white. The legal staff, once all white, is now mixed and he thinks the minority lawyers make out better financially than the white ones do. He says he hates the thought and he hates himself for thinking it, since fighting discrimination is what attracted him to the job in the first place.

He says he stays with the job because he can't stand the idea of "working to make the rich richer" in some well-connected law firm. Ideally, he would like to be able to "make a difference in the world," to have an impact on his times. He admits though that he also wants to make more money. He wants to hold on to his marriage with Abby. He says he loves her but he speaks of his warm and tender feelings for his client, Robin, the former Bryn Mawr literature major whom he is helping with legal advice. He says he needs the freedom to be with women. He cherishes the warmth and the intimacy of such relationships. "It's not only the sex," he claims, "but it just isn't possible to be truly close to someone unless the relationship has a sexual dimension." (His interview is sprinkled with words like "dimension" and "proclivity" and "process.")

He and Abby have an "understanding": He says his relationships with other women do not threaten their marriage. He is annoyed with Abby for putting off having a baby. He agrees that she should stay home and take care of a child until it is at least six years old. But he also admits he is used to having Abby working and bringing home a good salary. If she were home with a baby, he fears she would be more demanding, pressing him to stay home in the evenings. He has often heard her complain about her father "shortchanging" her mother by being away from home so much.

Unlike Abby, Mark does not have anxiety attacks. His temperament, he says, is different. He is neither as optimistic as she nor do his moods get as low. "But I walk around in a state of constant anger," he admits. "It's nothing serious. I'm used to it by now." A few minutes later he adds: "I value my freedom and independence more than almost anything I can think of. It is true, I'm asking for a lot. But I don't think it's too much. Sometimes I feel everything is shit. Everybody is out for himself. People don't really care anymore . . . If I had to calculate the odds I would say there is about the same chance I'll end up empty-handed as there is that I'll get what I want out of life. Maybe I'll give it all up and live in Maine. Robin has a brother with a house forty miles outside of Bangor, and we're invited to live there with him. I think I could build up a practice in Bangor. The more I think about it, the more tempted I am. If it weren't for Abby I think I'd give it a try."

(ii)

Abby repeats several times in her interview that she is distressed about her periodic anxiety attacks. I had the impression that she sensed a message was struggling to break through the surface—a message she does not want to confront. A remark about her mother's moralizing proved an effective way of deflecting my questions away from a threatening area of inquiry. Throughout the interview Abby, like Mark, implied that while she has many of the things she desires in life, she nonetheless feels up in the air about her life as a whole. Her decisions have a tentative character. Her commitments are qualified. She senses that she could withdraw from any one of them tomorrow—marriage, the prospect of children, living in an apartment in the city, even the editing career which challenges and stimulates her. She feels that the ground beneath her is not solid, that she is not firmly rooted.

She criticizes Mark for *his* lack of stability and commitment. Referring to his frequent suggestions that they move to another part of the country and adopt a different style of life, she says, "Everyone needs stable roots. You can't keep pulling the plant up by the roots every day to see how it is doing." Pointing to the orange tree in their sparsely furnished living room, she says, "What do you think would happen to that tree if I yanked it up and replanted it in another kind of soil and kept doing that over and over and over again? Even if the tree survived, it would be mess." As if reading Mark's mind—and not liking what she finds there—she says bitingly, "What kind of marriage is it if every day two people ask themselves, 'Should we stay married? Should we separate and divorce? Should we each go our own way?' "

Abby avoids taking a close look at her own choices because she finds it difficult to think about them clearly. Whenever she tries, she says she ends up frustrated and confused. I came away from the interview with her convinced that one source of confusion derives from the language she employs when describing her goals and wishes. She spins a web of words that trips her in its tangled threads.

In talking about herself she refers to her "emotional needs," her "sexual needs," her "material needs," her "need to be challenged intellectually," her "need to assert herself." When she discusses her "unfilled potentials" and her "need to keep growing," she seems to take these metaphors literally—almost as if she believes the process of filling her unmet needs is like filling a set of wine glasses at a dinner party: the more needs filled, the greater the self-fulfillment.

With this language of "need" she intermixes a sprinkling of words that carry a heavy burden of moral judgment. She condemns her own "selfishness" and "self-centeredness." Inevitably she turns to the trendy term "narcissism," endowing it with a moralistic meaning and using it in Lasch's sense to mean selfishness of an extreme form. Yet the great psychoanalytic writer Erik Erikson tells us not to forget that Narcissus after all was a good-looking fellow who derived genuine pleasure from glancing at his reflection in the water.

An excessive use of "need" language, borrowed from self-psychology, makes it hard for her to think clearly. She can't arrive at lucid judgments about her life in these terms. She can't understand her true choices—within the private world she has created for herself as well as within the larger world she shares with others.

(iii)

This brief sketch of Mark and Abby Williams along with the others in this book comes from a series of several hundred interviews I carried out, with the help of my associates, in various cities throughout the country. We worked in Dayton, Ohio; Dallas, Texas; Boston, Massachusetts; New York, New York; Omaha, Nebraska; San Francisco, California; Atlanta, Georgia; Des Moines, Iowa; Columbus, Indiana; Denver, Colorado; New Orleans, Louisiana; Seattle, Washington; Tempe, Arizona; Los Angeles, California; and other places. In these interviews I requested each person to describe what self-fulfillment and success meant to him or her in the most personal sense of these terms. The people I interviewed discussed their values, moral convictions and life goals. I asked them to contrast their own personal feelings about success and self-fulfillment with how their parents felt about these matters and pursued them in their own lives. I also asked each person to recount the risks he or she has taken for the sake of success and self-fulfillment, and the risks each has chosen to shun.

Most people talked freely about their goals and accomplishments. They spoke about the compromises they had made in their lives, and about their failures. They described what they have given up and what they have managed to hold on to. They forecast what they see ahead for themselves. And they related their own personal prospects to their sense of where the country is heading.

I did these interviews in order to evoke the complexity and individuality of people's lives. And yet, for a study such as this, life-history interviews are not enough. We also need larger, more scientific cross-section studies of the population as a whole. In recent years books based exclusively on life-history interviews have grown in popularity, and deservedly so. Books such as Studs Terkel's *Working* and *American Dreams: Lost and Found*; Kenneth Keniston's youth studies of the sixties, *The Young Radicals*, and *The Uncommitted*; Gail Sheehy's

Passages; Bernard Lefkowitz's *Breaktime*; Ellen Goodman's *Turning Points*, and many others succeed in showing the special qualities of individual life in a manner that no statistical survey, however subtle, can do.

But the methodological limitations of this life-history-interview method are severe. It is impossible from studies based only on small numbers of individual interviews to track changes in the culture at large. In what respects are the Mullers, the Williamses, the Agnolis and the Greensons unique? In what respects are they typical, either of a particular group or of mainstream America? Which of their beliefs or actions personify changes in the culture at large, as distinct from changes taking place in subcultures, or simply in their own lives? Life histories cannot answer such questions, but national cross-section studies can.

The value of combining the two methods—integrating findings from national studies with life histories—is that it enhances both: each is strong precisely where the other is weak. National survey data give the analyst a powerful solvent: with it he can separate from the rich ore of each life history what is representative of the society at large (or sub-groups within it) without destroying the irreducible uniqueness of the individual.

In this book, therefore, in addition to the life histories, I also draw upon a number of large national surveys. Some are in the public domain, others are not, and I have drawn on this latter group prudently. One of the national surveys based on a cross section of fifteen hundred Americans was conducted exclusively for this book; another national study of three thousand working Americans was re-analyzed in a special fashion for this book. I have used these and other surveys to illuminate the life histories, and used the life histories to illustrate the survey findings.

The survey data suggest that in most respects Mark and Abby Williams are not typical of the majority of Americans. Unlike Mark and Abby, most Americans do not subject their marriages, their jobs and their lives to a constant bombardment of doubt and reappraisal. There are, however, two respects in which our surveys show that the Williamses *are* typical. One is that their lives exhibit in an intense form the effects of the changing psychoculture that the majority experiences in a more attenuated form. Like the Williamses, the majority of Americans find themselves wrestling with the question of what they should give and what they can hope to get out of their marriages, their jobs, their lives —the giving/getting compact. They may not probe at these issues as frequently and relentlessly, but the dilemmas are clearly present. We saw these questions emerge in the histories of the Mullers, Agnolis and Greensons, and we will see them reflected again in other interviews and survey statistics.

Like millions of others, the Williamses are concerned with the meaning of money in the increasingly prevalent dual-wage-earner family. In earning more than her husband, Abby is decidedly atypical. And Mark is atypical in claiming that this does not bother him. (There are signs in the interview that at some level of consciousness it bothers him a great deal.) In our surveys we find that the meaning of money is changing for the majority of Americans. It remains as important as ever, but its symbolic and emotional significance is shifting. Money has many shared meanings, both practical and symbolic. Like sex in relation to love, the issue of money in relation to personal success is loaded with ambiguity. It is valued for the possibilities of enjoyment it opens up: one needs money for possessions, for travel, for leisure, for the "full, rich life." Money is also valued as a symbol of social worth. Money has been the main yardstick Americans use for judging other people's social standing—where they fit in the social hierarchy from lower-class poor to upper-class rich. It is this use of money as a measure for placing people in social strata that has been changing in recent years, especially as a growing majority of married couples depend on two incomes. We will come back to this theme in later chapters. It constitutes one of the most significant shifts in American culture.

Along with the majority of Americans, the Williamses are also affected by shifting sex mores, especially the meaning of sexual fidelity in marriage and what attitude to adopt toward it. In common with the majority they are also struggling with the meaning of fairness and unfairness in the division of effort between husband and wife, with the question of the proper amount of attention to be apportioned to child care, with finding a suitable life style, with defining work and career, and with many other themes associated with the new psychoculture.

The other respect in which the Williamses typify the majority of Americans is that they have more opportunity to shape their lives than their parents did. They welcome, indeed they rejoice in the freedom this gives them. Even with manifold uncertainties about their marriage, their jobs and themselves, they know that any family they might have would be small (one child), and that Abby would resume her career after seeing her child through infancy. Conflict-ridden decisions to be sure, but born of a freedom to adapt their lives to their own standards. In feeling that more choices are open to them than to their parents at a comparable age, the Williamses *are* clearly typical of the majority. This conviction is one of the defining features of the psychoculture and it is worth documenting.

To learn how people compare the choices open to them with those available to their parents I carried out a special survey among a national cross section of fifteen hundred Americans. The survey revealed that 73 percent of Americans feel they have "more freedom of choice" on how to live their lives than their parents did. Only 8 percent believe they have fewer choices; 17 percent report the same level of choice as their parents; 2 percent are not sure. Furthermore, an overwhelming 80 percent feel confident that they will be able to carry out these choices and live their lives the way they "truly want to live." An almost equal number (75 percent) claim that they are at least as happy as their parents or happier (only 20 percent say they are unhappier). Moreover, most demographic variations are negligible. These convictions are shared by men and women equally; by conservatives, moderates and liberals; by Catholics, Protestants and Jews; by whites and nonwhites and by people living in various parts of the country. There are a few slight variations by age and education. Older Americans and those without a college education report less confidence that they will be able to live their lives as they wish: they are less prone to state they are happier than their parents were, and fewer of them believe they have more freedom than their parents to choose how they will live. But even here the differences are not great: they do not drop by more than five to ten percentage points from the high levels of belief in greater choice registered by younger, better-educated Americans.

I consider this feeling of abundant choice one of the major forces shaping American culture today. Most Americans picture their parents' lives as having been hemmed in by economic, social and educational constraints which they themselves have fortunately escaped. It is a straightforward conviction, expressed typically from a variety of interviews in the following manner:

> "I have more choices than my parents did."
>
> "I can do what I want with my life; they couldn't."
>
> "I can afford to take chances they could never risk."
>
> "I have it easier than they did, and I appreciate it."
>
> "I haven't had to do without things the way they did."
>
> "I have a lot more than both my parents—and not just the tangibles."

"I'm getting more out of life than they did. For my mother, it was just family all the time."

"There was less of a gap between what they wanted and what they got than there is for me—but that's because they didn't have the choices I do."

"I have more possessions than my parents did, and more chances and choices. Times have changed."

"My parents operated in a different era. We have done more memorable things than they have. We can do more."

"My parents would say the same things I say, but they haven't *done* what I've done."

Americans who see their parents in this perspective do not necessarily think of themselves as better people, but they do believe they have more options to exercise than their parents did in the important domains of marriage, sex, family, work, travel, education, friends, possessions, where to live and how to live.

When it comes to making these choices, the majority have a much clearer sense than do Mark and Abby about what they want. Mark and Abby's ever-present conflict over what choices to make are decidedly atypical of mainstream America, but not their conviction that, unlike their parents, they have the freedom to choose.

(iv)

Although Mark and Abby are not typical of the majority they *are* typical of a special minority: people in whose lives the self-fulfillment motif stands out prominently. In interviews such people assert that self-fulfillment is vitally important to them, and their lives validate their claim. Because they are pursuing their self-fulfillment with great intensity, all of the conundrums and conflicts associated with the pursuit are as visible in their lives as the muscles of a weight lifter's body.

The Williamses portray the "strong form" of the self-fulfillment predicament whose most distinctive feature is that it ensnares people like the Williamses in a confusing triple bind. First, they find themselves presented with an abundance of choices about what to do with their lives, without, however, knowing how to make the right choices. Often they value their personal freedom so intensely that they regard each new choice and commitment demanded of them as a threat to their freedom and a challenge to other possibilities they might also exercise. The question of what to commit to and sacrifice for thus remains forever open, making their lives unsettled. This is the first bind.

Characteristically, also, they desire forms of self-fulfillment and success that presuppose a cooperative economic and social environment. Their goals take for granted continuing affluence, abundant career opportunities, flexible work arrangements, low-cost travel, diverse outlets for personal creativity, low burdens of responsibility, and so forth. Unfortunately, a low-growth, inflation-ridden and shortage-plagued economic environment with its troubling undercurrent of social/political stress creates conditions that are growing less hospitable to some of their self-fulfillment goals. This is the second bind.

The third bind concerns their interpretive framework: those most strongly absorbed in a self-fulfillment quest see the world and themselves through categories of thought borrowed from theories of self-psychology. They speak the tongue of "need" language: they are forever preoccupied with their inner psychological needs. They operate on the premise that emotional cravings are sacred objects and that it is a crime against nature to harbor an unfulfilled emotional need. This psychological attitude affects precisely those crisis points in their lives when their attention might more productively be turned outward— toward the world and its vicissitudes.

In 1979, Yankelovich, Skelly and White conducted a study among almost three thousand working Americans. As a representative sample of all those employed either full- or part-time, this study allowed our analysts to probe the values and motivations of the majority of adult Americans who now find themselves connected to the workforce. In the study we used a computer program called the Singleton segmentation procedure. The special virtue of this procedure is its objectivity: it locates factors that differentiate among groups of people without being "told" in advance what those characteristics might be.

The Singleton pattern showed one group of working Americans placing their personal self-fulfillment high above all other concerns— above money, security, performing well or working at a satisfying job. The computer analysis identified that segment of the American working population most thoroughly involved in the quest for self-fulfillment.

This group constitutes about 17 percent of all working Americans (approximately seventeen million people). They are younger than average, and more of them are professionals than among average Americans, while fewer are married or own their own home. In their politics they lean more toward the liberal than toward the conservative wings of

CHART A

THE STRONG FORM OF THE SELF-FULFILLMENT PREDICAMENT

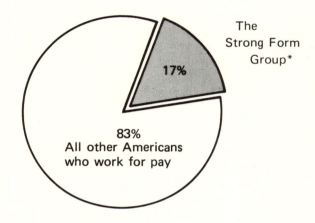

The
Strong Form
Group*

17%

83%
All other Americans
who work for pay

	Strong Formers	All Others
	(100%)	(100%)
Under 35 years of age	75	51
Some college education	51	35
Parents with some college education	42	21
Professionals	24	12
White collar	51	38
Married	47	65
Rent (rather than own) home or apartment	44	32
No religious affiliation	17	6
Liberal Democrat or Republican	61	43

* Because this analysis was conducted among Americans who work for pay, it ex-
cludes several large groups: housewives, full-time students, retired people, and the
unemployed. The proportion of strong formers among these groups is not known
since data are lacking, but it is almost surely smaller than among those who work
for pay since, except for full-time college students (4% of the adult population),
the other nonworking groups have lower levels of college education than the working population, especially the unemployed and the retired.

the Democratic or Republican parties. They are also the best educated of five groups differentiated by the Singleton procedure, with more than half (51 percent) having received at least some college education. And their parents have much more college education than the rest of the working population (42 percent to 21 percent).

Chart A shows the key demographic differences that differentiate this group from other working Americans.

The differences in age and education are perhaps the most worth noting. Clearly, the strong form of the self-fulfillment predicament affects the younger, better-educated elements of the population more than others. This is not surprising. In many studies we find cultural change linked with college education and with the perspectives people develop when exposed to the college subculture. American culture is split into many subcultures, each with its own set of beliefs, rituals and shared meanings. Many of us live in one or another of these subcultures for extended periods of time—the corporate world, the sports world, the labor movement, the military, the art world. The college subculture probably exercises the most powerful pull of all on those exposed to it, though not because it indoctrinates people with a cogent or unified ideology. The reason is simply that people are exposed to the world of higher education and its influences at an impressionable stage of their lives. Four years of life at a live-in college is for most people an indelible experience: attitudes and values acquired in college and graduate school—for good or bad—often last a lifetime.

Mark and Abby Williams are typical of the well-educated strong formers in several ways. They feel liberated from many of the economic and moral exigencies that dominated their parents' lives, but are thrust into their new freedom without a map to guide them. They find their freedom exhilarating, and they take seriously the responsibility of designing their lives according to a plan of their own choosing. But they embrace a theory of freedom that seems to presuppose that you are free only when you do not commit yourself irrevocably.

They are also typical of the strong-form group in being surprised and troubled by the possibility that the world may not cooperate with their desires. It is as if they had assumed that the obstacles to their self-fulfillment would always be internal—conflicts within their own psyches about what they "really want out of life"—the assumption being that once their goals were clear, accomplishing them would present few practical problems.

Often, like Abby, people in the strong-form group hold both an upbeat and downbeat view of their future at the same time—the paradox expressed by Abby as a feeling that "all doors are open to me . . . and yet at the same time they are closing." Exuberance is shot through with anxiety. Willfulness is coupled with a crippling sense of powerlessness. Decisiveness is undercut by confusion. And the warmth of self-acceptance is muted by an odd feeling of estrangement from the world. They are not sure how to choose and they are reluctant to risk freedom by making commitments that may prove irrevocable. They seek to preserve their freedom by failing to risk it. They do not see themselves as part and parcel of an ongoing social world, progressively discovering themselves in relation to their work, their friends, families and the larger society. Rather, they are isolated—some might say existential—units, related intimately only to their own psyches. People like Abby Williams might be readier to adapt to the tumultuous environment that confronts them if they realized that they do not have to regard their every "need" as sacred. Abby, for one, might even be relieved to hear it.

Chapter 6

———◆———

A Nonrebel in Rebel's Clothing

Whenever she speaks of her childhood, adolescence and twelve years of married life, Sara Lou Wellford recalls with astonishment her total conformity to the social norms with which she was brought up. In retrospect, she can hardly believe how thoroughly she played roles shaped by the expectations of others. In nearly all respects her present life repudiates the rules she was brought up to observe, and therefore she sees herself as a rebel. But, as we shall see, Sara Lou Wellford is not by temperament, character or inclination an authority-flaunting and rebellious person. Genuine nonconformity—violating the dominant social norms of the times—would make her so acutely uncomfortable that, like millions of other Americans, she would probably have chosen to endure and accept a lifetime of frustration had it not been for the large shifts in the country's cultural climate. Suddenly, the cultural climate seemed to encourage her rebellion instead of crushing her when she chose to act.

At thirty-six, Sara Lou Wellford has just come through four and a half years of frenetic activity that have transformed her life. Brought up in Birmingham, Alabama, by parents she describes as "quite conventional," she was "reared to be a Southern lady—pleasant, thoughtful and gracious. I was trained to please people, to do what others defined and not make personal choices or take personal risks."

A responsive child, she absorbed these and other lessons well. "The message I got from my parents said that success was how well one did in the eyes of others and what others thought of you. I was to marry well, which I did, and that was success to them."

For the twenty years she lived at home with her parents two motifs dominated her life: conforming to the wishes of others even to the point of playing a false role in order to please them, and learning to value success as defined by money and social position.

During her adolescent years she had dreamed of becoming a doctor, "to help humanity." Later she recognized this dream as "indulgence in self-glory" and, pushing it into the background, moved toward the acceptable compromise expected of a girl in her social circle. Instead of becoming a physician herself, she found one. "At age twenty," she says, "I married a doctor, and my family was delighted."

Actually, he was only a medical student, but he came from a good family and it was agreed that his prospects were excellent. Since his career was not yet launched, Sara Lou found a job and worked while raising a family. "I worked as a medical technician to put him through school. Then I worked so he could specialize. Then my children's opportunities came next: their education and social environment. That was twelve years of Blake's goals and then the children's. My role was as the giver. I accepted it because society expected it." In retrospect, she feels those years were "like being asleep."

She also went along with the prevalent sexual morality. "I grew up with a traditional approach to men and women and their roles. I liked male dominance and my own passive role. When I got married I assumed those sacred vows were not to be questioned. I never even thought of having an affair. When my husband told me he had affairs, I was hurt and angry. But, after all, he was a man. Wasn't it okay for a man?"

Her husband told her about his affairs in the fifth year of their marriage. She stayed with the marriage another seven years. In its last few years her discontent grew, and she decided to make a break. She had hesitated for years, yet once her mind was made up she acted swiftly. She and Blake agreed, more or less amicably, to separate. By then a prominent specialist, he agreed to generous child-support arrangements, but not to alimony. She accepted his offer, took the two boys, moved out of the big house in Birmingham into an apartment near the University of Alabama in Tuscaloosa, and immediately undertook a heavy course load to complete her college credits. Once she had her college degree, she applied to law school in Birmingham, was accepted, moved back into the city, worked "like a maniac" in her first year, made Law Review in her second year and was elected an editor. The following year she graduated from law school, found a "good job with a good firm" in San Francisco, packed her belongings and moved the two boys (now ages ten and fourteen) and herself to an apartment near the Bay.

The years following the separation were tense ones, the strain coming mainly from the tug between her children's needs and her own conception of self-fulfillment. In law school, after a brief stint at Law Review, the conflict grew so great that she decided to drop her editorship. "I finally decided to give up Law Review and the prestige that went with it. Time for my kids was more important . . . It was a hard decision but it was the right one and I'm glad I had the discipline to do it."

Of law school she says, "Those years took their toll on me. I was always doing a balancing act in order to have more time with the kids. Even so, I have a lot of guilt about my sons and their desire for me to be a P.T.A. mom. But I just can't do that."

The conflict was most acute over her decision to leave Birmingham. Her sons wanted desperately to stay, but she felt she had to accept this risk as well as all the other risks of the previous four and a half years. She says, "Leaving Blake, giving up my economic security and moving out of the house after twelve years of marriage was probably the first risk I had ever taken in my life. Going to law school was an even greater risk. The move to San Francisco when my kids and all my friends said I should stay in Birmingham has also been an enormous risk. Even meeting new and different people is a type of risk. I've had to say, 'To hell with the accepted advice of friends and family,' and go and experience something new."

Beyond the risks, she feels one other big drawback to her present way of life: "What I miss most right now is a good sex life. Shortly after I was divorced I started to express myself sexually. I went through a period of one-night stands, bedding with virtual strangers. Then I realized that while I don't need marriage for sex I do need respect for successful intimacies with others. Those casual relationships were self-destructive."

In contrasting her present views with those of her parents, Sara Lou observes, "My parents didn't agonize over self-fulfillment, or even discuss it. Success meant money to them and money meant self-fulfillment." But she vehemently rejects this syllogism. "My mother was tied up in traditional unthinking choices. She had to settle for less in life than I

have. She was constrained by her inability to take risks. It had nothing
to do with her. People had few choices in her day."

Where did Sara Lou's wider range of choices come from? What convinced her that she did not have to settle for her mother's "traditional
unthinking choices"? When did she sense she could afford to take risks
an earlier generation had forbidden? She explains these changes in herself in the language of the women's movement. She speaks of "becoming conscious" as if it were a single memorable event in her life, a
moment of blinding insight. But she makes clear that the process of
"becoming conscious" took place gradually over the final five years of
her marriage to Blake.

What did "becoming conscious" mean to her? She says it meant
the search for self, for the "real person" who was buried beneath layers
of role-playing and conformity to other people's expectations. "I used to
be naïve enough to think my identity revolved around my relationship
to other people. My identity used to be my role as wife and mother. My
earlier views toward success and toward myself were what other people
defined, not what was inside me. Now my identity is more as a person
in my own right."

In particular, Sara Lou cherishes her freedom to conceive of life
as a voyage of exploration, including self-exploration. Law school was
an adventure. The new job is an adventure. San Francisco is an adventure. She says that the idea of "fighting and winning new battles" fills
her with excitement and anticipation.

Recalling the struggles of the past four and a half years she sums
up with a sigh. "Finding self-fulfillment is not easy. It is a serious and
difficult pursuit." She adds quietly, "But it can be done. And I am
doing it."

(ii)

What finally leads people like Sara Lou to shift from long-suffering
acceptance to *act* on their dissatisfactions and to rebuild their lives from
top to bottom? The median duration of all marriages ending in divorce is
slightly more than six years; her marriage lasted twice that long. We do
not have to guess about Sara Lou's attitudes in the early years of her
marriage; we have her own clearly stated views. She says she accepted
the socially approved role of wife and mother as natural, comfortable
and fulfilling. She was "the giver" in the giving/getting compact, and
thus "very much a part of the mainstream." Only later in her marriage

did she experience this same role as alienating, demeaning and destructive of her "real self."

What caused the change? She says she was disillusioned by Blake's infidelities, but her marriage went on for seven years afterwards. She tells us that at a point late in her married life, she rejected her self-identification with her mother, whom she came to see as representing the passive, conformist side of her nature, and instead chose, as a deliberate act of will, to identify with her father. Her father symbolized vigorous action, self-sufficiency and control over life, in contrast to the victim role she assigned to her mother. Why did she decide as a thirty year old to shift her identification from one parent to another? The classic process of identifying with parents takes place at much earlier stages in the life cycle, in childhood and adolescence, and it develops unconsciously. Sara Lou did not behave as she did because she had begun to identify with her father. It was the other way around: she chose to identify with her father because she had decided, in her own words, "to act more like a man."

In an earlier era it would have seemed odd for someone with Sara Lou's upbringing to choose suddenly "to act like a man," to win other people's acceptance of this new role and to proceed, successfully, to carry out her project. This could happen only in a period and an atmosphere where stereotypes of "ladylike" behavior had begun to break down without being replaced by new norms unrelated to gender.

Had Sara Lou chosen, as in her mother's time and world of shared meanings, to "act like a woman" she would have had several options. She might have begun discreet affairs of her own. Or, she might have confronted Blake, insisting upon greater fidelity. (She says she never "really had it out with him," but just grew bitter.) Or she might have chosen to ignore the subject, resenting only Blake's telling her what she preferred not to know. All else failing, she might have divorced him and found herself "another Blake," preferrably one who played around less, but who fit comfortably into her way of life.

But she did none of these things. Acting with great vigor she re-created her life, virtually reversing all her former beliefs, identifications and values.

We have no way of knowing the "real" motives of Sara Lou Wellford. It would be easy, for example, to emphasize her psychological problems, for these play an important role in her life. She mentions that she is often anxious and depressed, she overeats and has more than once sought psychotherapy. Self-sufficiency and the need for control surface as recurring themes in the interview. Dependency on her husband made her feel vulnerable. Transient relations with other men also made her feel vulnerable and threatened her self-respect. She fears being vulnerable again. She suspects that new relationships will place demands on her she may be unwilling to meet. Psychologically speaking, she has her hands full. Maintaining a sense of balance and well-being under these circumstances can hardly be easy.

If we were concerned with Sara Lou for herself, a focus on her emotional problems might be legitimate. But this book is not about individuals. It is about the culture within which individuals form their goals and values. Only by bringing a perspective to bear that permits individual personality to recede into the background can we assess those characteristics influenced by culture and weigh their significance.

During the span of her still-young life, Sara Lou's cultural environment shifted in a decisive fashion. In her earlier years the message sent out to girls and women of her social class held unquestioned sway over her life. The message said: serve your husband and children; subordinate your desires to theirs; be a good mother, wife and hostess; be passive, gracious and feminine—and your husband will take care of you. In the later years of her marriage this intelligent young mother and wife, trained to respond to society's messages, started to receive new, conflicting signals. The new cultural message said: it is acceptable for you to have what successful men have—desires of your own; opportunities for self-expression, independence and recognition; actions on your own behalf; exercise of control over your own life; and pursuit of a career that does not force you to hide your intelligence behind "feminine" wiles.

In her interview Sara Lou tells us that in the middle years of her marriage she lived through a period of intense introspection. "Becoming conscious" took the form of questioning social roles dictated by her conformity to the expectations of others. When she speaks of "liberating the real person" buried beneath "artificial social roles," this is not her own voice. It is the language, metaphor and imagery of the women's movement and of popularized versions of self-psychology and existential philosophy. These influential voices have shaped the messages society conveys to people like Sara Lou about what is and what is not acceptable behavior.

Although she turned her life upside down, Sara Lou remains very much a conformist, although she is now conforming to a different social code from the one that prevailed when as a girl of twenty she married a promising medical student. The new rules give people who are not antisocial rebels the support they need to break loose from old life patterns. Against the background of changing cultural norms in the seventies, people like Sara Lou Wellford could dismantle and remake their lives and still remain within socially acceptable boundaries. Apart from their cultural context Sara Lou's *motivations* do not by themselves explain her *actions*. The missing part of the explanation is the transformation in psychoculture.

The rebellion of an intelligent and determined woman against the demands of a social role she finds stifling is an old story, the theme of countless novels, plays and films. In most of the stories, the women (from Hedda Gabler to Sissy Hankshaw, the heroine of *Even Cowgirls Get the Blues*) become social rebels. They reject their conventional roles as intolerable and go on to pay the penalty society exacts— and there is always a penalty. The anomaly in Sara Lou's private drama is that there is no great social penalty. Her story takes place in a culture in which the combined impact of the women's movement with new worldly possibilities reduces the penalties and expands the range of alternative social roles. Thanks to these changes, women with certain educational qualifications and cultural style (speech, mannerisms and mode of relating to others) have a variety of life choices that did not exist in previous periods of American life.

Many people feel uncomfortable with the identity society has dealt to them. They do not like being pigeonholed in a social role (bread-winner, housewife, teacher, middle-aged accountant, city dweller, student). What is new today is not the *feeling* of discomfort, but the urgency with which so many act to modify or discard the destiny pre-scribed for them by the old social roles.

Also new is the tendency to justify the change on psychological grounds. ("I must be true to my real self.") The resort to psychological justifications marks a sharp break with the past. In other eras people have changed the course of their lives because they could not make a living or achieve the social status, wealth and power they sought. Politics, religion and war have also uprooted people and transformed their lives. But ours is the first era when tens of millions of people offer as moral justification for their acts the idea that an inner and presumably more "real" self does not fit well with their assigned social role.

It is this matter of scope and scale that is crucial. Choices among life styles previously confined to tiny minorities—the socially privileged, or those who live at the artistic and cultural edges of society—are now available to everyone. Some of the options open in the past to these minorities—to the privileged because they were rich or famous and to those in the counterculture because they were willing to pay the price of social exclusion from the mainstream—are now open to the respectability-seeking middle class.

Sara Lou could not have acted as she did in the early years of her marriage without becoming a rebel. By the time her marriage soured, however, the social climate had changed so drastically that she was able to remake her life and still remain within acceptable social limits. She acknowledges that economic and institutional changes, as well as new social norms, played a major role in her life-transforming decisions. Without the influence of the women's movement she would not have decided to go to law school, and without her substantial child-support payments she could not have afforded it. She might have added that she could not have gone to law school if it did not accept large numbers of women, or people who had been out of school for some time, or that she would not have found a good job with a first-rate law firm if such firms did not offer jobs to women—as they did not just a few years earlier. Nor did she have difficulty in finding a good apartment for herself in San Francisco or in securing credit with a local bank without a husband as co-signer. All of these conditions did not exist on a wide scale before the 1970s, and they are still in the process of evolving.

Overall, Sara Lou Wellford typifies a new pattern in American life. She had the personal freedom to transform her life from one in which she was, after twelve years of marriage, firmly settled. When she made the change she did not feel déclassé, nor did she in fact become so: she was not disgraced by being divorced, nor ostracized for putting her own requirements ahead of her children's, nor condemned to shame and guilt because she slept around in the period following her divorce. And she made the change for essentially psychocultural reasons. Following the imperative of the self-fulfillment motif, she exchanged a life shaped by conventional social roles for one better suited to the needs of her inner self as she defined them. Ironically, though she is self-aware in many respects, she is not conscious of the extent to which her present life also fits a social role—a newer one, to be sure, but one increasingly acceptable in upper-middle-class American life.

Sara Lou now finds herself at a more advanced stage of the self-fulfillment predicament than Mark and Abby Williams. Like them, she places her personal fulfillment at the center of her life and above all other concerns, with the possible exception of her children's needs. Like the Williamses, she starts from the premise that having more choices than her parents, she has the opportunity—and the responsibility—to shape her life according to a design of her own choosing. Like Mark and Abby too, she pictures her self-fulfillment as a process of filling as many of her psychological needs and potentials as possible. Unlike them, however, she has chosen to act decisively, and for the most part circumstances and conditions have worked for rather than against her. In the years to come, however, she will have to confront all the confusing questions engendered by the triple bind.

Having accepted the responsibility for shaping her own life, what new moves and risks should she be taking in relationship to her two sons? What price, if any, will she have to pay in the future for having carried them off to San Francisco against their will? What accommodation should she be seeking with a man or men, and with women friends? To what constraints will she be subjected in her new career? How far will her formula of life-as-an-adventure carry her? How many more existential decisions about transforming her life will she make before a sense of rootlessness sets in? Will her strategy of "acting like a man, fighting and winning new battles," and the unapologetic placing of her own needs ahead of others continue to work for her in the future? What are the next moves in shaping a life for which there are no blueprints, no precedents and no traditions? In assuming that the object of the search for self-fulfillment is the finding of a "real self," what do you do with it once you have found it?

Chapter 7

...———◉———...

I Am My Own
Work of Art

Any discussion of self-fulfillment is confronted with a troublesome question of semantics. What is the relationship between self-fulfillment and success? Are the two ideas interchangeable? Do we seek self-fulfillment through becoming successful, and do we label as successful whatever brings fulfillment? The distinction between success and self-fulfillment may have been blurred in the past, but increasingly Americans are differentiating them. Indeed, the lives of some people embody a fierce conflict between the two concepts. To illustrate this conflict I have selected from my interviews a man in his forties who is old enough to have absorbed the more traditional meanings of success but who has grown preoccupied with some of the newer meanings of self-fulfillment.

Lyndon Hendries is busy juggling two goals—achieving worldly success as others define it and self-fulfillment as he defines it. He is unusual in the degree to which he has ruminated on the tension in his life between his success and his self-fulfillment.

Lyndon Hendries is older than Mark and Abby Williams or Sara Lou Wellford, and he has achieved more material success. A full partner in a rapidly growing public relations firm in Houston, Texas, he earns more than $100,000 a year, and is a star much in demand by the firm's clients. His marriage, however, is a dark spot in his life. Like Sara Lou, he has two young children, ages seven and nine, and he feels close to them. Unlike many of the men interviewed for this book, he enjoyed expressing his thoughts and deeper feelings. Because he experiences his worldly success as "hollow and meaningless," and because he has thought much about why his achievements don't satisfy his demands on life, he helps us draw the line between traditional success and self-fulfillment.

Asked how our society defines success, Hendries answers succinctly: "money and power." When asked, "What did success mean to your parents?" he says, "Giving children the maximum they could give, mostly material; being accepted in the proper social groups, and probably getting and staying married."

But as for success in his own terms, he says:

> "I have achieved success by the definition of others, but I am not yet self-fulfilled. I appear successful because success is externally measured. I have published, lectured, exceeded my income goal, achieved ownership, and a lot of people depend on me. So I've adequately achieved the external goals, but they are empty. They're empty because my measure of success is personalized, not externalized. There are times when I have liked those material and visible recognitions, but the personal price is way too high just for ego gratification."

In discussing whether he feels he is making headway toward self-fulfillment as he himself defines it, he says:

> "No; it may be unachievable, I don't know, I just work toward it. We all chase dreams and it seems that the grabbable ones are empty and only the ungrabbable ones are worth pursuing."

Compared with his clear definition of success, Hendries' conception of self-fulfillment trails off into a diffuse vagueness. Yet it is deeply felt and, as we shall see, it dominates his life. But it is less easy for him to define. Partly, this is because he conceives self-fulfillment as a process rather than as racking up specific achievements—amounts of money earned, possessions owned, status achieved. This "process of becoming" involves the unfolding of a self whose characteristics and expressions fascinate the audience of one who beholds them, Lyndon Hendries himself. But this self (and its "needs") often collides with the other selves, and proves wondrously elusive when one tries to pin it down in ordinary language.

Hendries' search for fulfillment creates many difficulties for him.

Asked if it comes into conflict with commitments and obligations to others, Hendries answers with a laugh: "Absolutely, unequivocally and often. But . . . I do basically and genuinely care about other people, so I often anticipate the conflict, and recognize and accept the consequences for myself."

The theme of conflict between the demands of others and his own self-fulfillment dominates the interview. Part of Hendries' self-fulfillment consists in shedding the burdens of having to respond to the needs of others. "I have an incredible number of people demanding things from me personally and professionally, and I am pleased when I can say no. I have grown more selfish in recent years, valuing myself more than family members, powerful peers, bosses or clients."

Asked in what areas of life the conflict between his self-fulfillment and commitments to others has been sharpest, Hendries promptly answers: "In my marriage, in my work and in a variety of family relations," and he is explicit about each.

With respect to his work he says:

> "It is paying off in terms of external rewards, but it inhibits self-fulfillment. Hard work means money and deferred benefits. But mostly, for me and for the culture, hard work has stifled individuality. It used to be axiomatic that hard work pays off; we were taught that hard work was its own reward. That is unequivocally bullshit. I still believe *good work* will be rewarded, although that's not big in our culture at the moment."

What bothers Hendries most about the demands of others is that they consume his time and therefore consume his "self." "Not having enough time becomes such an artificial and important barrier to people who want to live and experience. Our culture seems to treat time as the overriding consideration for everything—when a job is done, when to meet with somebody, how long to talk, how long to have fun. I am trying to get out from under that; but we are all controlled by it, so it is very difficult to do."

His marriage, he says, is the least fulfilling aspect of his life. He sees marriage as a relationship that calls on him to make more of an effort and commitment than he ever wanted to make. "It's taking a good deal more hard work than I ever anticipated. I don't think any of us build this constant work into our mental schedules." Later, referring to his marriage again, he says, "It has taken a superhuman effort to overcome first the disappointment experienced from earlier expectations and also to try to recognize the limitations. Membership in a family is not in-

evitable; it is made up of people, after all. A family is composed of individuals and is certainly not monolithic. It is a great institution but not
by definition."

Asked what he thinks will happen in his life over the next five to
ten years, he says, "I'll probably have to live alone at some point, and
perhaps totally reconstruct my expectations and my life style." Yet
when asked what he *hopes* might happen over the same period, he speculates about chances for salvaging his marriage under new terms. "I
would hope that my wife and I would share in new attitudes toward
our individual needs and our collective possibilities." Among these
individual needs, he says, is a relaxed attitude toward marital fidelity.
"Originally I thought fidelity was absurd, then I thought it made sense,
now I'm back once again to thinking it is absurd."

Lyndon Hendries shares with the Williamses an intense desire to
design his own life style, but he is under no illusion that this is an easy
or risk-free task. He says:

> "Our culture does not even come close to preparing us for the con-
> centration and pain involved with self-fulfillment. We have some
> idea of superficial pain and disappointment, but we are never pre-
> pared for dealing with ourselves. We are taught that we can be
> fired, that we can be sick, and we even have glimpses of the diffi-
> culties we encounter if we try to be individualists. But we have no
> idea how difficult it is to achieve our own personal scenarios. It
> involves lots of economic and personal risks."

Asked, "What is it about your present life that you find most fulfilling?" he says the greatest source of satisfaction in his life is his
children. "I would describe my relationship with them as perfect from
their standpoint and mine. It is not without hassles, of course, but there
is an incredible overriding affection and a communality of experience
and love."

Almost equally fulfilling are his travels abroad. He talks glowingly of
"the fascination and excitement I feel for people whose lives and cultures
are different." One of his dreams is to spend about half the year outside the United States.

He has also shortened his working hours, which makes him feel
that he has more control over his life. "I feel freer to have more time to
myself and that is immensely gratifying. But I still feel pulled by people
and events . . . on balance I am materially improving, intellectually stag-
nating, and in terms of intimacy, remaining basically where I am in proportion to my efforts."

Although he resents the demands that worldly success has made on him, he is not prepared to give up any of its benefits. He welcomes the advantages that come with having money. "Eating at good restaurants, sending my kids to good schools, travel, hiring people to do things that I don't want to spend my time doing; I like being able to lower my acquisition-frustration level." But the main advantage he sees to money relates to security in his old age. He says: "Economic security is extremely important to me, particularly as it relates to retirement. When one is in a weakened and powerless position, the only insulation you have is economic, and relying on the socioeconomic mechanism at that age is terrifying to me. As a society we do not really grasp what it is like to be old, particularly in a youth-oriented culture."

(ii)

In Lyndon Hendries' life, as in those of the Williamses, Sara Lou Wellford and Professor Agnoli, we see played out many themes of the strong form of the self-fulfillment predicament. Embracing the self-fulfillment ethos, particularly in its early virulent stages, creates a state of mind antithetical to the expectations traditionally associated with marriage and other relationships. Typically, any two partners enter marriage with expectations derived from the experience of their own parents. They may rebel against these, or they may accept them, but their expectations are necessarily defined by what they know, and, at least in a first marriage, what they know is what they have absorbed at home.

Marriages, therefore, are always rooted in the mores of the preceding generation. Even under the most stable circumstances, marital partners spend years adapting to the constant tiny surprises, many disagreeable, that come with living together. They learn how infinite the misunderstandings are that can arise between two people who think they understand each other. Successful marriages are woven out of many strands of inhibited desire—accessions to the wishes of the other; acceptance of infringements on one's own wishes; disappointments swallowed; confrontations avoided; opportunities for anger bypassed; chances for self-expression muted. To introduce the strong form of the self-fulfillment urge into this process is to take a broomstick to a delicate web. Often all that is left is the sticky stuff that adheres to the broom; the structure of the web is destroyed.

Perhaps the greatest threat to marriage arises from the question of sexual fidelity. Those in hot pursuit of self-fulfillment do not wish to deprive themselves of the exhilarating freedom and adventure that comes with sexual openness. The old restrictions seem to make little sense in light of the duty-to-self ethic. To insist implacably on monogamy appears hypocritical or old-fashioned or stubbornly possessive. The old double standard made a restricted concession to the male: his transgressions must be limited in number, they must never be flaunted, appearances must be maintained and responsibilities toward the family must not be jeopardized. The new ethos abhors this outlook as hypocritical and demeaning to women, and it is thoroughly rejected. But the new as-long-as-it-doesn't-hurt-anyone norm does not appear to work very well when it comes to extramarital affairs. The disclaimer, "we both agree we won't hurt each other" turns out not to apply: someone *is* hurt.

The truly committed seekers of self-fulfillment all expressed deep ambivalence on this matter. The subject made them uncomfortable. Like Hendries, most reported shifts in their own attitude, often moving back and forth several times. In principle, most endorse greater sexual freedom for both partners. But in practice, they acknowledge that such freedoms strain their marriage.

Strong formers often do better with children than with sex. The battle of egos stirred up by the self-fulfillment urge is usually fought so as to exempt the children—at least partially. It is as if spouses split their self-fulfillment requirements into two unequal portions: a full measure laid on the other partner, a half measure on the children—on the grounds that the kids did not enter into the giving/getting covenant as consenting adults, and so must not be made to bear its full burden. The Wellford, Agnoli and Hendries children all bear part of the brunt of their parents' search for self-fulfillment—for all are the children of strong formers. But in each instance, at least one of the partners is willing to curb his or her desire for fulfillment so that the children will suffer less.

These kinds of differentiations—"I'll sacrifice for the kids but not for her (or him)"—characterize many forms of self-fulfillment negotiation. The party-of-the-first-part grows preoccupied with how to reconcile his desires with the demands made by the party-of-the-second-part —spouses, children, employers, friends, others. The result: a complex edifice of adjustments, accommodations, exceptions, balances, strategies and conflicts that keep the party-of-the-first-part busy full-time holding it all together.

We see this process at work in Lyndon Hendries' efforts to secure for himself the benefits of worldly success (travel, comfort, security) *and* familial success (protecting the children, salvaging the marriage) *and* self-fulfillment (creativity lavished on the self). Keeping it all going takes an immense effort. It is constantly threatening to come apart, imposing a strain of anxiety and loneliness on his life. But he is not ready to settle for less, nor does he know how he would choose if choice were required. In this respect he is typical of those caught in the triple bind.

The key to the triple bind is that the old self-denial rules have lost their normative power. No moral virtue is attached any longer to the idea that it is good to curb the imperatives of the self. Under the old ethic, self-denial was assumed to have virtue for its own sake; under the self-fulfillment ethic self-denial makes no sense.

Characteristically, therefore, strong formers find themselves ill at ease with their heritage of moral values. They cannot wholeheartedly accept their parents' ethos because they regard the parental focus on self-denial as outmoded. They feel their parents had no choice, while they do. With intensity, they act on the conviction that they are free to shape their own lives, even though their actions push them on to unknown territory without the guidance of tradition, custom and conventional rules. They know their risk is high.

Often they themselves see the strand of egoism and greed ("pigginess") in their actions, and it troubles them. But something drives them on. The new duty-to-self norm is energized not merely by self-centeredness but also by another impulse. Significantly, strong formers cherish what they call "creativity," particularly the creative adventure involved in shaping one's life. It brings satisfactions lacking in older conceptions of success.

To understand what creativity means in the context of the search for self-fulfillment we turn to national survey data.

(iii)

The Singleton analysis described in Chapter 5 compares the strong form group (17 percent) with the majority (83 percent) of the working population, and it shows unmistakably the high value strong formers place on being creative in the way they think about and live their lives. In the survey, 60 percent of the strong formers described themselves as having powerful creativity needs, while among the rest of the population only 29 percent so characterized themselves. People were asked if they had the choice between living "more creative lives" or being "better off financially," which option they would select. Their answer could hardly be more unequivocal. By two to one (67 percent to 33 percent), the majority selected financial gain. But among the strong formers, the opposite pattern prevailed: by two to one (65 percent to 35 percent) they chose the more creative life.

Though strong formers claim to value creativity more highly than money, like Lyndon Hendries most of them seem not yet prepared to face any genuine conflict between a creative life and an affluent one. (A majority of them say they need to add more possessions to the things they now own.) This does not mean they are hypocrites, for if they were forced to choose, undoubtedly many would opt for personal creativity. But they assume they do not really have to choose. They want both creativity and the things money can buy, and assume they will have both. However, there is a trace of doubt, and it makes them anxious.

What does creativity mean to someone strongly committed to self-fulfillment? The survey findings show that it means so many different things that we may be tempted to dismiss the term as meaningless. But this would be a mistake. There is a pattern unifying the many items, large and small, that make up the meaning of creativity for the strong formers. Let us look at the specifics.

Far more than the majority, strong formers describe themselves as "spending a great deal of time thinking about themselves" (67 percent to 40 percent) and "searching for ways and means to acquire a higher level of self-knowledge" so that they will know themselves better (58 percent to 34 percent). Strong formers say that much of their satisfaction in life comes from shaping themselves to meet their own ideals, while the majority say their satisfaction in life comes mainly from home and family (56 percent to 29 percent). The strong form group is somewhat younger than the majority, but when we hold age constant we find that it does not essentially change this pattern.

More than the majority, strong formers also want to be outstanding in their field of work (62 percent to 42 percent). And by a larger margin they insist on having something meaningful to work toward (77 percent to 59 percent). More than others they also want to make sure they have enough time and energy to pursue their off-the-job personal interests (80 percent to 67 percent).

More of them feel the need to be well read and well educated (58 percent to 39 percent), to seek excitement and sensation (71 percent to 52 percent) and to "restore romance and mystery to modern life" (70 percent to 52 percent). We have here a clue about why money is important to them and how they want to spend it. More of them than among the majority say they prefer spending their money on experiences such as travel and vacations that will enrich their lives, rather than on acquiring physical possessions (71 percent to 52 percent). But once again their ambivalence about money comes to the fore. Most people say that being a "well-rounded person" is much less important to them than making a living, but by a two to one margin (52 percent to 25 percent) strong formers reject this idea. They do more painting, drawing, sculpting and ceramics (36 percent to 15 percent) than the majority, and also more writing (45 percent to 18 percent), photography (22 percent to 10 percent) and baking their own bread (20 percent to 9 percent). They are more likely to try new restaurants (36 percent to 20 percent) and new foods (56 percent to 36 percent). They prefer a world full of variety and change to one settled and stable (46 percent to 26 percent).

They are enthusiastic advocates of natural foods, preferring wheat germ, sugar substitutes, natural foods high in fiber, foods made out of soy beans, and particularly organic foods (50 percent to 27 percent). But in another mood, they also opt for the occasional elegant meal with wine and candlelight (86 percent to 59 percent). More than the majority, they would like to belong to a literary discussion group (34 percent to 15 percent), an art discussion group (29 percent to 12 percent), to take language courses (42 percent to 24 percent), or to enroll in a cooking school (41 percent to 20 percent).

The sharpest differences are found among their efforts to seek self-understanding, such as reading books to "help me understand myself better" (79 percent to 54 percent), joining self-discovery programs such as encounter groups (43 percent to 19 percent), engaging in meditation and introspection (48 percent to 25 percent), analyzing one's dreams (57 percent to 28 percent) and, if needed, seeking out psychotherapy (41 percent to 19 percent).

They are more concerned than the majority with their bodies and their diets. More of them exercise to improve their muscle tone (71 percent to 50 percent), or to build their bodies (50 percent to 29 percent), more shy away from fattening foods (62 percent to 45 percent) and concern themselves with nutrition and a well-balanced diet (60 percent to 40 percent).

They are much more inclined to eat yogurt (27 percent to 8 percent) and raw vegetables (38 percent to 22 percent), and to seek out ethnic foods such as Japanese (41 percent to 23 percent), Indian (30 percent to 14 percent), Russian (34 percent to 15 percent), Greek (41 percent

to 20 percent) and French (58 percent to 35 percent). But, being diet
conscious, they avoid potato chips and other junk foods more than the
majority does (32 percent to 16 percent).

They are more involved in yoga and TM (43 percent to 19 percent),
and their sporting life conforms to a different profile from the norm.
They prefer skiing (26 percent to 13 percent), tennis (40 percent to
23 percent), hiking (44 percent to 22 percent), biking (51 percent to
35 percent), taking long walks (59 percent to 41 percent) and even
saunas (22 percent to 9 percent).

In contrast to the majority, more of them enjoy rock music (64
percent to 40 percent), dancing (67 percent to 44 percent), works of
art (74 percent to 46 percent) and sleeping on water beds (44 percent
to 25 percent).

Far more than the majority they value tolerance and individuality,
holding (by a 58 percent to 39 percent margin) that "people should be
free to look, dress and live the way they want, whether others like it
or not."

Chart B presents some of the key differences between strong formers
and the mainstream majority. The chart summarizes what this group of
self-fulfillment seekers means by "creativity" as a life style.

By now it will come as no surprise that in contrast to the majority,
strong formers agree that "self-improvement is important to me and I
work hard at it" (66 percent to 39 percent).

And here, of course, we have a key to the force behind the fabulous
outpouring of energy into self-fulfillment. Strong formers stand squarely
in the mainstream of the traditional American pursuit of self-improvement. Only when it comes to the *object* of self-improvement do they veer
sharply from tradition. In the past the purpose of self-improvement was
to better oneself in the tangible, visible ways associated with worldly or
familial success. But for these strong formers the object of their creative
energies is . . . themselves. Self-improvement is pursued more for its
own sake than for external rewards. "I am my own success story and
my own work of art. I lavish on myself the riches of Western civilization
and the accumulated affluence built up by earlier generations of
Americans," they seem to say.

The continuity with the past is inescapable. The classic American
theme of self-improvement stands out prominently, as does faith in education, and an evangelical streak of earnestness that runs throughout the
American saga. We find the same outpouring of creativity, practicality,
individualism and ingenuity. What is new is the shift in the object of
all this energy, a shift from the external to the inner world.

CHART B

"CREATIVITY" AS A LIFE-STYLE

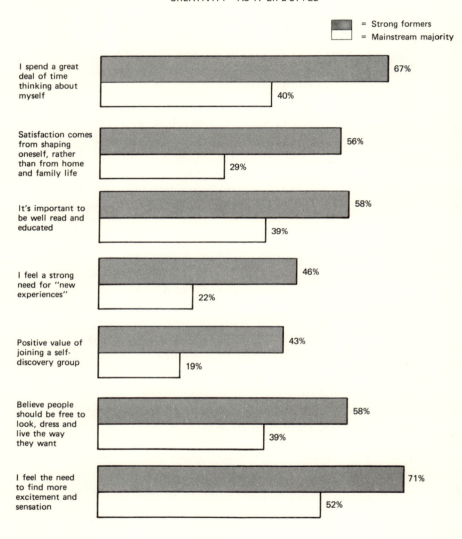

CHART B
(Continued)

"CREATIVITY" AS A LIFE-STYLE

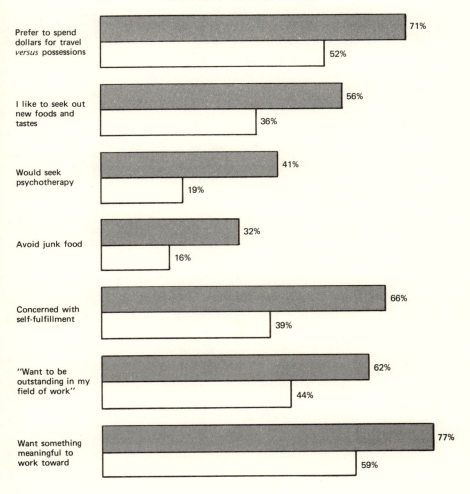

Prefer to spend dollars for travel *versus* possessions — 71% / 52%

I like to seek out new foods and tastes — 56% / 36%

Would seek psychotherapy — 41% / 19%

Avoid junk food — 32% / 16%

Concerned with self-fulfillment — 66% / 39%

"Want to be outstanding in my field of work" — 62% / 44%

Want something meaningful to work toward — 77% / 59%

CHART B
(Continued)

"CREATIVITY" AS A LIFE-STYLE

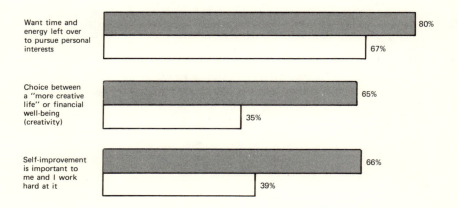

Want time and
energy left over
to pursue personal
interests
80%
67%

Choice between
a "more creative
life" or financial
well-being
(creativity)
65%
35%

Self-improvement
is important to
me and I work
hard at it
66%
39%

Chapter 8

—◉—

New Norms: Being Obliged to Do What You Want to Do

As the survey findings in the previous chapter make clear, many of the activities pursued in the name of self-fulfillment express self-improvement energies, not simple pleasure-seeking. If the zeal devoted to them were channeled into worldly aims—building new industries, solving the energy problem, devising new modes of health care—we would not label them as hedonism or narcissism.

Why are the energies of so many millions of talented, well-educated Americans being lavished on themselves rather than on the world? For strong formers like Lyndon Hendries a high rung on the socioeconomic ladder has not proven satisfying. In the new system of values it represents a lesser form of success: it may be success as others see it, but it is not self-fulfillment, and indeed, clashes with it. Old-style success required subordinating the self to external goals, while self-fulfillment seems to require that the self be cultivated, not denied. It is in this conflict between denying the self and nurturing it that we find the key to the normative transformations of our era.

A psychologist friend told me an anecdote which had amused—and bemused—her. A patient in psychotherapy with her, a woman in her mid-twenties, complained that she had become nervous and fretful because life had grown so hectic—too many big weekends, too many discos, too many late hours, too much talk, too much wine, too much pot, too much love-making.

"Why don't you stop?" asked the therapist mildly. Her patient stared blankly for a moment, and then her face lit up, dazzled by an illumination.

"You mean I really don't have to do what I want to do?" she burst out with amazement.

Ordinarily we think of norms in opposition to desires—dictating what we should do (wake up early, work hard, buckle down, use moderation), as distinct from what we would like to do. It had never occurred to her, my friend admitted, that norms could support desires and that people could come to feel it was their moral duty to yield to their impulses. Her psychological thinking had been influenced by Freud, and she had come to think of social norms as outgrowths of the parental dos and don'ts people internalize in early stages of development. She made no clear distinction between individual conscience and social norms, or rules.

Yet it is useful to distinguish sharply between them. Conscience is a "property" of the individual. Norms are social phenomena, referring to the unwritten rules and mores of a society, expressing its social authority. In a democracy, vast social authority resides in the expectations of the community. The expectations the majority hold about what is or is not appropriate behavior carry considerable moral weight, as do the expectations of any subgroup of which one is a part—a youth gang, a church congregation, a college faculty, a management team.

Logically, there is no reason why norms should not apply to desires if the social group endows them with moral authority. In such circumstances the pursuit of a desire would become a social duty, with the same power to goad the individual as other, more traditional norms.

Norms are social glue. They hold things together. A normless society could not exist. Norms are what keep us from degenerating into that nightmare of solipsistic anarchy Hobbes described as "the war of each against all and all against each."

Norms belong squarely in the domain of psychoculture because they are a species of shared meanings—those that happen to carry special moral force. The norm "a woman should marry and have children" translates readily into the shared meaning that being a "real woman" involves the experience of marriage and childbearing. The norm "a man should hold the door for a woman and let her go first" translates into one of the shared meanings in our culture of being a gentleman. Visiting Americans are often startled in Japan at the sight of exquisitely courteous Japanese men stepping ahead of Japanese women in order to get through a door first. Clearly, for the Japanese, being a "gentleman" conveys a different shared meaning than it does in our culture.

The Japanese psychiatrist, Takeo Doi, describes his first visit to America and his first overnight stay at the home of an American colleague. His colleague's wife told him he was welcome, and then urged him to feel free to help himself during his stay with them. He reports that upon hearing these words he felt desolated and a wave of loneliness and isolation overcame him. In Japan to tell a guest that he must help himself is to reject him. One helps an honored guest; under no circumstances must he ever feel that he must resort to helping himself.*

The shared meanings of moral norms vary greatly from culture to culture, and within a culture from one period to another, but they penetrate to every corner of our social existence.

Though moral norms in America have changed in the past few decades, I must add that virtually no norm is so "old fashioned" that it cannot find millions of Americans who continue to adhere to it—or at least pay it lip service. For example, most Americans now reject the idea that women should be restricted to mothering and homemaking, leaving it to the men to work outside the home and "run the country." But 37 percent of American *women* still agree with precisely this notion. Most Americans reject the old double standard of sexual fidelity in marriage. Yet 14 percent of all Americans (more than 22 million adults) still subscribe to the view that it is all right for husbands, but not for wives, to "play around," and 35 percent continue to believe a woman should be a virgin until she is married.

Many norms that once enjoyed universal support no longer do. But they continue to be endorsed by large minorities. Women should not work if they have men who can support them. Married men with homosexual urges must keep them strictly suppressed. Women should carry the main burden of marital fidelity. Such norms are far from obsolete, though they are no longer as prevalent as they once were.

Over the past several decades the rules of social behavior have expanded, moving us from a society with relatively homogeneous definitions of family, sex roles and working life toward an explosive pluralism on these and other fronts.

Virtually all the recent normative changes in America have moved toward greater tolerance, openness, choice and a wider range of ac-

---

* Takeo Doi, *The Anatomy of Dependence,* trans. John Bester (New York: Kodansha, 1973), p. 13.

ceptable behavior. The shifts are not uniform and stable; as in all periods of cultural ferment, people contradict themselves and often change their minds. But there is a clear pattern of change. From universally held prescriptions of what is and is not appropriate behavior for a man, woman, husband, wife, son, daughter, friend or relative, most norms have shifted toward looser, freer codes of behavior. In the past, and the recent past at that, one could hardly escape the icy disapproval of friends and neighbors for even small infractions of social norms—a man who failed to mow the lawn, or a woman who told dirty jokes. Now it is easy either to ignore the neighbor's disapproval, or to move a few blocks or states away and find new neighbors who will remain benignly neutral to social behavior that would have scandalized most Americans just a decade or two earlier.

As norms shift from rigidity to flexibility, the meaning of "right" and "wrong" (which underlies all norms) has itself undergone transformation. Traditional concepts of right and wrong have been replaced by norms of "harmful" or "harmless." If one's actions are not seen as penalizing others, even if they are "wrong" from the perspective of traditional morality, they no longer meet much opposition. A majority of the public today would not fault a single woman who decides to have a child if she can care for the baby properly, or criticize an unmarried couple for living together "if they really love each other."

The one major change that the Middletown III researchers found in Muncie, Indiana was this increase in tolerance and loosening of norms. Asked in 1924 whether "Christianity is the one true religion" and whether "everyone should be converted to it," an overwhelming 94 percent of Muncie residents agreed. Confronted with the same question in 1977, only 41 percent concurred, a massive change in the norms governing religious tolerance.*

And when the Lynds asked Middletown teenagers whether being a good cook and housekeeper were the two most desirable qualities of a mother, a 52 percent majority of teenage girls in 1924 insisted that this was so; by 1977, however, the vast majority (76 percent) had dropped these requirements.†

Before documenting the shifts in traditional norms that have now swept through our culture, it may be useful to keep in mind some of the norms that have not changed. Chart C presents a profile of moral values

---

* Theodore Caplow, "The Measurement of Social Change in Middletown," *Indiana Magazine of History* (December 1979).

† Howard M. Bahr, "Changes in Family Life in Middletown, 1924–1977," Middletown III Project Paper #6 (1978).

CHART C

TRADITIONAL NORMS

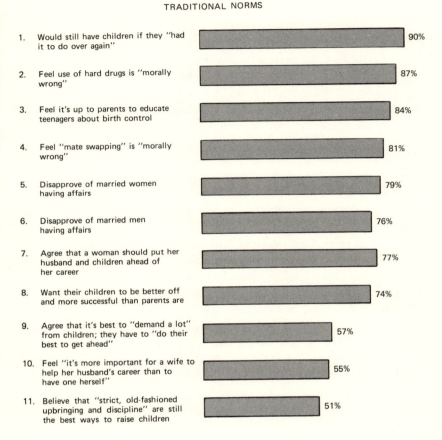

1. Would still have children if they "had
    it to do over again"   90%

2. Feel use of hard drugs is "morally
    wrong"   87%

3. Feel it's up to parents to educate
    teenagers about birth control   84%

4. Feel "mate swapping" is "morally
    wrong"   81%

5. Disapprove of married women
    having affairs   79%

6. Disapprove of married men
    having affairs   76%

7. Agree that a woman should put her
    husband and children ahead of
    her career   77%

8. Want their children to be better off
    and more successful than parents are   74%

9. Agree that it's best to "demand a lot"
    from children; they have to "do their
    best to get ahead"   57%

10. Feel "it's more important for a wife to
    help her husband's career than to
    have one herself"   55%

11. Believe that "strict, old-fashioned
    upbringing and discipline" are still
    the best ways to raise children   51%

SOURCES

1976–77 General Mills American Family Report: Raising Children in a Changing Society — Nos. 1, 8, 9

1978–79 General Mills American Family Report: Family Health in an Era of Stress — Nos. 3, 11

TIME Magazine/Yankelovich Survey; July, 1977 and March, 1978 — Nos. 2, 4, 5, 6, 7

NORC General Social Survey, 1977 — No. 10

and beliefs that a majority of Americans continue to adhere to. Thus far these have escaped the transformations wrought by the shifts in the plates of culture.

(ii)

The strong form of the search for self-fulfillment comprises one end of a continuum, characterizing Americans who are self-consciously building their lives around norms that make a moral virtue of self-expression. In the center of the continuum we find the majority of Americans struggling with the weak form of the self-fulfillment predicament. Most of them do not agonize over their inner needs and potentials. They do not fuss daily over existential life-decisions as if these were worry beads to be fingered at fretful moments. These people, especially if they are over thirty-five years of age, have mostly settled into stable commitments to family, work, friends, community and leisure. These commitments rather than creative forms of self-expression, fill their life space. Their inner lives are rarely subject to upheaval. The pressures that tear at the strong formers also tug at them but do not dominate their lives. The majority retain many traditional values, including a moderate commitment to the old self-denial rules, even as they struggle to achieve some measure of greater freedom, choice and flexibility in their lives.

Mrs. Greenson, whom we met in Part I, illustrates the majority. Most aspects of her life are settled into a traditional mold: stable marriage, conventional household arrangements and relationships to children, a history of accommodation to the needs of others. All her decisions emanate from commitments in which she is thoroughly enmeshed: these impose incessant demands on her—but support her as well. Her house is, as it were, already built. She may be redecorating a metaphorical corner of it; but unlike the strong formers, she is not razing it to the ground in order to rebuild it on a new foundation.

In these next few chapters I want to discuss the concerns with self-fulfillment that average Americans who are not strong formers have. The majority embrace both older success goals and newer self-fulfillment ones, but, as we shall see, at a lower pitch of intensity and in different forms of expression than Lyndon Hendries, for example. Their commitment to self-fulfillment is weaker, and therefore they exhibit weaker forms of the self-fulfillment predicament.

We should also recognize, however, that the continuum has another end. There are millions of Americans who remain unaffected by the new self-fulfillment values and are attached exclusively to more traditional goals. Before discussing individual lives, it is important to gain a statistical overview of this continuum and of the changes in cultural norms that affect the nation as a whole and not merely the 17 percent strong-form minority.

Estimating the number of Americans in the center of the continuum is a somewhat different task from identifying those at the extremes. This is because a person may have a conventional outlook in most respects, and yet be engaged in the search for self-fulfillment in one part of his life—his work or marriage or leisure. Therefore we must count as expressing the weak form of the self-fulfillment search all adult Americans who do not belong either with the strong-form minority or, at the other extreme, with the minority of Americans totally uninvolved in the search for self-fulfillment. Ten consecutive years of national studies conducted by Yankelovich, Skelly and White between 1970 and 1980 reveal that by the outset of the nineteen-eighties only 20 percent or so of adult Americans remained unaffected in their philosophy of life, untouched by the great shifts in culture.

This group of approximately 34 million Americans includes many older people, particularly in rural areas. It includes Americans who are conservative in their cultural outlook. And it also includes some poorer Americans, black and white, who, having been excluded from the affluence of the past, nonetheless do not question the merits of the old giving/getting compact. Owning a fine car and home, living in a nice neighborhood, maintaining an intact family life, working hard for these goals, sacrificing self-expression for the sake of an education or for the family—these remain their unqualified values. Their life styles and philosophy have not changed from the outlook that dominated America in the nineteen-fifties and earlier periods.

This leaves 63 percent, or more than 100 million adult Americans, in the middle of the continuum to be counted as involved in the weak form of the self-fulfillment search. Since this is the majority, most of us fit here. We have many other concerns in our lives than the search for self-fulfillment—family obligations, work, inflation worries, health cares, kids with school problems, crime, what the Russians are up to, the football game. At the same time, we, too, are raising questions about the giving/getting compact, Some of us question it on the domestic side —what we should be giving to our family life and getting from it. Others of us confine our questioning to work, what we should be getting out of our jobs and what commitments we should be making to them. And others focus on the question of whether the old rules still make sense. Once people begin to question social rules, they find it difficult to draw the line. Our studies show a strong increase in recent years in aimlessness, especially among young people, and also in hedonism as people find themselves abandoning the old rules without having as yet adopted new ones they can believe in.

Chart D identifies twenty major normative changes that have taken place in America in recent years as documented by survey research. These are changes in how Americans feel about marriage, women, abortion, work, religion, government, etc. In some instances, we have trend data going back to the nineteen-thirties, in others the comparisons go back only ten or twenty years or even less, and in a few instances, there are no previous measures and we must infer from other evidence that a change has taken place.

The list of twenty changes could easily be expanded to several hundred. These twenty are not necessarily the most important ones. They simply are ones that have been measured. But compositely, they show in a striking fashion that however much continuity exists in American culture, there have also been far-reaching changes in the normative rules.

Though the shifts in norms applies to the full sweep of American psychoculture—from the type of clothes one wears to one's obligations to God and country—I want to focus here on changes in domestic norms, i.e., norms relating to marriage, childbearing, giving and getting in relationship to children, sex roles and sexual behavior.

I gathered my first evidence of the strength of marriage norms in a study conducted in the late 1950s among women in their teens and early twenties. At that time all the single women interviewed in the study assumed they would marry and have children. All those already married who did not have children stated they planned to have them; most wanted three or four or more. All mothers interviewed in the study were married, and each pronounced herself thoroughly satisfied with this state of affairs. Several admitted they had become pregnant without intending to, but no one felt comfortable saying outright that she did not want to have a child. It would not have been respectable to say so— or even think so. In several instances I suspected that a woman had had an abortion, but I never found out whether this was true: in the fifties, few women would admit such a lapse from respectability to a stranger.

When I pressed the younger women to tell me why they cherished marriage, family and children as their inevitable destiny, some spoke glowingly of the joys of family life and the fulfillment for a woman that comes with having children. Many, however, were rendered tongue-tied. My questions struck them as unanswerable, meaningless. "You get married and have children," they said, "because that is what you do. What

CHART D

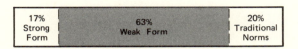

| 17%
Strong
Form | 63%
Weak Form | 20%
Traditional
Norms |

CHANGES IN SOCIAL NORMS

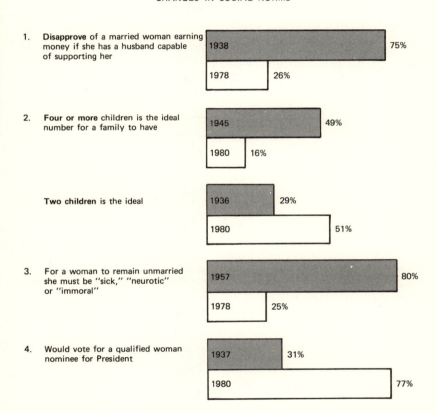

1. **Disapprove** of a married woman earning money if she has a husband capable of supporting her

   1938 — 75%
   1978 — 26%

2. **Four or more** children is the ideal number for a family to have

   1945 — 49%
   1980 — 16%

   Two children is the ideal

   1936 — 29%
   1980 — 51%

3. For a woman to remain unmarried she must be "sick," "neurotic" or "immoral"

   1957 — 80%
   1978 — 25%

4. Would vote for a qualified woman nominee for President

   1937 — 31%
   1980 — 77%

CHART D
(Continued)

CHANGES IN SOCIAL NORMS

5. Condemn premarital sex as
    morally wrong

| 1967 | 85% |
| 1979 | 37% |

6. **Favor** decision making abortion up
    to 3 months of pregnancy legal

| 1973 | 52% |
| 1980 | 60% |

7. **Agree** that both sexes have the
    responsibility to care for small
    children

| 1970 | 33% |
| 1980 | 56% |

8. **Approve** of husband and wife
    taking separate vacations

| 1971 | 34% |
| 1980 | 51% |

9. Agree that "hard work always
    pays off"

| 1969 | 58% |
| 1976 | 43% |

10. **Agree** that "work is at the center
    of my life"

| 1970 | 34% |
| 1978 | 13% |

CHART D
(Continued)

CHANGES IN SOCIAL NORMS

Men

11. Would go on working for pay even
    if they didn't have to

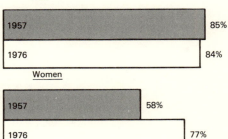

1957   85%

1976   84%

Women

1957   58%

1976   77%

12. Increase in level of anxiety and
    worry among young Americans
    21—39 years of age

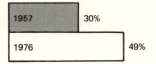

1957   30%

1976   49%

13. **Agree** that "the people running the
    country don't care what happens
    to people like me"

1966   26%

1977   60%

14. **Agree** that they "can trust the
    government in Washington do
    do what's right"

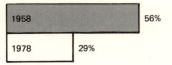

1958   56%

1978   29%

15. Experience a "hungering for
    community"

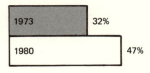

1973   32%

1980   47%

CHART D
(Continued)

CHANGES IN SOCIAL NORMS

16. Americans with a "sour grapes" outlook on life

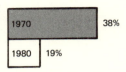

1970   38%

1980   19%

17. **Agree** that it is morally acceptable to be single and have children

1979   75%

18. **Agree** that interracial marriages are not morally wrong

1977   62%

19. **Agree** that it is not morally wrong for couples to live together even if they are not married

1978   52%

20. **Agree** that they would like to return to standards of the past relating to:
    — sexual mores
    — "spic and span" housekeeping
    — women staying home and only men working outside the home

1979   21%

SOURCES

The Gallup Opinion Index — Nos. 1, 2, 4

NORC; The University of Chicago — No. 1

Institute for Social Research; University of Michigan — Nos. 3, 11, 12, 14

The Roper Organization; for Virginia Slims — No. 4

Yankelovich, Skelly and White, Inc. — Nos. 5, 7, 8, 9, 10, 15, 16, 17, 18, 19, 20

Harris Survey (ABC/Harris) — Nos. 6, 13

else would a woman do? That is what a woman's life is—getting married, having children and raising a family. It is not a matter of 'want' or 'like to' or 'choice.' Why talk about things that are as natural and as routine as breathing?" In answer to my question about why she wanted to get married and have children, one woman said sarcastically, "Why do you put your pants on in the morning? Why do you walk with two feet instead of one?"

In the late fifties, a University of Michigan study asked a national cross section of Americans what they thought of anyone, man or woman, who rejected the idea of marriage. An overwhelming majority (80 percent) severely criticized those who preferred the single state, stigmatizing them as "sick" or "neurotic" or "immoral." The remaining 20 percent were neutral, neither condemnatory nor approving. Fewer than 1 percent had anything good to say about the unmarried state. By the late seventies, the country's interpretation of what kind of person would deliberately choose to remain unmarried had shifted dramatically. Condemnatory attitudes shrunk from 80 percent to a mere 25 percent— from virtual consensus to minority standing. A three-fifths majority (61 percent) swung into the neutral column. And a significant number of Americans (14 percent) praised the choice of the unmarried state as a valid and positive way of life. In other words, in the late fifties, 80 percent of all Americans held that being unmarried was an unnatural state for a man or woman: to be "normal" was to be married. By the late seventies, a mere generation later, virtually the same massive majority (75 percent) had totally changed their normative premise. Moral contumely was withdrawn from the unmarried state. Not that marriage was deemed bad; quite the contrary, most Americans continue to favor the married condition. But in keeping with the trend toward pluralism and the definition of morality as not doing harm to others, it is becoming as "normal" to be unmarried as to be married. According to Elizabeth Douvan, a Michigan researcher associated with the study, "norms about marriage and parenthood have changed dramatically over the last twenty years. Today marriage and parenthood are rarely viewed as necessary, and people who do not choose these roles are no longer considered social deviants."*

Furthermore, and also in contrast with the past, it has become normal to think of marriage as enduring less than forever. When an Associated Press/NBC poll asked Americans in 1978 whether they

---

* *ISR Newsletter*, Vol. 7, No. 1, Institute for Social Research (Ann Arbor: The University of Michigan, Winter 1979).

thought "most couples getting married today expect to remain married for the rest of their lives," a 60 percent majority said no. In this same poll a two-thirds majority (68 percent) concluded that as a consequence of these and other changes the institution of marriage is growing much weaker than in the recent past. Sheila M. Rothman writes in *Woman's Proper Place*:

> An expectation of impermanence now seemed normal within a marriage. If the experts of the 1920s counseled women to find fulfillment in an intensive and all-consuming intellectual and sexual relationship with one man, their counterparts in the 1970s told them that fulfillment was not a unitary, once achieved/always achieved state, that different stages demanded new relationships. In the 1950s as in the 1920s, diamonds were "forever." In the 1970s diamonds were for "now."*

Lest there be any doubt about the power of norms to influence behavior, a handful of social facts should allay it. As I noted in the Preface to this book, single households (defined by the Census Bureau as men or women living alone or with an unrelated person) have had an explosive growth rate, increasing 66 percent from 1960 to 1980. During this same period single-parent families, mainly women but now including more than a million and a half men, also grew rapidly—from 9 percent of all households in 1960 to 14 percent now. Together, these two categories constitute nearly four out of ten households. Marriage and "traditional" family life are growing less universal all the time.

Between 1960 and 1977 it is estimated that the number of unmarried couples living together more than doubled—from 439,000 to 957,000. Here is how one woman, a twenty-seven-year-old graduate student living in Kansas, described her parents' reaction to the news that she was living with a man.

> "When I first told my parents I had a new roommate, they immediately knew what was going on. My mother's first words were, 'Don't do all the cooking and cleaning.' "†

Since the advent of sanctioned wedlock, some individuals have always opted to forego the ceremony and mate in accordance with their own rules—or with no rules at all. But such people were always recog-

---

* Sheila M. Rothman, "Family Life as Zero-Sum Game," excerpt from *Woman's Proper Place* (New York: Basic Books, 1978), *Dissent* (Fall 1978), p. 397.
 † *Time* 11/21/77.

nized as deviating from the norms the society at large held sacred, or at least important. Now, what used to be called "living in sin" translates into the more neutral "living together." When Yankelovich, Skelly and White asked in its surveys for *Time* whether people thought it was "morally wrong for couples who are not married to live together," more than half (52 percent) answered no, that this was now morally acceptable.

The loss of normative power carries over to childbearing as well. From the once universally held norm that a childless woman was, by definition, "barren," and "not a complete woman," we have moved to a widespread acceptance of childlessness without stigma. A YS&W study shows that virtually all Americans (83 percent) now believe it is acceptable to be married and not have children. A majority (59 percent) even rejects the weaker version of the concept: "People who do not have children are selfish." (We sense here some hesitancy, a lingering feeling that while childlessness may be acceptable, it is not necessarily praiseworthy.) In the same tolerant spirit three out of four Americans (75 percent) say it is now morally acceptable to be single and have children—an astonishing turnabout in mores when one recalls the aura of scandal and disgrace formerly associated with having a child out of wedlock.

Here too, changes in behavior parallel the shift in norms. In recent years the fertility of American women has followed a steady downward trend—from 118.3 births per 1,000 women in 1955 to 66.7 in 1975. In the 1955–59 period, a woman in her childbearing years could expect to have 3.7 births; in the 1965–69 period, 2.6 births; in 1977, 1.8. In the 1950s married young women who did not want babies were reluctant to admit it. Now I often encounter the reverse situation: many young women when interviewed deny any interest in having babies; only when pressed do they admit to harboring a "curiosity" about the experience of childbirth and mothering.

So much has been written in recent years about changing sexual norms that we need not dwell on them at length. A few survey findings sum up the story. As recently as 1967, a Yankelovich, Skelly and White survey for CBS News found that most parents of college-age youths (85 percent) condemned all premarital sex as morally wrong. Now, a majority (63 percent) condone it ("If two people love each other, there's nothing morally wrong with having sexual relations"). Nearly the same majority (57 percent) reject the norm that a bride should be a virgin when she gets married. And, as we have seen, most Americans now reject the old double standard that "if a husband plays around a little, that's excusable, but a wife never should."

For the first time in American society, only minorities of adults report discomfort at "having friends who are homosexuals," and while slim majorities still feel that homosexual relations may be morally wrong, there is a declining willingness to allow laws restricting the sexual preferences of consenting adults; and barely one quarter of the population (21 percent) expresses a desire for a "return to traditional standards regarding sexual relations."

The double standard lives on, however. Its existence can be documented in the mere 45 percent plurality of Americans who find male nudes in women's magazines acceptable as compared to the nearly 60 percent who accept female nudes in men's periodicals. The divergence is merged again, however, in the nearly doubled acceptance of total nudity in films and plays in the last ten years.

Not surprisingly, normative changes relating to sexuality, childbearing and marriage carry over to affect the man-woman division of effort in the family. Changing norms of what a woman is "supposed to do" as wife and mother and what a man is supposed to do as husband and father are transforming the institutions of the workplace and the family. Probably no set of shifting norms carry greater significance for the culture.

Norms affecting whether a wife should work outside the home have, within a single generation, reversed themselves. It should be kept in mind that some women in America have always worked outside the home. The number of working women has increased in recent years, but the phenomenon is not novel. What is new is the cultural meaning of women working. In the eighteenth century, and particularly in the nineteenth, it was not unusual for the whole family—the husband, his wife and his children to work for pay outside the home. In the late nineteenth and early twentieth century, as the nation industrialized and its wealth grew, it became a source of pride for a man to be so successful as a provider that his children and even his wife no longer had to work outside the home. In the early post–World War II years the majority of women with children who worked were blue collar, not blue stocking. When middle-class women worked outside the home, a clear understanding existed between husband and wife. Even if the wife earned as much as or more than the husband, the norm insisted that rent and food money come from *his* salary. It was acceptable to use the wife's income for "extras," to pay for a housecleaner once or twice a week, or a baby-sitter, or even a vacation, but not for the necessities of life. For a man to depend on his wife's income carried a social stigma that diminished a family's status in the eyes of others. The law supported this norm. A wife's earnings could not legally be counted in calculating how large a mortgage the bank would give a family. (Cynthia Muller's mother was correct.) The mortgage was geared to the man's income alone. In the eyes of the bank, a wife's income did not exist, even if it was larger than her husband's.

In practice, the norm that middle-class wives did not work to earn money—like so many social rules—was often breached. When this happened, the couple spun elaborate rationalizations to insure that the husband's position as chief breadwinner would not be undermined in his own eyes or in the eyes of others. In its social meaning, to have a working wife meant that the husband was incapable of providing for his family. To be less than a good provider meant that one was less than a man.

This shared meaning, equating manliness with earning power, has persisted in the culture with great force; until the late 1960s it was held almost universally. One of my favorite survey questions is to ask people what they mean by a "real man." Up to the late 1960s, an 85 to 90 percent majority defined a "real man" as someone who is a "good provider" for his family. Other meanings—sexual potency, physical strength, being a responsible and caring human being, being handy around the house—always fell far behind this root cultural meaning. In recent years, however, the definition of a real man as a good provider has declined from the number one spot to the number three position, and had slipped from 86 percent in 1968 to 67 percent a decade later. The cultural definition persists, but in attenuated form.

Even more strikingly, the work patterns of women reflected a marked shift in cultural meaning. Whereas it was mainly blue-collar women who once worked for pay, now it is the better-educated, upper-middle-class women who increasingly work outside the home, seeking satisfactions that include but are not limited to financial ones.

The cultural meaning of a woman working outside the home has shifted subtly from an act that diminishes the manliness of the "head of household" to one that enhances the status of the woman without adversely affecting the man. As recently as 1970 only a minority of Americans (42 percent) wanted unstintingly to strengthen women's status in our society. By the end of that decade, a two-thirds majority in a Harris poll (64 percent) approved this notion, and work outside the home has become the key to achieving this goal.

In the abstract, the idea that women ought to have a choice—an alternative to housekeeping—is now almost universally endorsed. Three out of four Americans believe that if a woman finds housekeeping unsatisfying, she ought to be able to get out of the home to develop her interests even if her husband has to do more around the house. Just as many men as women express this sentiment. In practice, however, norms relating to women working for pay outside the home are still in transition.

Most men, in particular, remain ambivalent about their wives working outside the home, but they are coming to accept and even to depend on it. In a typical interview, a middle-aged insurance salesman recalled, "At first I didn't want my wife to work at all. I wanted her home when I got there. Then, when she started to work, I insisted that we live within *my* means, on *my* salary. Now, we live on both paychecks and I don't know how in the world we would live any other way."

As more women work, the norms governing the division of effort within the home continue to loosen. In the single decade of the seventies Americans who believe that both sexes should share responsibility for cleaning the home has almost doubled (from 24 percent to 42 percent). Similar increases have also been registered for the idea that both sexes should share responsibility for shopping for groceries, cooking and taking care of small children. But in the domain of housekeeping, the new norms are honored more by lip service than action. Men agree in principle that they should share the housekeeping, and most men do help more than they used to, but their assistance around the house remains largely an ineffectual expression of good will. As Princeton sociologist Suzanne Keller observes:

> Things have worked as well as they have because the women have taken on multiple burdens pretty much without protest. Should women refuse to do so in the next decade, romantic relationships would suffer even more than they do now.*

Our research indicates that husbands and wives have different perceptions of the stresses caused by women working. A substantial 25.

* *The New York Times,* 9/14/79.

percent of working wives say their husbands are bothered by having them away from home so much; only 1 percent of the husbands admit to being so bothered. One out of five working wives claim their husbands are disturbed that their homes are not as neat and clean as before the wives went to work, but virtually none of the husbands say this bothers them. Husbands, on the other hand, do admit to disliking the pressure to help around the house. They say their wives underestimate the discomfort to the whole family caused by the fact that they (the wives) work for pay.

Happily or unhappily, the dual-earner family is rapidly becoming the norm, now accounting for a majority of upper-income households. Although economic need pushes many women to paid jobs, it is not easy to define economic need. In many families, husbands and wives both work to maintain a standard of living that they have come to enjoy and expect, though they hardly "need" it in a literal sense. Indeed, an impressive 67 percent of women who work say that they do so for self-fulfillment reasons as well as economic ones.

In the 1950s most married women rated the housewife's job as an important, interesting and challenging task. A majority of women (including those who work at paying jobs *and* those who stay home) now state that the woman who is truly fulfilling herself manages a career as well as a home. Today, the proportion of women who rate housewife's work as dull and boring exceeds the number of those who find it interesting by a large margin (34 percent to 20 percent). A woman I interviewed in Los Angeles was typical. "I'm a housewife and mother," she said, "and if you make a success of it it can be a fulfilling job. But very often I'm bored and I'm torn; I've got to have more time and more identity to myself. I feel trapped."

As with so many norms, the path of change proceeds along the lines of age and education. Most of the women over fifty-five feel comfortable with the traditional sharp cleavage of responsibilities between men and women, while only a minority of those under thirty-five like the rigid divisions. Similarly, a minority of those wth some college education (37 percent) endorse the old roles, while the majority (57 percent) with a high school education or less do so.

One of the most far-reaching changes in norms relates to what parents believe they owe their children and what their children owe them. Nowhere are changes in the unwritten social contract more significant or agonizing. The overall pattern is clear: today's parents expect to make fewer sacrifices for their children than in the past, but they also demand less from their offspring in the form of future obligations than their parents demanded of them. Measures of these attitudes in previous eras do not exist, largely because no one thought of the parent-child bond as anything but permanent. But the data now available is unmistakable. In a series of studies on the American family carried out by Yankelovich, Skelly and White in the 1970s for General Mills, the following key findings came to light:

· Nearly two thirds of all American parents (63 percent) reject the idea that parents should stay together for the children's sake even if the partners are unhappy with each other.

· A similar majority (66 percent) feel that "parents should be free to live their own lives even if it means spending less time with their children," and an almost equal number of parents (63 percent) endorse the view that they have the right to live well now and spend what they have earned "even if it means leaving less to the children."

· On the other hand, most parents recognize that in the name of fairness, if they reduce their level of sacrifice for their children, then their children should not be burdened with future obligations to them. Sixty-seven percent believe that "children do not have an obligation to their parents regardless of what their parents have done for them."

There is one survey finding in particular that encapsulates the ambivalence Americans feel about these sweeping normative changes in marriage, family life and the parental relationship to children. These changes fill most Americans with sadness. They look back on the "old days" of stable family life with longing. The changes create a feeling of loss, almost of grief, and give rise to many inconsistencies and contradictions. The same large two-thirds majorities that say parents now have a reduced commitment to their children and their children to them also say they wish to see "a return to more traditional standards of family life and parental responsibility." Why the inconsistency? A related survey finding provides the key: majorities may claim in the abstract that they want to return to the family life of the past, but when it comes to specifics, only one out of five (21 percent) has any hankering to go back either to traditional standards of sexual relations, to the "spic and span" housekeeping norms of the past, or to the male monopoly on working outside the home. Americans long for the warmth and closeness they associate with family life in earlier decades, but not if it means going back to the old rules. How to preserve warmth and closeness while at the same time holding onto the new freedom to choose?—this is the preeminent question the culture confronts on the domestic scene, and it is the testing ground of most life experiments made in the search for self-fulfillment.

Chapter 9

———◉———

The Old Epochal Experience

Early in January 1979 I found myself sitting through a three-hour NBC News special entitled, *The American Family: An Endangered Species?* I marveled at how the producers were unable to resist showing among fourteen "typical" American families, a lesbian couple with five children (from previous heterosexual marriages); a young woman who later died as part of the ghastly ritual in Guyana where a crazed Jim Jones led more than nine hundred of his "family" to mass suicide; a circle of about forty friends whose shared activities were said to constitute a family; and a group of old people who had acquired an "instant" family upon paying the admission fee to what seemed, in effect, a "rent-a-family" retirement home.

But among the fourteen, one portrait lodged itself in my mind precisely because it was not as exotic as the others. On the contrary, it lingered because of its very ordinariness, and because of what it says about the normative changes in American life.

Halfway through the show the camera settled on a married couple in their early thirties living in a trailer in Youngstown, Ohio. The wife, whom I will call Mrs. Youngstown, is a slightly dumpy woman, with an oval face and a body that has just begun to sag. She is feeding a jar of baby food to one of her two sons, an infant in a highchair. Her other son is sitting contentedly nearby playing with a ball.

Mr. Youngstown, standing in the background, is an attractive young man with a mustache, who wears his hair a trifle longer than is the current fashion. Along with thousands of other steelworkers, Mr. Youngstown is unemployed, laid off from Youngstown Sheet and Tube, one of Republic Steel's main plants in Ohio. Like other American steel companies, Republic has had difficulty competing with imported Japanese products, and as a result, for the first time since the Great Depression of the 1930s, mass unemployment haunts the town.

We see immediately that Mr. Youngstown is angry, restless, at loose ends. He acknowledges that unlike his father, who lived through severe layoffs a generation ago, he can count on sizable benefits in the form of unemployment insurance and union payments. These keep his sons in baby food and other necessities. But he does not like the idea of accepting these benefits without working for them. "I wasn't raised to take money for nothing," he says. "You feel like you are taking it out of someone else's pocket."

He reflects on what his work means to him: "It's your job—the man's job—to provide for the family. To protect them. Without a job you can't provide and you can't protect . . . it is a devastating experience."

Looking to the future, he lets himself dream a little. "I don't like it in the trailer. I want to have my own home. I'd like to have a few acres . . . maybe breed a horse or two." Abruptly, the interviewer brings him back to the bleak reality of the trailer and his joblessness: "How would you feel if your wife found a full-time job in case you don't go back to work as quickly as you would like?" the interviewer asks. He answers without hesitation: "If my wife had to go to work full-time, I don't think I could take it. It would be humiliating."

Then it is Mrs. Youngstown's turn. She observes that her husband's joblessness creates heavy financial and emotional pressures on both of them. "He shouldn't be home all day," she says firmly. "It's not the right place for him." She rebuffs the interviewer's question about finding a job for herself. "The best place for me is here at home with the baby, watching him grow." She says she never had any desire to work outside the home and had always assumed she would get married and raise a family. Now everything is threatened by her husband's prolonged joblessness. Anguish creeps into her voice and into her body language. She appears to droop. Her face is drawn, almost visibly darkening.

Then, abruptly, her mood changes. The look of anguish passes. Quietly but with unmistakable force she says: "I will make it work. I will make it work no matter what I have to do. I don't want to lose it all." For an instant her determination lights up the screen, suffusing it with dramatic intensity.

The episode is over. The screen fills with a peanut butter commercial, then with a portrait of another "typical" American family, a middle-aged single white man who has adopted a black child and a Korean child for whom he is both mother and father. We are back in TV-land. But for one small moment we glimpsed an authentic American epochal experience, illuminated in the solidity and gravity of a woman's life. Even though her husband spoke at greaetr length, it was the electricity of the woman that crackled across the tube. We knew we were witnessing, and in some sense sharing, one of those acts of determination that shape a person's life, giving it direction and meaning.

Mrs. Youngstown's reality resides wholly in her family life—her children and husband and home. Perhaps the trailer is a stopgap, but for her it is home nonetheless. This is what she has and this is all she has. Further, it represents what she wants: to be the person who stays home and watches the children grow, doing what she can to nurture that growth along. She is where she belongs. During the day her husband does *not* belong at home. He belongs at work, "providing and protecting."

Why, in its succinct normalcy, does this incident stay so fixed in my mind? Other vignettes are more colorful. The portraits of a "blended" couple with built-in children from previous marriages, and of an unmarried couple who live together because both were married before and now prefer the more limited commitment of life without a marriage license are more contemporary and "with it" forms of family life. In an odd sense they arouse interest but do not jar. They blend unobtrusively with TV's standard evening entertainment.

I suddenly realize what startles me about the experience of the Youngstown couple. As "normal" as they are, they too have become atypical, almost as exotic in today's America as the lesbian couple or the single male parent of two adopted children.

The Youngstowns belong with that 20 percent minority of Americans who have managed to ignore the great cultural changes sweeping over the rest of the nation. Their lives preserve the older epochal experience intact. In it, the self-denial ethic plays a central role as the binding force that holds the structure of their lives together. In this respect the

Youngstowns are at the opposite end of the continuum from the Williamses, Sara Lou Wellford, Lyndon Hendries and other strong formers.

The Youngstowns interpret their experience within a traditional pattern of shared meanings: what it means to a man to be unemployed ("a devastating experience"), to think about having one's wife work for the essentials of life ("humiliating") and to accept money for not working ("like taking it out of someone else's pocket"), and what it means for a woman to stay home ("where I belong"), to have her husband at home during the day ("not the right place for him"), to be married, have children and raise a family ("my whole life").

In Mrs. Youngstown we see exemplified the full meaning of the American epochal experience as it once existed on an almost universal scale. Think how drastically the Youngstowns' predicament differs from that, say, of Mark and Abby Williams and how much more severely their lives are threatened. Mrs. Youngstown risks losing everything that holds meaning for her life, because these things *do* have meaning. Many aspects of the risk do not lie within her control but in external circumstance (e.g., the fate of Youngstown Sheet and Tube). It is the objective reality of the predicament that differentiates it so sharply from that of the Williamses. Mrs. Youngstown raises no existential questions about who she is, what she believes and what is worth sacrificing for. She knows every inch of the ground on which she stands. She lives according to a clear set of rules. And she knows what they are. She knows what winning is and what losing is. She may lose, but not if her will and determination are decisive. Circumstances may yet claim her as a victim, but her battle is with circumstances and not within herself or with her husband or her children. The battle is fought within tightly prescribed constraints. Under the rules she follows, she wins by having her husband return to work, not by finding a job for herself. Her experience is played out within definitions imposed by a psychoculture that is now passing from the scene.

The changes in that epochal experience and the strains these changes create in people's lives is nicely illustrated in one of the interviews Ellen Goodman reports in her insightful book, *Turning Points*. She describes a couple who are the same age and come from the same kind of socio-economic background as the Youngstowns, but whose response to our changing psychoculture is far more typical of today's trends.*

* Ellen Goodman, *Turning Points* (New York: Doubleday, 1979).

Paul, a thirty-year-old printer, and his wife, Sandy, have three children. Paul is a firm believer in separate "spheres" for men and women: he is the husband, father and provider; Sandy is the wife, mother and homemaker. Paul has an enormous emotional investment in this role; in many respects it is the central meaning of his life.

Paul makes what he regards as a good living. But it is no longer enough to fulfill his aspirations for his family: college for his kids, a secure future and a material standard of living he and his wife see as the rightful heritage of middle-class Americans.

He tells Sandy that to make ends meet he intends to take a second job at nights in a local print shop. In this "traditional values" solution, Paul confirms his role as the good provider, the "real man"—at the cost of giving up time with his family and diminishing his quality of life. But Sandy vehemently rejects the idea. In fact, her objections lead to what he later describes as the first real argument of their marriage. She makes a countersuggestion: she will find a job. She says this is what she wants to do anyway, to get away from her regime of children and housework.

At first Paul rejects her suggestion out of hand, as unthinkable. But cultural norms *have* changed, and his male co-workers reassure him. They tell him it isn't a bad idea; the extra money helps. Not that it's really necessary, mind you. But it helps. Gradually Paul's resistance weakens. Sandy finds a part-time job, and he doesn't protest. It boosts their income to a level that is sufficient to meet most of their goals.

But then, almost imperceptibly, their positions within the household shift. Sandy becomes more independent; she makes decisions on her own which in the past she would have left to Paul, or at least shared with him. Life changes in many small ways. Paul sees that the kids are given breakfast and sent on their way in the morning. He learns to drink instant coffee, if not to like it. He accepts the change but he is not nearly so comfortable with it as his wife appears to be. Goodman quotes his reaction:

> "It's not what I grew up thinking was the family type of thing . . .
> A family to me is the man working and the woman at home. Okay.
> Now, you can't afford that, and I know it. Then I know that Sandy
> likes being out of the house, which I'm not sure I understand, but
> there it is. What bothers me is something different. When I was
> growing up everyone looked up to my father. My mother, us kids.
> Whatever you say, a man likes to be looked up to. Made to feel
> important. Not in a bad way, not that anyone is afraid of you or

anything like that. But looked up to. When the man brought the money in, that was it. But when the woman is bringing the money in too . . . it's just not the same."*

No, it isn't the same—not for Paul, not for Sandy, not for their children and not for the society either. Paul and Sandy had a choice, more of a choice than Paul's father had. A tradition-minded person, Paul holds fixed views and a conservative outlook. And yet he accepted, though reluctantly, a solution modeled on the newer self-fulfillment outlook, rather than on the older pattern of husbands who make the living and wives who stay home. But the solution exacts a psychic cost. The old giving/getting covenant might have required Paul to exhaust himself moonlighting for the extra money he needed for his family, but there would have been compensations. His self-denial would have gained him a status the loss of which he now keenly feels. The new cultural rules sadden and discomfort him, but he accepts them, though reluctantly.

We do not learn what Sandy thinks. Did she take the job out of economic necessity, or because it opened up outlets for self-expression she did not find in her traditional role of housewife and mother? It does not matter what the precise weight of these factors may have been. The fact is that Americans today are subject to many conflicting pressures. New ones say, "fulfill thyself"; traditional values say, "deny thyself for the sake of others"; current awareness says, "take heed: stormy weather lies ahead."

The life goals of both families, the Youngstowns even more than Paul and Sandy, exemplify what was until the early nineteen-seventies the dominant meaning of success in American life, a form of success I have referred to earlier as "familial success." More than in any other domain of psychoculture, changes in the meaning of familial success are reshaping our rules of living.

Most Americans still define their life goals in relation to familial success. A minority, like the Youngstowns, accept it without change. The vast majority, like Paul and Sandy, partly endorse it, but partly modify one or another of its key terms.

The concept of familial success clusters around three sets of shared meanings: the intactness and well-being of the family; enough money

* Goodman, op. cit., p. 36.

to provide some of the luxuries of life as well as security; and a hankering after respectability and acceptance. In my interviews and surveys these three components of familial success are most clearly described when people speak about their parents' lives.

When asked what success meant to their parents, people said:

> *Success meant being good parents—*
> "Providing for the family."
> "Making a home for the children."
> "Giving children the maximum you could give them—mostly material things."
> "Raising children and seeing them grow into healthy and happy adults."
> "Caring for the family."
> "Having a stable family life."
> "Trying to create a happy home life."
> "Giving us the chance to get what they didn't have."
>
> *Success meant money—*
> "Getting it, holding onto it, buying things with it—especially a car and house."
> "Gaining security from money."
> "Enjoying independence because of money, acquiring luxuries with it, flaunting it."
> "Handing money on to one's children."
>
> *Success meant social standing and respectability—*
> "Being accepted by the right people."
> "Staying married."
> "Caring about how others see you."
> "Having the respect of those who count."
> "Having the right car and the right house."

In almost all instances people differentiated between familial success and self-fulfillment in their *own* lives but said these goals were synonymous for their parents. In describing what self-fulfillment meant to their parents, typical comments were: "I don't think they were concerned with it," or "they never talked about it." Or "they didn't have time to be concerned with it; they were too busy making a living." These comments came both from young people whose parents are still alive and are relatively young, and also from people in their fifties and sixties, most of whose parents had died. Strikingly, though many had difficulty in saying what self-fulfillment meant to their parents, no one had any difficulty in stating what *success* meant to their parents.

One can visualize the shared meanings of familial success—maintaining the intactness of the family, making money and earning the respect of others—as forming a mutually supportive triangle. Until recently the epochal experience of most Americans took place within the region defined by the triangle. Life's satisfactions and its crises came from how one experienced these meanings. If success meant being married, having children, making a good living and having everyone know about it, then the epochal experience of the individual played itself out within the range of possibilities implicit in these meanings.

Within the meaning of familial success, only one form of family life was highly esteemed: the nuclear family with clearly prescribed roles for husband-father, wife-mother and children. Both parents were expected to sacrifice for their children. It was assumed that successful family life required such sacrifices—the wife subordinating her own desires to the needs of husband and children, the man willingly accepting the frustrations of the workplace as long as the job paid well.

The pursuit of money formed the second side of the familial success triangle. To afford a free-standing home in the suburbs and the material possessions that went with it—an automobile, dishwashers and freezers to make mother's job easier—were believed to be an ideal foundation for successful family life. Husband and wife functioned as a unit, he on the job, she at home, to acquire the products and services that made life more secure and comfortable. If, through lack of educational opportunity or "bad luck," one's standard of living failed to improve year by year, one could at least work hard to insure that the children would receive a good education so that they could attain a higher plateau of material well-being than their parents.

Respectability formed the third dimension of the triangle and depended on the other two. To raise children and to move ahead economically entitled one to recognition—in one's own eyes as well as in the eyes of others. Consumption and respectability went hand in hand. Expensive cars, diamond rings, fur coats and silver flatware gave tangible evidence of success, as did tended lawns, floors so clean "you can eat off them" and sheets that could be washed "whiter than white."

Even more important than physical possessions in conferring respectability was one's success in keeping the family intact and well behaved. A family broken, except by death, diminished one's respectability. A divorce meant failure, even shame. Abortions were hidden from public scrutiny, particularly if unmarried daughters were involved. For the middle-class majority, joblessness and dependence on welfare meant a sure loss of status, even more than in the nineteen-thirties.

Men did not voluntarily drop out of the workforce. If the husband made a "good living," a wife who chose to work at a paid job threatened the grounds of the relationship and the husband's self-conception of his own manliness.

These social values are now under seige.

Chapter 10

···——◆◉◆——···

"Otherwise the World Is One Big Factory"

Of the three sides of the familial success triangle, we are least familiar with the one labeled "respectability."

What is respectability? Is it as old fashioned as it sounds? What is its fate under the influence of the shifts in culture? Has it disappeared as a shared meaning, or does it retain its old significance, though perhaps garbed in new semantics? There is no way to understand today's cultural shifts without comprehending the changing meaning of respectability.

In the late seventies, Bernard Lefkowitz wrote a fascinating book about people (mostly men) who decided to give up working for a living.* He describes his father's experience a generation earlier as a worker in New York's garment district—and mentions his father's horror at the idea that any man would deliberately choose not to work and to live instead on charity or welfare. To the author's father such a man was not a *mench* but a poor slob devoid of both self-respect and respectability in the eyes of others.

Coming from a different region and another milieu, Sara Lou Wellford tells us that in the genteel Southern background of her upbringing,

---

* Bernard Lefkowitz, *Breaktime: Living Without Work in a Nine to Five World* (New York: Hawthorn, 1979).

respectability was all-important to her family—as important as to the elder Lefkowitz, although it assumed a different form of expression. Sara Lou was brought up to conform to the expectations of others, and among these the social significance of "marrying well" figured prominently.

In fact the theme of respectability is prominent in every interview I conducted. Mothers of college-age men spoke of their embarrassment over what to do when their sons brought home a girl friend for an overnight stay. How to handle the question of separate bedrooms without seeming gauche or straight-laced? What to say to him? To her? The attitude of most was, "I don't care what they do there [at college]. Under my roof they are going to behave." The mothers automatically assumed that the couple were sleeping together. They did not need to disapprove of such behavior to know it would not be "respectable" for them to allow it openly in the parental home. Attitudes of parents of college-age women were more varied. Most were unwilling to concede that the daughter and her boy friend were sexually active. Therefore, fewer questions arose about sharing the same bedroom. Respectability alone mandated the decision.

My associate, Florence Skelly, refers to the many expressions of respectability that emerged from our studies of the fifties, sixties and seventies as "respectability badges." People wore them openly, since the purpose of a badge is that it will be seen by others.

Skelly observes that our culture, up to now, has proven wondrously ingenious at providing respectability badges, so that almost all Americans can, if they wish, preserve some element of respectability and therefore think of themselves as successful. Postwar America was highly competitive but it was also an era in which the symbols of respectability were available to the majority rather than to the select few. Most married Americans could observe the preordained sex roles in marriage; have children and sacrifice for them; afford to buy a car; own a TV set; keep lust confined to their hearts—and in doing these things participate in a culturally-defined consensus on the nature of respectability and success. Moreover, success symbols were clear-cut and concrete. Respectability could be achieved through such visible symbols as a home in a good neighborhood; a neat, clean appearance; eating out in restaurants; traveling for vacations; and sending children to college. People found it easy to know when they were successful, and to let others know as well—no small virtue for a symbol.

We come here to one of the main sources of confusion about the meaning of success in America—the overlapping meaning of respectability and social mobility. It is in the nature of respectability that it can, in principle, be shared by all, regardless of social position. There are no inherent limits to the number of respectability badges a society can create, and no basis for limiting them to a select class or group. On the contrary, in a society such as ours most members will pursue and win respectability even at the cost of other goals. Social mobility is another matter. By definition, it is limited. The search for higher status takes place in a hierarchical world. In what we have called the old epochal experience—the characteristic experience of the American majority in the two decades following World War II—both respectability and status were pursued with vigor; each interacted predictably with the other.

Here, abstracted from my interviews, is the case of a young man whose experience may clarify the difference between social mobility and respectability by showing the source of each.

His story belongs in the center of the continuum, characterized by the weak form of the self-fulfillment predicament. It moves slightly away from the old epochal experience personified by Mrs. Youngstown, yet it remains rooted in the classic American tradition of familial success, tinged with certain aspects of self-fulfillment that create a predicament quite different from those of the strong formers.

(ii)

Tom Wheeler is twenty-two-years old and the youngest of six brothers. His five older brothers are married and live close to each other and to their parents in Columbus, Indiana. The family moved to Columbus from West Virginia seven years earlier because Tom's father thought job opportunities would be better there for himself and his sons.

Tom works as a crewman in the maintenance department of McDonald's. He expects to be appointed assistant manager of the department in a few months, and thinks he has a good chance of being accepted into the company's management training program. He started at McDonald's while still in high school, but at his father's urging left to take a job at the same factory where his father and brothers work because the factory pay was better. After a year on the job he found factory work "drove me up a wall," so he quit and went back to McDonald's, at a sacrifice in pay. He is planning to be married in June, and is saving most of his salary toward a down payment on a house. He says he has "big plans" for the future. "I want to get into management. I think I have the potential."

His decision to leave the factory sparked an argument with his

mother and father. "They wanted me to be like them and stick to something safe." His mother accused him of wanting to "get rich quick." He
says that "she is worried that I have big ideas." Of his father and
brothers he says, "They have no vision. They don't care whether they
are getting something out of their work or not as long as the paycheck
comes in. They're not really trying to improve themselves. But it's important to me to get something out of what you do. Otherwise the world
is just one big factory."

Tom says that for his parents, success means "money. Economic
security. Providing. Making ends meet. I don't think they even dream
of satisfaction from what they do as long as my dad makes enough
money to support the family." But for himself he says:

> "Success means having a job that gives me personal satisfaction. It
> means a happy family life. Success is not just money. I want to
> have my own business and make enough to get along and be com-
> fortable. My five brothers are all factory workers. I'm not trying
> to be better than them. But I'm not satisfied personally with fac-
> tory work. I plan to get ahead. I want to be my own boss.
>
> "I also never expected to get married so soon. But I can't see liv-
> ing together. I want to make this commitment—have the security
> of marriage and a home. I'm close to my own family even though
> we don't agree on everything. I'm proud of my family—how well
> we get along and how close we are. Most big families split and the
> kids live in all different states. We stick together. It is important to
> us to be close to one another."

But he anticipates some friction in his own married life: "My job
has bad hours—I work from one to ten in the evening. My fiancée gets
upset. She wants a husband with a nine to five job who is home with
her every evening. But I've got to try for this management job. It's
important to me. I get a little stubborn with my fiancée. But I know I
have to learn to give in more if I want our marriage to work."

Several themes emerge with sharp clarity from the interview. Tom
wants to construct his marriage and family life with the same warmth,
closeness and intimacy he shares with his parents and brothers. But
at the same time factory work holds a different meaning for him than
for the other members of his family. He sees the factory as a trap: a
world in which men settle for a daily life devoid of meaning and satisfaction in exchange for the money to support a family. He thinks he
can do better: receive inherent as well as monetary satisfaction from
his work.

Most other meanings that shape Tom's life he shares with those closest to him: the meaning of a family, of being formally engaged and having a fiancée, the security of settling down, owning a house, working hard and loyally for a good living and giving in to the needs of others so that marriage and family life will work.

On only one set of meanings does he part company with his family and his fiancée. He has "plans" and "dreams" to avoid the fate of his father and brothers who he thinks lack vision. His family is upset because they fear he is putting on airs and trying to show that he is better than they. His fiancée is distressed because carrying out these plans may interfere with his coming home on time—and perhaps with other family commitments as well.

Though he receives little support for his plans from family and fiancée, the values, norms and meanings conveyed by the larger culture come to his rescue. In seeking to "better himself" through hard work, to get ahead and improve his lot through training and developing his "management potential," he gets support from one of the strongest sets of shared meanings in traditional American culture.

The dramatic possibilities of Tom Wheeler's life are contained within the shared meanings communicated by the psychoculture. The messages are mixed and inconsistent, creating conflict. The message from his mother says: "Stick with what is safe. Settle for a good-paying job at a factory whether you like the work or not. You will make a living and provide for your family." The message from the social structure, transmitted by teachers and books and his first boss at McDonald's who supported and encouraged him, says the opposite. "This is the land of opportunity. If you work hard and are dedicated and loyal you can improve your lot. You can better yourself. You can be part of management or own a business and be your own boss. The world is more than a factory. If you have vision you can succeed."

Still other messages have come through to Tom from the cultural values associated with the self-fulfillment motif, and their influence is substantial. Although Tom clings to traditional concepts of sexual morality and family life, his attitudes toward work are similar to those of the self-fulfillment group. He looks to his work not simply as a means for carrying out his responsibilities as a good provider, nor solely as a method for achieving upward mobility. Enthusiastically, he embraces the new meanings of work that have entered the culture. Like millions of other young Americans of all social classes Tom has come to believe that work should be "meaningful" and satisfying in its own right.

Our research shows that what people mean by "meaningful, satisfying work" is closely related to the self-expressive needs of the individual. Work is seen as a source of personal challenge and opportunity for growth. For Tom the world of the factory is depersonalizing and alienating. In the factory, one is not recognized as an individual or treated according to one's own unique personality. In his deeply felt and threatening image of "the world as a factory," this meaning comes through clearly.

In most people's lives respectability and social mobility are so tightly linked that the distinction between them seems artificial. Within the Wheeler family, however, Tom's parents and presumably his brothers have no need of improved social standing to guarantee their respectability. As with Mrs. Youngstown, what is important to them is that the family be sustained in its economic and emotional well-being. Characteristically, it was Tom's mother who expressed fears that his "big ideas" and "get rich quick" ambitions pose a threat to the unity of the family. To Mrs. Wheeler, representing the entire family except for Tom, to expect nothing but economic benefit from work is a realistic sacrifice unqualifiedly worth making for the sake of family well-being.

Tom's parents exemplify the criteria of familial success—the tightly integrated triangle of family security, money enough to provide the necessities and some of the luxuries of life, and respectability. Respectability comes from the fidelity with which each member of the family carries out the roles prescribed by the larger society—the roles of breadwinner husband and homemaker wife-mother. The yearning for social mobility expressed in Tom's life is not a *necessary* part of the respectability sought by other members of the family, not even by his own fiancée.

Here we begin to grasp the deep roots of the meaning of respectability. It draws its strength from the emotional power of the need to belong, surely one of the most potent of all human drives. To be human is to belong, to be part of an entity larger than oneself—a family, a tribe, a neighborhood, a religion, an ethnic group, a social class, a profession, a society, a civilization. The forms of respectability represent the symbolic links binding the individual to the larger entities of which he or she is a part. A respectability badge is a sign of belonging. It says, "I am a wife and mother in good standing," or "I am an American," or "I am a respected physician," or "the other members of the church receive me with fellowship."

Historically, belongingness has dwarfed the individualism we associate with our present society and the tradition of modernism. Meanings associated with belongingness dominated the cultures of our forefathers as they still dominate most of the non-Western cultures of the world. Even in the West until the recent past, individualism could express itself only within the confines established by rigid norms governing respectability, norms that varied mainly with social class.

The gifted philosopher of ideas, Isaiah Berlin, traces back to Johann Herder the insight that the immense power of nationalism in the modern world derives from its ability to bestow the gift of belongingness on people whose affiliation with other groups (the guild, the church, the community, the family) had been weakened by modern industrial society. The nation-state filled the vacuum created by the dislocations of industrialism.

> One of the fundamental needs of men, as basic as those for food, shelter, procreation, security and communication, is to belong to identifiable communal groups, each possessing its own unique language, traditions, historical memories, style and outlook. Only if a man truly *belongs* to such a community, naturally and unselfconsciously, can he enter into the living stream and lead a full, creative, spontaneous life, at home in the world and at one with himself and his fellow men; enjoying a recognized status within such a natural unit or group, which itself must command full unqualified recognition in the world at large; and thereby acquiring a vision of life, an image of himself and his condition in a community where concrete, immediate, spontaneous human relations may flower undistorted by neurotic self-questioning about one's true identity, and free from the crippling wounds inflicted by the real or imaginary superiority of others.*

The satisfactions of individualism come at an incalculable price, and a telling history of Western culture could be written around the theme of the dialectic conflict between individualism and belongingness. Because psychologists focus so sharply on the *individual*, their writings imply that each person must achieve psychological well-being through his or her inner resources. They often underestimate how dependent we are on the larger society to create the conditions—social, economic, political and cultural—in which well-being can be nurtured. For most of this century, and in particular in the quarter century following World War II, the values of most Americans drew support from powerful sym-

---

* Isaiah Berlin, *Against the Current: Essays in the History of Ideas* (New York: Viking, 1980), p. xxxvi.

bols of respectability which "delivered" some of the essentials of psychological well-being. In particular, these symbols gave Americans a sense of self-esteem and identity, a feeling of effectiveness and a conviction that their private goals and behavior also contributed to the well-being of others.

The badges of respectability—money, family, possessions, education, position in the community—were powerfully reinforced in the 1950s and 1960s, as more people moved into the middle class through better education, a booming economy and a steady rise in the median income of all but the poorest 20 percent of the population.

If the word "respectability" is too mundane to carry so heavy a psychological burden, there are other phrases that more directly convey belongingness, such as "social acceptance," "social identity" and "earning the respect of others." Even the old-fashioned term "honor" might more vividly delineate this dimension of familial success. Yet, I am satisfied to stay with respectability despite its thinness, because it belongs so appropriately to the epochal experience of the era that is now beginning to pass from the scene. Faintly old fashioned, it suggests a concern for appearances. It is precisely this concern for appearances—in both the literal sense of appropriate dress and the figurative sense of how one will appear to others—that is changing.

To the extent that the search for self-fulfillment emphasizes the inner person, external appearances no longer count as much as they once did. The shared meaning of respectability diminishes, and belongingness loses ground to individualism. As respectability badges disappear, or count for less, the visible marks of belongingness grow more subtle and intangible. Without tangible symbols of respectability it is difficult to send others the instant message, "I am a successful (i.e., respectable) individual." Having a family without a record of divorce, maintaining a well-kept home, exhibiting one's children as well-mannered and neat and clean in appearance have all been drained of much of their symbolic significance. As a consequence, it becomes harder to demonstrate respectability to oneself or to others.

As respectability grows more elusive, the incentive to pursue it diminishes. Respectability is a relentless taskmaster. It is never easy, the elder Lefkowitz tells us, to be a *mench*—to drag one's frail body every day and every year to a low-paying job controlled by an exploitative indifferent boss. But that is what being a *mench* is. Self-denial and respectability walk hand in hand; no one ever said you were *supposed* to enjoy your obligations. Quite the contrary, being a *mench* is the acceptance of self-denial for the sake of the obligations that bind the individual to others—the family, the religion, the race, the community, the nation. As the norms supporting self-denying respectability weaken, inevitably the sense of belongingness must weaken too.

There is a sense, then, in which a society's symbols of respectability are sacred—they have no instrumental value, but they celebrate and reinforce the human community. This is the meaning of Mrs. Wheeler's fears: she does not want the family to lose Tom, nor does Tom want to lose his family whom he cherishes. But he feels he must take the risk in pursuit of *his* freedom, *his* adventure, *his* self-fulfillment. Otherwise the world is one big factory.

Chapter 11

·····◆─◉─◆─·····

Feliciano's Bicycle

It is not a coincidence that the Youngstowns and the Wheelers come from the working class. Culturally, working-class groups are often the most conservative, holding on to traditional values after "conventional" behavior has been abandoned or transformed by other social classes.

Even in an age of easy communication, shifts in meanings do not travel through our culture uniformly. Typically, such changes move along lines of social class, age, and to some extent geography. Smaller towns get the word more slowly than big cities. The West Coast and the East Coast usually reflect cultural changes before the middle or southern states do. The young are more susceptible to cultural shifts than the old, the well-to-do more than the poor, and the better-educated more than those with less education. Though far from invariant, the process follows this route often enough to alert us to the likelihood that younger people living in coastal cities and educated at the nation's most prestigious colleges will usually prove to be the pacesetters of cultural change. Time and again we find that ideas cropping up in these groups reappear within a five- to ten-year period in diluted form among older, poorer, less well-educated groups living in the smaller cities and towns of the Midwest and South.

But not all ideas entertained by the well-educated young inevitably spread to the population at large. Most, in fact, do not. In the sixties, long hair, jeans, rock music and casual sex moved swiftly across social class and geographical barriers to be adopted by virtually an entire generation of youth; but radical politics, new sex roles for men and women in marriage, and counterculture attitudes stayed bottled up in campus-based enclaves, largely rejected by working-class youth. One cannot generalize casually from the values of college students to predict the nation's values in the future. Many such extrapolations in the past have proven disastrously wrong.

Nor can one look at working-class life as if it were a museum preserving an American culture that had already disappeared from other strata. Such a viewpoint is condescending and false. Social class superimposes its own realities on the culture, realities that cannot be ignored. The best way to gain perspective is to look first at the common themes of American culture, and then to examine the variations imposed by social class and age. Age and social class are the two axes along which cultural variability is most pronounced. Intersecting with each other they jointly determine how the shared meanings of the culture will be expressed. A Smith College graduate in her late fifties who is also the wife of a well-to-do surgeon will express her self-fulfillment yearnings differently from Tom Wheeler's fiancée, though the yearning may be equally strong in both.

There are many subcultures in America shaped by ethnicity, geography, profession and religion. These superimpose still further variations on the forms of expression taken by the self-fulfillment urge. But age and social class make, as it were, the primary claims on culture, and therefore express the minimum level of complexity we need to take into account.

Social science is more familiar with the variations created by social class than with those shaped by age. In recent years, however, excellent studies on life span development have been done, showing how our concerns change as we move through the adult stages of the life cycle. This work was pioneered by Carl Jung and Erik Erikson, and further developed by Daniel J. Levinson, Bernice Neugarten, Jane Loevinger, George Vaillant and others. Popularized for the public by journalist Gail Sheehy in the best-selling book *Passages*, this perspective emphasizes how lifecycle changes interact with general cultural patterns.*

Passages suffered from a tendency to overemphasize the effects of the life cycle, and to understate the effects of changes in culture. Sara

* Gail Sheehy, *Passages* (New York: Dutton, 1974).

Lou Wellford, for example, discarded her old life and struck out on a new path not because she had grown a few years older and had moved into a new phase of the life cycle, but because changes in cultural norms relating to marriage, divorce, women's roles and self-fulfillment strongly supported her own stirrings. Without these cultural changes, Sara Lou's changing attitudes as she grew older would have taken different forms. Yet, despite its one-sidedness, *Passages* served a valuable purpose: it made technical research on the life cycle accessible to millions of people, making them more aware than they had been before of stages of development taking place in postadolescent years. Freud and Piaget had made us conscious of the developmental stages of childhood, suggesting by implication that once the child and adolescent was formed development ceased, to be replaced by aging—a process of deterioration, not growth. The life-cycle framework enriches our understanding of how one's psychic economy shifts with each new stage in life, producing new interests, preoccupations and values. One reason I have selected many of my examples from people in their thirties and early forties is to minimize the added complexity of taking into account these changes in the life cycle. Americans in their thirties and early forties are old enough to have experienced the dominant culture of the post–World War II era, and yet young enough to have received full blast the new cultural meanings.

With these thoughts in mind, let us observe the self-fulfillment theme as it expresses itself in the life of a working-class man who is in about the same stage of life as Mark and Abby Williams and Sara Lou Wellford. His life reflects many common elements shared by Americans pursuing their self-fulfillment, and also shows the variability created by social class. We encounter here a significant difference in what it means to be successful in America.

(ii)

Miguel Feliciano, thirty-three, was born in Puerto Rico but moved to New York with his parents a few days before his first birthday. He grew up near the docks on the lower West Side of Manhattan in an area appropriately named "Hell's Kitchen." Recalling his school friends, he says, "Almost all the people I went to school with are junkies now."

At the time of our interview he had been married for two years, and his wife was six months pregnant. He obviously cares deeply about her and delights in the prospect of fathering a child. He works as a mailroom supervisor in a large Manhattan brokerage firm for a salary of $14,000 a year. Since his wife does not work, his family's income is below the national median.

Like virtually everyone interviewed in this study, he defines his ideas about success and self-fulfillment in opposition to those of his parents. "Success to my parents meant survival," he says quite simply. "Just making enough money to raise the family was success. My father was a waiter and held two jobs. He worked day and night just so we could survive." He contrasts this outlook with his own view. "I don't think like my parents at all. I don't worry about surviving. I know that if my job fails I'll find something else. I can afford to look for ful-fillment."

Recalling his parents' life of self-denial, his own sacrifices dwindle to insignificance. He constantly reminds himself how much better off he is than his parents were. "I recently took a vacation in Florida. My dad never took a vacation in his life. Also I went to Puerto Rico to visit my ninety-year-old grandmother. It was so beautiful . . . I've been able to have what I want. I have more time to do what I want. I'm not strug-gling to survive. I have never had to say, 'I can't.' "

Toward the end of the interview, he comments on how he person-ally has experienced the cultural changes of recent years. "It's becom-ing easier, especially for people of my ethnic background, to find fulfillment in this country. We are accepted more now. Racial prejudice isn't as strong. I belong, and I don't feel as insecure. Before, even money couldn't get someone like me security or friends or a job. Now things have relaxed. It's a new generation. People aren't as old fashioned. My parents used to tell us not to mingle with American girls. Now people don't listen to their families. It's more relaxed and open."

Like most others, he feels he has more choices open to him than his parents did, and that these choices have shaped his life. "I volunteered to go to Vietnam because I wanted to go and see and experience. It was a risk but I wanted to fulfill my desire for travel. I've always wanted to go to the unknown. Vietnam was the unknown."

But it was more than adventure that drew him to Vietnam. "I also enlisted for Vietnam so I could get an education. My family could never have sent me to college."

After leaving Vietnam and the Army, he worked for several years at the Post Office. But he didn't like the job. "I quit because I couldn't stand being treated like an animal. I wanted some respect."

After the Post Office he worked for a short time as a salesman—with some success. But he quit that job too. "I earned more money selling than at my present job, but I didn't like the crazy life of running around."

He is struggling to make do with modest means in New York City, not an easy task. At first he minimizes the need for money. "Money isn't important to me. I've never valued money. And possessions aren't important either. If I didn't have them I'd be just as happy." But in the next breath he adds: "My wife and I have a color TV. It's the first one in either family. It's not important, but it does symbolize something for the families. They enjoy it."

In Vietnam he had a chance to learn about electronic cameras, and the experience crystallized a project in his mind. He decided then that he wanted to become a nature photographer, and the desire persists. "My present job is in the city, and it isn't what I would choose. I really wish I could work somewhere outside the city as a nature photographer and earn enough to live."

He says he knows his dream is not realistic, and that he accepts a certain amount of fatalism as one of the givens of life. "I've had a lot of experience with accepting. I lived with my mother for a long time after my father died because she needed the money I earned at my job. I would have liked to move out of the city. I had a chance to move to California and do nature photography but I didn't go because of my mother." He says he is not bitter about the decision.

Other regrets and missed opportunities come to light as well. Despite the Vietnam GI Bill of Rights, he did not go to college. "I'm dissatisfied I didn't get a college education. When I watch a football game on TV and they mention that one of the players is from such and such a college, I feel very sad. I can't say I'm from any college. I went to New York City Community College at night, but I don't have a degree and I don't have a school I can identify with."

Unlike his other missed chances, this one inspires some guilt because it is one over which he felt he had control. But Miguel doesn't brood long over "might-have-beens." After several false starts he found an outlet for his self-fulfillment that fills him with joy.

He pours his energy into bicycle racing. "I value my bicycles because they are my tools for expressing myself," he says. "I keep getting better and better at it. Even though I'm past the age where I should be improving, I still am. I spend at least two hours a day at it. I love it. Riding in the city is dangerous. But it's like a race car driver. The danger is part of the challenge." After a pause, he concludes, "Riding and my marriage are the most fulfilling parts of my life."

The story of Miguel's life is classically American. Unlike his parents, he does not have a language barrier or a major problem of cultural adaptation, so he has had a better chance than they did to "make it" in American society. Within his own definition of personal success, he *has* made it, and he takes pride in his achievement. Yet his story has a familiar ring in quite another respect. He has scaled down his dreams: the lost opportunity to leave the city and go to the promised land (California) because his mother needed him in New York after his father's death; the lost opportunity to get a college degree; the lost opportunity to pursue his dream of making a living as a nature photographer in some rustic setting instead of dragging himself daily to and from a job in a city he does not like.

Miguel is operating within a narrower sphere of possibilities than the Williamses, Sara Lou Wellford or Lyndon Hendries. But within his constraints he has found, at least momentarily, two routes to fulfillment —his bike racing and his embryonic family life.

The bike racing symbolizes concretely what Lyndon Hendries defined as the essence of self-fulfillment—a set of wholly personal, subjective standards by which a person measures his or her own achievement, and, like Hendries, either finds it wanting, or like Feliciano, finds it satisfying. Like Hendries, Miguel Feliciano is caught in the cross pressures of two competing conceptions of success. Hendries' conflict lies between self-fulfillment and wordly success. Feliciano has taken himself out of the worldly success game, but he is torn by the conflicting demands that separate self-fulfillment from familial success.

As the interview proceeds, we see just how acute the conflict is. The themes of Miguel's bike racing and his obligation to his wife and unborn child take shape as the two dominant forces in his life. Bicycle racing is clearly on his mind when he explains what fulfillment means to him. "Fulfillment is being good at what you like, whether that is work or sports. If you achieve just one field to be good in, that's enough. You don't have to be good at everything. You can be successful without having it relate to money. That describes me. I can identify with being successful in a sport."

But bike racing also creates problems for him. "Last year we moved to New Jersey so I could have a place to train. But now I have more than four hours of commuting a day, and that is really draining. I get up every morning at 4:30 to train. My riding also upsets my wife. She's not excited by racing, and she also worries about the danger." After a long pause he adds, "But she tries to understand. She comes to my races."

Once he begins thinking about his wife and unborn baby, Miguel's conception of fulfillment shifts from the personal to the familial. "For me my wife is number one, cycling is number two. If my home life isn't happy and secure, nothing would be good, so that's why it's number one." Yet, a note of ambivalence remains. When asked about what he finds most fulfilling in his life, he talks only about his cycling.

"In the future I will get more involved with cycling. I hope to reach a higher plateau in my bike racing before I reach my limits. I also hope to have more children. I want at least three. I look forward to the future because I am just starting my family and getting settled. I've only been married two and one half years. *Later our marriage will be more relaxed*." [Emphasis added.]

Asked about sexual fidelity in marriage, he reflects: "I used to think it was wrong to have extramarital affairs. I've changed my view. Even though I haven't yet had one, I'd have one just to ease the tension that builds up. It's like flavors of ice cream. I'd like to taste more. I'd never get serious with anyone else though, because I'd never leave my wife . . . I used to think that once you got married you lived happily ever after. Now I think marriage isn't enough."

He knows he faces more conflict ahead, torn as he is between the demands of his wife and the demands of his cycling. He doesn't know how the baby coming in three months will affect the balance of his life, but he is anxious about it. He suspects that his wife, reinforced by the presence of the baby, is not going to surrender to a bicycle the devotion she regards as due her and a child. But his racing has assumed a powerful symbolic meaning for him. As long as he excels at it, he can think of himself as someone who has achieved success in the sense of personal fulfillment: he need not depend for self-esteem on a prestigious job or a big paycheck. The baby-versus-bike predicament looming in the future is likely to cause him trouble.

Miguel depends heavily on the respect and nurturance of his wife. Being protected by women, and receiving care from them—first from his mother, now from his wife—has grown into an indispensable source of emotional stability ("I stay near my mother . . . my wife is very important to me"). At the same time, his concerns about achieving personal fulfillment and preserving a masculine identity as a free and adventuresome soul are tied up with cycling. It is not clear how he will reconcile these conflicting forces as his physical stamina diminishes and the demands of family life increase. Through bike racing he has expanded his sphere of personal freedom. Through the attentions of a nurturant wife he has met his emotional needs for family life. He wants both, he needs both. But he may not be permitted to have both.

(iii)

Miguel Feliciano's life permits us to see both the features of the self-fulfillment predicament that transcend the lines of social class and also to trace the kinds of variation that social class creates. For Miguel, as for the educated and professional legions around him, the self-fulfillment predicament is rooted in his conviction that he has a greater choice of goals and life styles than his parents had—a conviction as we have seen that is shared by most Americans.

Inevitably, however, such new conceptions of fulfillment bring the individual into conflict, either with the goals of familial success or with the goals of worldly success (e.g., Lyndon Hendries' strong attachment to the trappings of wealth and status).

In all instances, the structure of the conflict is similar, whatever the social standing of the people involved. But the variables created by social class are both subtle and powerful. Consider, for example, the cultural meaning of work. Miguel Feliciano seeks work that is emotionally satisfying when he dreams of nature photography in a bucolic setting. A more traditional meaning is that hard work is seen as a means for "bettering oneself." Often the two go together and form a powerful combination: practicing law for Sara Lou Wellford, being a professor for Agnoli before his disillusionment, being a manager at McDonald's for Tom Wheeler. The *desire* for such work—either the emotionally satisfying type, or the status elevating type, or the two combined—is widely held in America, among both men and women and in all social classes. But there are clear differences along the lines of social class, as individuals appraise their chances of securing such work. Those from upper-middle-class backgrounds with degrees from prestigious colleges regard work that combines satisfaction and prestige as a virtual entitlement; those from blue-collar backgrounds may desire it but often assume it is not for them because they lack the educational prerequisites, and they often fail to pursue it vigorously.

Tom Wheeler opposed both his family and his fiancée to get the kind of work he wanted. He also took a cut in salary from his factory job, because he had heard of the McDonald's management training program. (Not knowing about such opportunities is often a major obstacle keeping people of working-class backgrounds from realizing opportunities they desire.) Miguel Feliciano, on the other hand, was easily deflected from his opportunities: the sales job (it didn't satisfy him); the chance to go to California (family obligations); the opportunity to secure a college education (he let it pass). It is almost as if he is saying, "This kind of success is not for the likes of me." His regret about not going to college did not focus on the lost chance for social mobility; it was the lost chance at social identification that haunted him. ("I feel very sad. . . . I don't have a school I can identify with.")

Upper-middle-class youth, on the other hand, have learned to be confident about realizing their hopes because their experience with reality encourages them to do so. Research shows that the factor most strongly associated with acquiring a good college education and with getting ahead economically in America is the family background which launches the individual into social competition.* Someone from an upper-middle-class family background will more readily translate his worldly desires into action in order to acquire education and other credentials than will someone from a working-class background.

The working-class American more often hesitates to risk abandoning a familiar path for one that poses hidden dangers, an attitude that comes at least partly from reality-testing associated with social class. The self-confident conviction that the world will cooperate with one's plans—so characteristic of a Sara Lou Wellford or a Lyndon Hendries —is not shared by the Miguel Felicianos, the Wheelers (except for Tom) or the Youngstowns, because their own and their family experience suggests the opposite, namely that the world does not usually cooperate. Therefore, "Why take a chance?"

In the upper reaches of societies everywhere, upper-class contenders start out with great worldly advantages—money, family, education, contacts, savior-faire—so individuals are freer to pursue their conception of fulfillment in defiance of, or with indifference to, prevailing cultural norms. The theme is a staple of the literature of manners— English, French and American. What is different about contemporary American culture is precisely the fact that private conceptions of fulfillment hitherto confined to the upper crust have become democratized and now find their way into all social classes.

Miguel Feliciano, even more than Tom Wheeler, shows us the intimate link between self-fulfillment and the psychological structure of self-esteem. To the extent that the definition of success in any culture

* Christopher Jencks et al., *Who Gets Ahead? The Determinants of Economic Success in America* (New York: Basic Books, 1979).

follows the rules of a competitive zero-sum game—if you win, I lose—
it is difficult for the losers to maintain their self-esteem, especially in a
society founded on social mobility. If people believe that success can
be won through hard work, intelligence and effort, then those who fail
must somehow or other come to feel that they are personally responsible, and therefore are in some fundamental sense, unworthy.

One great virtue of the norm of familial success was that it reduced
the zero-sum penalties of the success game. Most of those who accept
the discipline of work and family life—the subordination of self to
society's social definition of employee, husband, wife, father, mother
—can in an expanding economy be winners in the familial sweep-
stakes. The majority of Americans in the post–World War II era
accepted these rules and still do. They played the familial success game,
and won.

Americans have come to believe that they can loosen the discipline
on the self and give more attention to the expressive side of life. Fulfillment, measured by one's private standards of satisfaction and achievement, finds its perfect symbolic expression in Feliciano's bicycle—it is
adventure and danger and freedom and self-improvement and machismo
all wrapped up in one convenient object. Small wonder he resists claims
on him that might make him give it up.

Chapter 12

·····➤◉◀——···

"With a Little Bit of Luck"

Miguel Feliciano rejected social mobility as his route to fulfillment, choosing instead his bicycle and his family. The Wheelers also rejected social mobility, choosing instead the secure world of the factory and a close-knit family life. Tom Wheeler, on the other hand, is taking his self-fulfillment risk within the familiar tradition of bettering oneself by means of social mobility. What, in today's America, is happening to social mobility and the competitive drive to succeed? How have the shifts in culture loosened this building block of America's social structure? Let us now consider what shared meanings underlie the search for social status in America and how they are changing. We cannot understand the new cultural rules until we see them in relation to these more traditional issues.

The blunting of competition in American life is an elusive and yet far-reaching effect of shifts in our culture. It is elusive because the evidence is so mixed. Anyone wishing to prove that competitiveness remains alive and vital in America will easily find supporting evidence. At the same time, the idea of self-fulfillment achieved according to one's own internalized standards implies a shift away from winning in harshly competitive contests with others.

In the nineteen-fifties when I was Tom Wheeler's age, his choice—pursuing competitive opportunities to better one's situation—would have seemed inevitable to people brought up as I was. That, after all, was the point of the sacrifices our parents made. They had worked and saved and pushed themselves to the limits of endurance so we could go further than they had gone in our standard of living, education and position in the world. For the men, this meant occupational success; for the women, it meant marrying and having a family, preferably with a man who could make a good living. The pressures on Sara Lou Wellford to marry well were not confined to the South or to her social class; they were universal in our culture.

But today, Tom Wheeler's choice of social mobility over other alternatives seems less inevitable. Indeed, it is a choice questioned and challenged from all sides. As we have seen, the 17 percent or so of Americans in the strong form of the self-fulfillment predicament question it radically. But even the majority questions it, though in a more moderate way. Hugely successful self-help books like Wayne Dyer's *Your Erroneous Zones* define personal fulfillment in opposition to social mobility. Dyer's message is: you do not have to make it in the world to be fulfilled and to feel good about yourself. People who have eliminated their erroneous zones

> . . . are not afraid to fail. In fact they often welcome it. They do not equate being successful in any enterprise with being successful as a human being. Since their self-worth comes from within, any external event can be viewed objectively as simply effective or ineffective. They know that failing is merely somebody else's editorial opinion and not to be feared since it cannot affect self-worth. Thus, they will try anything, participate just because it's fun, and never fear having to explain themselves.*

William Irwin Thompson, a guru historian searching for the spirit of the New Age, landed, early in his career, conventionally as a teacher at M.I.T. In a televised interview he described to Bill Moyers his encounter with M.I.T. and social mobility, and he tells how he responded to its temptations:

> "Everything that I am now doing and thinking in the relationship of mysticism to science and politics comes from that experience of

* Dr. Wayne W. Dyer, *Your Erroneous Zones* (New York: Avon, 1977), p. 241.

being in the Vatican of engineering at M.I.T. . . . My boss said,
'Look, you've made it, you're a success, this is Cambridge, this is
the intellectual capital of the world; why are you restless; stay
here, we'll promote you, don't go off to Canada.' And I said, 'No,
this is Ur, and I'm going into the land that He will show me.' "*

Other Americans reject the blandishments of promotion no less
firmly than Thompson. But why this ambivalence about getting ahead?
Why does it trouble so many? Why is it under seige? What do people
feel is wrong with "making it" in America? The answer to this question
goes to the heart of those forces that underlie the shifts in our culture.

(ii)

Social scientists from various disciplines—political science, economics
and sociology—have endlessly studied the reward system of American
life and the role played in it by competition and social mobility. Some
of those concerned with this touchy subject confine themselves to collecting and analyzing data, keeping their political convictions to themselves. Others display their convictions, hoping to shape the way
people think. The most influential grouping in the universities, where
most inquiries into social class are carried out, are probably the egalitarian reformers or "redistributionists." Their research findings show a
huge spread between the haves and have-nots in America. The mag-
nitude of the disparity outrages them, and they argue urgently for
redistributing income to achieve greater equality in American society.

Most of these social critics are intent on making three points: that a
rigid class structure exists in America and has existed for a long time;
that the system violates our cherished norms of social justice; and that
only through redistribution of income can equality be restored.

Since much of the public's understanding of social class and mobility
derives from the work of such critics, we have grown accustomed to
equating social class with social injustice and inequality. The term
"social class" conjures images of the evils of poverty, of racial and
other prejudices, of a rigid caste system and of privilege zealously
protected; images of a system that violates the traditional American
ethos. Egalitarian reformers urge that the present system of getting

* *Bill Moyers' Journal*, Show No. 408, "At the Edge of History: A Conversation with William Irwin Thompson," PBS air date March 26, 1979, © 1979 Educational Broadcasting Corp.

ahead is antithetical to the true spirit of American life and that we can be faithful to that spirit only by redistributing the rewards that have accrued to Americans through the system as it now functions.

In contrast to these reformers, most Americans do not hold a well-defined position on the topic of social class. They are uncomfortable with the term: "social class" carries overtones that make people cringe and think of societies whose inequities they or their ancestors left behind in favor of a "free" America. Also, the public is well aware of the gap between rich and poor. Americans say they dislike the idea of hierarchy based on money, and know the system is pockmarked with prejudice and discrimination which they would like to see eliminated. But they strenuously resist efforts at redistributing income and they reject the redistributionists' theories about how the system actually works.

Thus, we have a confusing situation in which egalitarian reformers write about social class in ways that make their case against the inequities of our social system, but largely ignore the concerns harbored by the American public itself. The public has its own quarrel with the system, but it is not the same quarrel, and the public, furthermore, does not write books and articles, so its concerns can easily be mistaken for those of the egalitarians. It is worth sorting out the two critiques: one relates to the country's political agenda, the other to the question of cultural change in America.

At the heart of the egalitarian position is the assertion that our class structure is not truly open. Real equality of opportunity, according to these critics, does not exist. Their research findings show that Americans who enjoy class-related advantages manage to pass them on to others in the same social class—their offspring, their friends, their classmates— leaving only the scraps for those who start the competitive race from disadvantaged origins including such "out-groups" as blacks, Hispanics, Native Americans, the very poor, the physically handicapped. (Sometimes the inventory of out-groups includes women and everyone who is not a middle-class-white male. But this addition confuses the issue.)

Among the social scientists with an egalitarian bent, one of the most proficient at gathering and analyzing data is sociologist Christopher Jencks. For a number of years he has been conducting studies to learn how social mobility and competition actually function in America. In his first major work, *Inequality* (1972), Jencks and several colleagues found, by examining the body of research material then available, that neither family background nor education could account for all the variations in income and status among Americans. Economic success, he concluded, was explained not so much by birth, striving or "competence" as by a number of other unmeasured variables, which he described collectively as "luck."*

On this statistical finding he based his redistributionist case. He argued that if getting ahead depends largely on chance, then it is surely unfair for some to end up with so much wealth and privilege while others are mired in poverty. For Jencks, the key flaw in our system of social mobility was its dependence on mere chance.

In the years following the publication of *Inequality*, Jencks was stung by the criticism that his emphasis on luck might be merely an artifact of his research methods. Unable to account for the differences between successful and unsuccessful people in any systematic way, perhaps he had attributed to luck what might be the role of other factors, such as personality, drive, ambition and skill, factors not easily reduced to statistical measures.

So Jencks organized a new research team and spent five years analyzing a new and more sophisticated set of data. Then in 1979, he and a number of colleagues at the Harvard Center for Education Policy Research published *Who Gets Ahead?—The Determinants of Economic Success in America*. The book examined eleven different studies, conducted from the early sixties to the mid-seventies.

The new portrait drawn by Jencks and his colleagues in *Who Gets Ahead?* places less emphasis on luck than the earlier study. But his portrait of America is bitterly one-sided. It is a picture of a class-ridden America in which being born into the "right" family is all-important, a rigid America in which a man's test scores in the sixth grade shape his expectations of himself and those of others toward him (none of the eleven surveys included women), a superficial America in which a man's surface characteristics such as college credentials or the color of his skin count for more than what he is really worth as a person, and a unidimensional America in which only making money and achieving occupational success seem to count in life.

In comparing his conclusions in *Who Gets Ahead?* with those in his earlier work, *Inequality*, Jencks meets his critics part way. He acknowledges that in *Inequality* he overstated the roll of luck and understated the impact of family background on income and on occupational

---

* Christopher Jencks et al., *Inequality: A Reassessment of the Effect of Family and Schooling in America* (New York: Basic Books, 1972), p. 8.

status. He also acknowledges that his research approach in *Inequality* was "fundamentally flawed." But lest his critics rejoice prematurely, he states emphatically that despite the flaws, his study's major policy conclusion was nonetheless correct, and he repeats his call for redistribution. In the very last paragraph of *Who Gets Ahead?* he concludes that liberal reforms aimed at making education and other opportunities for improvement available to everyone ("equalizing men's personal characteristics") is "an unpromising way of equalizing peoples' incomes" because that approach has not worked: "*Inequality* argues that past efforts at equalizing the personal characteristics known to affect income had been relatively ineffective. This assertion, sad to say, remains as true as ever." Summing up he says: "Thus, if we want to redistribute income, the most effective strategy is to redistribute income."*

Egalitarians like Jencks raise issues that are and will remain at the center of our political struggles for years to come. But the perceptions of egalitarian reformers, including Jencks, of how the system works and what is good and bad about it bear almost no resemblance to the shared meanings of getting ahead, fairness, luck, equality, competition and social class that really do turn up in American psychoculture.

(iii)

A recent book, *Social Standing in America*, written by two prominent sociologists, Richard Coleman and Lee Rainwater, discusses the public's attitudes toward social class. Their research consists of several studies conducted in Boston and Kansas City in the early and mid-seventies, supplemented by a national survey conducted in the late seventies.

Coleman and Rainwater tried to find out whether and to what extent Americans are "class conscious." Do Americans picture our society as rigidly organized into classes, and what do terms like "social class" and "class standing" mean to them? Where do they place themselves and other people in a "social hierarchy?" How do they feel about the idea of social class?

The authors conclude that Americans are less comfortable with the term "social class" than with the phenomenon itself; the term bothers them because it implies a rigid caste system into which one is born and

* Christopher Jencks et al., *Who Gets Ahead?—The Determinants of Economic Success in America* (New York: Basic Books, 1979), p. 311.

from which one cannot move. It was for this reason that Coleman and Rainwater settled on the term "social standing," since it seemed to them to carry less of a connotation of rigidity, and to be more compatible with the idea of social mobility.

Virtually everyone they interviewed held a class-conscious picture of himself and fellow Americans as occupying a rank in a social hierarchy ranging from high to low, with many gradations in between. People had no difficulty locating themselves and others in the hierarchy according to "the relative desirability of life situations,"* that is, who gets what.

Americans do not therefore reject the idea of a social hierarchy as such, despite its implications of inequality. Most people merely say they wished social class could be based on something of intrinsic worth like moral goodness rather than on money and material possessions. But they know it will not be so in this life. The authors conclude that Americans believe there is such a thing as social class in America if by social class people mean how they and others are rated and treated in the community.

How does the public's attitude toward social class differ from that of the egalitarian critics? The egalitarians fault the system on three grounds: they see an unjustifiably large gap between rich and poor; they believe equality of opportunity does not really exist; and they conclude that social mobility is difficult for those who come from the wrong side of the tracks.

We learn something important about our psychoculture when we realize how totally most Americans reject this diagnosis. Whatever we like or dislike about our social mobility system, we care very little about reducing income inequality, especially at the higher end. About 15 percent of the people in the Coleman/Rainwater study said they wanted to get rid of poverty by placing a floor under people's incomes. But even among this minority who want to elevate the low end of the scale virtually no one expressed any interest in lowering the high end of the income scale.†

My own studies show that many Americans favor leveling *up* under certain conditions but are unalterably opposed to leveling *down*. They do not want the rich to be deprived of their riches—provided that they have acquired them according to accepted rules of the game.

---

* Richard Coleman and Lee Rainwater, *Social Standing in America: New Dimensions of Class* (New York: Basic Books, 1978), p. 17.
† Coleman and Rainwater, loc. cit.

In recent years there has been much talk about a tax revolt by Americans. Public opinion polls have confirmed public hostility toward the existing tax system. Yet, when one digs into the findings, the pattern of tax resistance shows little "soak the rich" sentiment. Two-to-one majorities, for example, would reduce the capital gains tax and give other incentives to assist those already well-off to invest their money.

Overall, the public's attitude reflects the sentiment "there but for the grace of God go I." The attitude suggests, "who knows, one day I may be in a position to invest. . . . I may move up in income brackets so that I too can benefit from the capital gains exemption."* But whatever the reason, the majority of Americans do not want any redistribution that can be interpreted as taking away from the successful the fruits of what they have earned. The national psychology holds that those who play the game according to the rules (and the rules include luck, hard work and "good connections"), are entitled to their success, and should be able to reinvest liberally what they get.

Egalitarian critics find such public attitudes frustrating and brush them aside, relying instead on their own moral intuition about right and wrong, fairness and unfairness. They insist on reducing the extremes at both ends of the income scale, whatever the "false consciousness" of their fellow Americans may dictate. But the reason Americans not only tolerate but insist upon preserving income disparities is central to American psychoculture and to traditional American values.

People's image of the social hierarchy is not that of a ladder—what Disraeli called the "greasy pole." The dominant image is that of a giant arena in which Americans compete for an amazing variety of rewards, small and large, and where the rules for winning are clear and the contest is open. Indeed, Coleman and Rainwater describe this conception as "the nation's motivating force for individual achievement."† The opportunity to acquire rewards associated with improvement of social standing—money, recognition, respectability, interesting and challenging jobs—is the engine that drives it forward.

When people locate their own standing in the social hierarchy, they put themselves in the highest position they can justify either by the money they earn, the education they have accumulated or the work

* Daniel Yankelovich and Larry Kaagan, "Proposition 13 One Year Later: What It Is and What It Isn't," *Social Policy,* Vol. 10, No. 1 (May/June 1979), p. 19.
† Coleman and Rainwater, op. cit., p. 25.

they do. These are the visible signs of accomplishment in life, and they acknowledge them with pride. People often exaggerate their accomplishments to build their social standing, thereby reinforcing their self-esteem and enhancing their image in the eyes of others.

Most Americans freely acknowledge the factor of luck in getting ahead, but unlike Jencks, they approve of this feature of the system. Luck says to everyone, "the die is not cast; the outcome is not fore-ordained; the wheel of fortune may spin again, and this time you may be the beneficiary." But Americans believe that luck alone is never enough; even though a little of it never hurts. To most Americans, luck has the very opposite property from that with which Jencks endows it. For Jencks, luck or chance is antidemocratic because it may produce unfair results. But to the average American, luck is profoundly demo-cratic: it is color-blind, race-blind, IQ-blind and even merit-blind. With luck, it is never too late for thee and me. If Americans had to choose between a society that excluded luck but guaranteed equitable results and one which allowed for a large dose of chance with somewhat ragged results, I am reasonably sure on the basis of my studies that they would pick the latter.

(iv)

Most Americans believe in the reality of social mobility in America, confident that opportunities for "bettering oneself" exist in abundance. Americans are not blind to injustice, unfairness or privilege. They see these obstacles to getting ahead all around them, just as the egalitarians do. But the majority weigh them differently; they regard them merely as roadblocks to be bypassed.

The average American bases this appraisal on parental and per-sonal experience. Most people see themselves and their parents as Exhibit A: direct beneficiaries of the American social mobility system. This perception is itself a social fact of great importance.

The Coleman/Rainwater research found, as I have found in my own work, a nearly universal perception among Americans that they had been able to improve on their parents' lot in life. Their research shows that 91 percent of their survey respondents see themselves as better off than their parents, divided into two subgroups. The larger group, 60 percent, report that they occupy a higher socioeconomic rank than their parents, while the other 31 percent say they have the same social rank as their parents but they live better (e.g., "my life is a lot easier . . . I have more free time . . . I live a better life").*

For those who assess their social standing several notches above their parents', these "proofs" are offered: a higher-paying job than their father held, a better home and neighborhood, and more money for education or leisure pursuits such as travel, vacations and second homes. Most gauge their progress in terms of higher income, and about a third mention a higher level of education, mainly to explain how they got their higher income.

Americans love to answer questions comparing their own lives to their parents'. It gives them an opportunity to cite their parents' desires and dreams for them, and to express pride in themselves for having been able to make these parental dreams come true. This is the central feature of what people think of as the "story of our lives." They recall with satisfaction how their parents postponed and sometimes sacrificed their own well-being so that they, the children, might enjoy a better life. The children acknowledge their debt; they *are* living a better life. They think about this aspect of their relationship to their parents in a rush of nostalgic warmth and their pleasure in their own accomplishments is powerfully reinforced.

Their satisfaction derives not only from recalling their parents' self-denial, but also from appraising their own role in achieving a higher standing than their parents and they give themselves credit for this accomplishment. Most Americans believe that social mobility is won mainly through personal effort. "Anyone who really wants to can better himself or herself"—this conviction still serves as the traditional American article of faith. Asked "What is the most effective way for a person to improve his social standing in America?", most people cite parental encouragement, a good education, ambition and plain hard work. Underlying these answers are two premises: that ample opportunities for advancement existed for them personally and that these are also available to people with the requisite education and willingness to work hard.

Of the two requirements—education and hard work—people regard education as a necessary but far from sufficient condition for taking full advantage of their opportunities. Education is merely the price of admission. Social critics sometimes define our system as a meritocracy where careers are open to people of special talent or intelligence. But this is not the popular view. America gives little credit for success to

* Coleman and Rainwater, loc. cit.

merit in the form of talent or special qualities of mind. Most of the credit is given to drive and ambition—including the ambition to go to college. The average American would argue that whether or not a person goes to college is up to the individual, not to his family. If someone has the drive and the will to get ahead, he can do so regardless of family background, a belief the Jencks research does not contradict.

In the past, people from higher-income families were far more likely to go to college than those from poorer homes. As long as access to higher education depended on whether your family could afford to send you to college, this correlation had to be strong. In the past decade or so, however, since the bulk of the research on which Jencks draws was done, access to college for lower-income families has dramatically improved. For most young Americans, limited family income is no longer a significant barrier to access to a college education. People who wish to go to college have available to them a wide array of federal government grants, state government subsidies, loans and scholarships. This is one of the great unheralded social accomplishments of the 1970s. Choice of college is, to be sure, still restricted by income. If you can't afford the tuition, you do not go to an Ivy League college unless you are gifted and receive a scholarship. But Jencks' research shows persuasively that what counts in getting ahead is not which college you attend, but the fact that you completed four years and received the all-important degree as a credential.

In evaluating the role of education one should also keep in mind the difference between occupational success and income success. Coleman and Rainwater suggest that occupational status may no longer be as useful an index of social standing as in the past. They emphasize that no group took as much pride and satisfaction in its social standing as those who, lacking a college education, nonetheless made enough money to achieve the style of living to which they had aspired. "For most Americans occupation seems to be playing a less important role in determining social standing than formerly," note the authors. They cite as a typical response the view that "If you can afford to live in a nice neighborhood no one really cares what you do for a living."*

What do Americans dislike about the social class system? Up to now, they have had no fundamental quarrel with who gets what—not at least during the long post–World War II period when incomes were rising.

* Ibid.

But now we are leaving behind a half-century of political agreement built around economic growth and the use of government policies to increase consumption, pay special attention to the vulnerables of our society and place a floor of minimal security under everyone. We are entering a new, more restrictive era whose consequences have yet to become apparent. One clue, however, to America's future direction lies in understanding that the quarrel the American people do have with social mobility has little to do with the political system.

But what, then, is this quarrel?

Chapter 13

···➤◉◄···

What's Wrong with Getting Ahead?— The People's Critique

Unlike the egalitarians, the average American's quarrel with the social mobility system is more cultural than political (though Americans *are* distressed that social mobility does not always work as an open system with equal opportunities for all who desire to take advantage of them).

The average American closely identifies "getting ahead" with the goals, values and meanings of familial success. Familial success implies an emphasis on family life and an ever-improving standard of living. For the quarter-century following World War II, this blend seemed like the perfect arrangement. If I worked hard, observed the rules and learned to keep my personal desires mostly suppressed, I might find myself well rewarded—with moral self-esteem for my self-denial, with the acceptance of others for my respectability and with worldly goods from an affluent economy.

These are very substantial rewards, and in the ascendant period of familial success, in the 1950s and 1960s, a majority of Americans believed that they were well worth the price they exacted. Both objective conditions and our cultural heritage encouraged the goals of familial success. Material rewards were available in abundance, giving a powerful stimulus to a nation whose material wants had been scanted during the Depression of the thirties and the world war that followed. Because the individual's pursuit of these rewards served the society so well, a consensus prevailed that economic growth was good for the country. Thus, the pursuit of material goods was legitimized by the culture with a powerful reinforcing effect. For those Americans who had lived through the Depression the price of "success" did not seem excessively high.

But now we confront a new phase in our economy and our culture. As we have seen, self-denial has lost much of its normative appeal, and in some parts of our culture (among the strong formers) it has been turned upside down; if I have a duty to myself, satisfying rather than denying the self becomes the ascendant norm. In its sweeping transformation of the norms relating to marriage, family, sex and children, the culture has already weakened one side of the familial success triangle, thereby destabilizing the other two sides. A traditional family life is no longer the prime symbol of respectability; conversely, you no longer lose your respectability if you are divorced, choose to live alone, refuse to have children, belong to a household in which both spouses work or engage in discreet sexual experimentation. To be the exclusive provider for the family no longer drives the male to endure the frustrations of an unsatisfying job, and the housewife-mother role is less often esteemed by society, or by women themselves.

As traditional domestic norms falter, so do the motivations for getting ahead. People interviewed in the Coleman/Rainwater study and in my own studies say that so far they have done better for themselves than their parents, but they are concerned about their future and the future of their children as changes in the economy make an ever-improving standard of living more problematic. The steady and rapid economic growth pattern of the post–World War II years no longer seems likely. And several decades of affluence have sated some of the hunger that once made the acquisition of a home, a car, a washing machine and a TV seem worth sacrificing for.

It is in this context that questions about mobility have grown more acute. For many years our popular culture has acknowledged the disagreeable side of the competitive struggle. The "rat race" is a stale phrase precisely because the phenomenon has been around so long. What differentiates today's American from even his own self in the recent past is the feeling that there may now be alternatives to the rat race that "real people" can pursue.

Here from my interviews are some brief portraits of Americans, who, having participated in the rat race, later got out of it.

* * *

Samuel Moscowitz, now fifty-six, owned and managed a hardware store with his brother-in-law near the University of Chicago for almost thirty years. The store was successful, and it enabled him to own a home in a neighborhood far from the store, and to send both his son and daughter to private colleges. But the store also drained him physically and emotionally, making him, he said, "a nervous wreck." He developed high blood pressure and complained of constant headaches. He was mugged twice and the store was broken into three times. On vacation in Florida six years ago, he developed a passion for bird watching and a deep attachment to the swamplands of southern Florida. Two years ago he sold his interest in the hardware store to his brother-in-law in exchange for a small weekly stipend to continue as long as the store remains profitable. He moved to Florida, where he found part-time work as a guide in the swamplands. Since his children are, as he says, "off the payroll," he could afford to make the move by drastically simplifying his life. He has few regrets about the move; "I was totally fed up with the break-ins and the threat of violence. I've paid my dues to middle-class respectability, and now I'm ready to do something for myself." Between his salary as a guide and the small income from the hardware store he is not afraid of economic insecurity. But he is also counting on Social Security to keep pace with inflation.

The only drawback to his new way of life is his wife's attitude. She likes Florida but misses her friends and her old way of life. She is concerned that something will happen to the hardware store and that they will be unable to live on her husband's meager earnings as a guide. She talks vaguely about finding a job, but she has never worked outside the home and is apprehensive about doing so. "Slumming it," as she refers to their present way of life, attracted her as a vacation from "regular life," but it does not appeal to her as a life style. Her husband says she misses middle-class life more than he does, and that makes him uneasy, clouding what otherwise would be a serene and fulfilling life.

Dan Turner, at thirty-eight, has worked as a physical therapist and coach, and has risen to chairman of the physical education department at a state-supported community college in upstate New York. Raised and educated in northern Michigan and committed to outdoor living and nonurban values, he has worked hard and successfully to add imaginative outdoor programs of the "outward bound" type to his departmental curriculum.

With limited time and capital, Dan bought a small parcel of land in Vermont and built an A-frame cottage on it. Originally he built it for family vacations, and in anticipation of his retirement. During the time Dan was building the cottage, the state education department, under financial pressure from the legislature, began cutting back on "nonvital" programs at state-supported schools. Shuttling back and forth to the state capital, Dan lobbied against the dismembering of his program and his department. One by one, members of his staff were dismissed, and his instructions were, as he says, to "make do with what you've got left." At first he tried to hide his frustration: he didn't want his family to see him as upset as he clearly was. He felt his professional world being pulled out from under him by what he called "a bunch of uncaring bureaucrats who think that physical education is just a bunch of idiots kicking a ball around for college credit. They need to save money, so sure, let's cut phys ed, it's not important anyway."

He described the budget cuts and staff reductions as "eating my guts out. My own job was secure, but my life's work was being undone."

Rather than swallow his frustration, as he says his father had done all his life, Dan quit his job and moved to Vermont with his family, "retiring" a quarter-century before he had intended to. He has cut back on his living expenses. He works part-time as a physical therapist at a mental hospital nearby, his wife works part-time in a doctor's office and the whole family spends a great deal of time and energy trying to adjust to rural life and a low income: storing up firewood, growing and preserving vegetables in Vermont's short growing season, insulating the house properly against the severe winters. He enjoys his new life, and most of the time feels he made the right decision. But he sorely misses the "challenge of the work I had been doing." Occasionally he speculates on what it would be like to come back and resume his old job.

Jane Coates, born and raised in Dallas, had been married to a successful real estate broker there for twenty years. The Coateses have a son, seventeen, with whom Jane shares a close and affectionate relationship. For a long time Jane felt that she, her husband and all their friends were living lives organized around values that made her feel "like a shallow person, living out some script," even though she admits enjoying the comfort of the big house, the big cars and the country club.

The more Jane began to suspect that she had lost touch with her husband, who disagreed utterly with her ideas about self-fulfillment and "being true" to herself, the more she began to think about divorce. She hesitated for several reasons. Concerned primarily about how her son would react, she was also "more than a little nervous" after twenty years of economic security about giving up the material comforts of her married life. She had always dreamed about operating a small restaurant, but "it had always been just that, a dream."

The conflict within her persisted as the distance between her life and what she felt was her "true self" lengthened. "The only way to become myself," she said, "was to shed my married life, whatever the costs." Several years ago she divorced her husband. "I was taught that you had to stay married for the kids, but I found out that kids living in an unhappy home are worse off than if there was a divorce. My son's attitudes, his grades and his outlook on life all improved when the final break came, even though he was angry with me at first. I wouldn't hesitate to do it again. People used to be afraid of losing or failing. In this day and age we don't live in such a narrow world; we can take risks and bend rules."

After her divorce, Jane took the modest financial settlement she received from her ex-husband, borrowed a considerable amount of money from the bank and opened a restaurant. She was pleased with her success, but she sold the restaurant and took a job as a hostess at another nearby restaurant when she realized that ownership was a day and night involvement. Total absorption was not self-fulfillment to her. "I went into a business I knew almost nothing about; I succeeded and sold out. I have always felt that too many people say, 'Oh, if I had my life to live over I'd do this and that.' Well, no one gets that chance, so you've got to do it now . . . and I did."

Now her son is away at school and she is living with a man whom she likes but does not intend to marry. She is relaxed with him. He is the kind of "down to earth," unpretentious person she says she enjoys being with. But although he is important in her life, the relationship with him is not the essence of her self-fulfillment.

For Jane Coates self-fulfillment is intangible and somewhat mysterious. At the core of her concept of self-fulfillment is the idea of "authenticity," which means many things to her:

"Accepting myself as I am and accepting others for what they are, not who they are.

"In being down to earth, admitting my likes and dislikes—the strengths and weaknesses in myself, I find a certain happiness.

"Fulfillment to me means being my own person.

"It isn't what you do that makes you successful but how you feel about it. If you feel that you are self-fulfilled then you are a success."

She sums up her attitude: "I took a big risk in order to strike out on my own and find a life more suited to me. And as a result, my quality of life has improved, if I use happiness and fulfillment, rather than money as a yardstick. I am getting what I want out of life."

Each of these individuals has chosen, for different reasons, to opt out of the rat race as he or she defined it, whether running a store in a racially troubled section of Chicago, maintaining "creativity" in a program against the opposition of a bureaucracy that places a low value on what you are doing, or maintaining the façade of a marriage built around symbols of wealth.

A rat race implies meaningless competition and effort, being manipulated like a laboratory animal regardless of one's own needs and "well-being." Moscowitz, Coates and Turner reacted strongly against these constraints. They did not walk out because the economy forced them out. They quit because their values told them not to sacrifice themselves for economic security or social standing or respectability. All three people express the weak form of the self-fulfillment predicament: they belong with that vast 63 percent majority of Americans whose lives and values are conventional in most respects, but who, in one or another corner of their lives have permitted the values associated with the search for personal fulfillment to take precedence over the traditional goals of worldly or familial success.

We have already seen that in 1970, 38 percent of adult Americans responded like losers in the competitive battle; my associates called them "retreaters." Their sour attitude toward themselves and others derived from injured self-esteem: according to the standards of familial success, they found themselves wanting. Either their families had not proven supportive or grateful enough for their sacrifices, or they had not accumulated as much material comfort or security as they felt they should, or they believed they had not received the full measure of respect and recognition to which they aspired.

For them, the giving/getting compact of familial success had not worked out. They were well aware of the price they had paid in self-denial, but according to their calculations, it had not been worth it. Significantly, though, they did not renounce familial success itself. Indeed, more than most younger Americans they fully accepted its rules and lived by them. Even as self-defined losers, they were not rejecting the rules; they were simply grousing about the outcome of the competition. They felt cheated, but they would not change the rules.

Unlike Moscowitz and the others, these true "retreaters" responded passively to the tensions of the rat race without reconsidering their personal values. They simply became resentful. Significantly, by the start of the eighties, the incidence of these victims of the competitive rat race—these retreaters—has been cut in half (from 38 percent to 18 percent). Today, Americans in all age brackets challenge the rules of the rat race more actively than they once did.

Yankelovich, Skelly and White studies show that 75 percent of Americans no longer find acceptable the prospect of working at a boring job "as long as the pay is good"; 65 percent feel that an employee has a right to refuse to move to another city if the company asks him to; 63 percent feel that the employee also has the right to refuse promotions; 78 percent say they would refuse to leave a job they like for one that pays more. A majority (56 percent) say they no longer believe as their parents did that "a man with a family has a responsibility to choose a job that pays the most rather than one that is more satisfying but pays less."

These survey findings also show how weakening one side of the triangle of familial success weakens the other sides as well. As long as a man's self-esteem derived from his role as provider, it hardly mattered whether his job was boring or not. Being bored was an acceptable part of the cost, the price a man was expected and generally willing to pay for the extrinsic rewards of the job—the money, the security and the status. Today people still want their jobs to pay well, but they are no longer as willing as they once were to trade satisfaction on the job for money and status.

For some, this unwillingness takes the form of seeking work rich in inherent satisfactions. As we have seen, those in strong pursuit of self-fulfillment goals stress the creative potentials of their jobs. For others, however, the unwillingness takes a different form. If they see an opportunity for work that is less tiring or stressful than their present job, they may well accept a reduction in status, money or future opportunities, as with the automobile workers in Tennessee where unexpected thousands submitted requests to trade their higher-paying jobs on the assembly line for somewhat poorer-paying, lower-status custodial jobs.

This is a striking example of new attitudes toward competitiveness. The custodial jobs were considerably less stressful and tiring than the line jobs, and thanks to union scale, the drop in income, while real, was not catastrophic. The auto workers are simply one example of the myriad ways Americans are seeking to blunt the harsh competitive edges of social mobility.

(ii)

Even in the fifties and early sixties when the ideal of familial success dominated the culture, Americans were fully conscious of the high psychic cost of competitiveness and conformity. During this period one book after another criticized this aspect of American life. Sloan Wilson's *The Man in the Gray Flannel Suit* helped make Madison Avenue the symbolic home of the rat race. William H. Whyte's *The Organization Man* analyzed what he called the organization ethic—the tendency of large corporations to support cultural norms that "would rationalize the organization's demands for fealty and give those who offer it whole-heartedly a sense of dedication."* Whyte showed how the pressures of society worked to legitimize self-denial in the service of the organization —the corporation, the economy, the community.

The pathos implied by the title of David Riesman's book, *The Lonely Crowd*, helped make it one of the most influential books of its era. Riesman said that American social character had changed to accommodate the new tasks our society was being called upon to perform. In an earlier America, when it was a matter of mastering the physical environment, the virtues of self-reliance, hard work, stamina and rigid adherence to principles of right and wrong formed the dominant American social character, what Riesman called "inner directed." With the growth of large-scale organizations and the beginnings of a service economy, competitive success called for less rugged individualism, and instead rewarded what Riesman called the "other directed" character which could receive signals from others rather than take direction simply from one's own inner gyroscope. The society came to reward the persuasive person, the popular one who could work co-operatively with others.

So ambivalent were the fifties that although Riesman saw many attractive features in other-directed behavior, most readers regarded it as a loathsome development, less attractive than either the stubborn strength of earlier inner-directed Americans or than what Riesman called the "autonomous" social character, a blend of the best features of both types, less conformist and more independent-minded than the other-directed type, but also less rigid and more sensitive to the needs of others than the inner-directed American.

In 1954, the historian David Potter showed perceptively that Ameri-

* William H. Whyte, *The Organization Man* (New York: Simon and Schuster, 1956), p. 6.

can social critics were preoccupied with the darker aspects of the success ethic. In analyzing three influential works of the period (Riesman's *The Lonely Crowd*, Karen Horney's *The Neurotic Personality of Our Time* and Margaret Mead's *And Keep Your Powder Dry!*), he showed that all three condemn a harsh competitiveness as the decisive influence on the American character. To Mead and Riesman the struggle for competitive success shapes the less-attractive features of American social character and distorts the cultural scene. And for Horney the cultural trends that induce "neuroses in our time" also center on individual competitiveness. Horney said that competitiveness is not confined to economics but spreads to personal values such as popularity and attractiveness and extends over the full life span of the individual: "competitive stimuli are active from the cradle to the grave,"* she wrote.

Potter's criticism of these observers is that their analyses don't go deep enough. "To take culture as a given factor," he writes, and to explain character in terms of culture "without considering the forces that shape the culture . . . interferes with the fullest and deepest understanding of society."† Potter traces the competitiveness of American life back to its economic roots: he argues that economic conditions shape our culture and have always done so. Specifically, he argues that our economic abundance in its various forms—the frontier at one time, the exploitation of natural resources at another, our manufactured wealth at still another—has shaped American culture. "Rapid social change paced by economic abundance is," he writes, "at the heart of the matter."‡

(iii)

Potter and many other students of the American character in the nineteen-fifties all converged on the same gloomy diagnosis: competitiveness dominated American life, and was creating an unhealthy tension in it.

Having lived through that period as a young adult, I recall vividly my own personal brush with getting ahead. I cannot judge how healthy or unhealthy the encounter was, but I do know that it exerted an all-pervasive influence on my own youth and on my friends.

The roots of my personal experience go back to the thirties. My father struggled to exhaustion during that period and afterward to eke

---

* Quoted in David Potter, *People of Plenty: Economic Abundance and the American Character* (Chicago: University of Chicago, 1954), p. 56.
  † Potter, ibid., p. 59.
  ‡ Potter, ibid., p. 69.

out a living. In the early thirties my mother died unexpectedly, and to make matters worse my father lost the property he had acquired with great effort in the previous decades. He never fully recovered from either loss. A man much given to reflecting on his experience, he ruminated on the problems of making a living and raising a family under such trying conditions. Preoccupied with his obligations, he brooded over what he regarded as his ethical and practical failure to make it easy for his children to do better than he had done.

He wanted me to become an engineer, a line of work for which I was fantastically ill equipped. In his eyes, engineering combined just the right amount of respectability, security and income to permit one to be of use to society and to carry out future obligations to others. Fortunately for the engineering profession, he did not press the matter. I suspect he felt he did not have the right to do so since in his eyes he had not fulfilled his own obligations. By the time he died—he was almost ninety—he had long forgotten his dream of genuine respectability for his only son, and he accused me of having imagined it when I raised the subject. But I recall his earlier urgings well: the engineering profession symbolized the aspirations of many parents in that period, particularly those who were first- or second-generation Americans, as my parents were.

Many of my friends whose parents were more successful in directing their sons did not escape as easily from an occupational fate that ill-suited them. Under their parents' influence several of my boyhood friends eventually became successful dentists, though they were as little drawn to dentistry as I was to engineering. As a consequence they never developed a wholehearted commitment to their profession but instead devoted their energies to an awesome array of hobbies and outside interests.

I was reminded of these friends when, in the midst of writing this chapter, as I tried to recall the spirit of the fifties I chanced upon the obituary section of *The New York Times*. I was impressed but not surprised to learn that a Dr. Theodore Kazimiroff, a prominent Bronx dentist, was the founder of the Bronx Historical Society, and that his love for archaeology traced back to his youth. The obituary revealed that in his home he maintained a collection of Indian artifacts including fifty thousand arrowheads, clay pipes, war clubs, pieces of pottery, stone tools and harpoon points. Dr. Kazimiroff also helped to found a wildlife sanctuary, and was a frequent lecturer on the ecology of the Bronx River, serving as a consultant to the Museum of Natural History. He had an interest in botany, geology, mineralogy and zoology, and he wrote widely for scientific and general interest publications.* Undoubtedly, he was an excellent dentist as well. But I could not help wondering whether, like my own childhood friends, he had been persuaded to abandon his early scientific interests for the practical advantages of dentistry. Had he been born a generation later he might have pursued his boyhood interest in archaeology as a career. At least he would have had the choice.

And this, of course, is the point. If no choice exists, one does what one must. For the exceptional or rebellious few there are always choices. But the majority accept the world as it is: they neither seek to bend it to their will, nor does it accommodate them with special favors. I know that for my boyhood friends who became dentists, the decision was the fruit of an uneasy compromise they eventually came to accept and make the best of—a career chosen as a sacrifice of self-fulfillment at the altar of practicality. They had entered the competitive race, and had emerged as winners. But all of them harbored a sense of loss of early selfhood that, not surprisingly, surfaced much later in their own lives or in the lives of their children.

I intend, of course, no slur on dentistry. The dentists I have met as an adult are wonderfully dedicated to their profession—especially my present dentist. My memory of reluctant dentists is a private boyhood one, but it represents for me the ambivalence of my generation toward the competitive struggle. Many of us undertook the challenge of the competitive game knowing that we were giving up something precious. We could not name it precisely, but we valued it nonetheless. To be sure, many of my generation had no conscious reservations at all about the competitive struggle. Those who did have reservations eventually overcame them because, apart from the shortage of alternatives, the price of success was not intolerably high, considering the substantial rewards of family life, respectability, material well-being, the rootedness of social identity—and the opportunity to find symbolic expression for the self through other outlets.

I introduce this personal note with some reticence. But I believe it helps to make concrete what is perhaps the most subtle of the contemporary changes in American psychoculture: a small but decisive shift in how we regard competitiveness. This is not to say that we have rejected competitiveness as such, for Sam Moscowitz was, after all, in his mid-fifties before he left the hardware store, Jane Coates was in her forties and Dan Turner in his late thirties and not really sure he

* *The New York Times,* 3/24/80.

had made the right decision. But these cases and especially the survey findings do suggest a shift in priorities. In a highly nuanced fashion, the terms of the unwritten giving/getting contract have changed. The rewards for fighting to get ahead seem to have grown a shade less appealing; the inner price exacted, a shade more costly and less worth the sacrifice.

(iv)

The conflict that the competitive struggle creates between self-expression and self-denial is strikingly similar to what we encountered when we explored the domestic norms relating to marriage, family, sex and children. The majority of Americans still yearn for the comforts and satisfactions of marriage and family life, but they try harder than before to stretch the limits of these institutions to make them more receptive to enhanced freedom for individuals and less demanding of self-denial.

The conflict over getting ahead reflects a similar pattern. Just as most Americans continue to value the family and wish to preserve it in some form, the majority continues to value our system of social mobility and wishes to preserve it. We must not lose sight of the American devotion to the principle that competition for social rewards is inherently good. In describing people's objections to the competitive scramble, I referred to its dark underside. But there is also an attractive and bright side, and for most people it still predominates.

This positive aspect of competition enjoys a place of honor in the rules of American life. Indeed, our highest ideals are implied by the honor paid to equality of opportunity and the incredible array of rewards American life offers to all who wish to compete for them. We compete vigorously in our sports; we compete in our educational system; we compete for jobs, honors, recognition and scientific achievement. We honor "best sellers" in all domains, and our world of entertainment is dominated by the "star" system in which some shine more brightly than others. We divide people into winners and losers, and logically so, for the system works toward such allocations.

The most severe indictment made by egalitarian reformers is that our society's competitive aspects do not work fairly. Certain groups—blacks, women, Spanish-speaking minorities, gays, undocumented workers, Indians, the physically handicapped, older people, ex-mental patients, ex-addicts, ex-convicts—are discriminated against in the competitive arena. Moral exhortation, consciousnesss raising, and increasingly, the force of the law itself are brought to bear to equalize conditions so that all individuals and groups will have a fair chance to compete for society's prizes. Although some egalitarian reformers have despaired of achieving real equality of opportunity with its implied emphasis on competition, the American people have not. In general, they approve of the competitive system. But as with the family "system," when competition is seen as either unfair or destructive of the self-expressive side of life, many of us now seek to change our circumstances, though without abandoning the system itself.

But we protest less about the rules by which we compete than we do, for example, about sex roles in marriage. For most Americans feel that the objectionable features of the competitive system are diminishing, and that the rigidities of getting ahead in America are withering away. In particular, young people believe this. Almost 90 percent of those under thirty in the Coleman/Rainwater report say they believe that "social class is getting less important than it used to be," and for the most part, Americans are enthusiastic, even elated, by this change.

Americans find it easy to identify the unattractive features of our status system and to welcome their decline. They perceive less of the kind of racial and ethnic prejudice that keeps minorities from access to jobs. They point to the wider availability of higher education ("a person can get as much education as he wants"). They sense that the workplace is growing fairer and more objective ("if you can do the job you are hired, if you can't, you are not"). They see and applaud progress in uncoupling jobs from income: they know that working-class jobs (plumbers, welders, sanitation workers, truck drivers) are no longer synonymous with low income, and hence with low status. They see that the middle class has grown more affluent, blurring the lines between middle-class and upper-class privileges such as a higher-priced car or travel abroad.

People also point to the relaxation of norms relating to proper dress codes. They associate the old norms about dressing appropriately for each occasion (e.g., the prohibition against women wearing slacks outside the home or supermarket) with the social-class system. "There are no set rules anymore," they say. "Attitudes are more relaxed. There is less keeping up with the Joneses."*

People recall with amazement how awed their parents were by the doings of "society people" reported in the newspapers. They emphasize the distance between themselves and the previous generation in not taking as seriously status pretensions based solely on wealth.

---

* Coleman and Rainwater, op. cit., p. 298.

The dentist-with-hobbies represents the compromise my generation made between the conflicting demands of self-expression and those of familial success. We chose familial success and sought self-expression within it through symbolic means (those "hobbies"), or vicariously through our children. The present generation is less willing to accept that accommodation. They are testing the system to see if it will yield the rewards of success (money, security, good jobs, recognition) without exacting the penalty in self-denial that once accompanied these rewards.

To the extent that it can adapt itself to these new cultural demands, the social mobility system will evolve peacefully and even unobtrusively. As in family life and marriage, there is room for elasticity, especially under conditions of affluence. But just as we have seen how the new cultural norms create stress points in marriage and family life, the rigidities and constraints of the social mobility structure are also fertile sources of tension.

The interplay between economy and culture is an extraordinarily complex matter. For the materialist historian, David Potter, the causal arrow points in only one direction: the economy shapes the culture. But I would urge that now the causal arrow also points in the opposite direction: if the changing economy alters the psychoculture, it is also true that the changing norms and meanings of the psychoculture influence the economy. Now, as perhaps never before, causality shifts back and forth.

In *The Cultural Contradictions of Capitalism*, Daniel Bell writes of the "disjuncture" between culture and social structure. What he means is that Americans are choosing to live in ways that may not benefit our economy. The system, as he conceives it, presupposes that individuals will want to compete for the rewards society provides—good jobs, security, products, honors. Cultural changes that weaken the urge to compete also weaken the economy. This creates tensions, the consequences of which are still unclear.*

In the nineteen-seventies we Americans pressed our demands for goods and services and new modes of social life as if there were no external realities to limit us. We assumed we lived in a world so rich and flexible that it could easily supply all that we wanted. But in the reality of the current world, to which we turn in Part III, the ability of our economy to meet our demands is severely limited. We do not yet know where the encounter between expanding cultural demands and a troubled economy—the world turned upside down—will lead.

* Daniel Bell, *The Cultural Contradictions of Capitalism* (New York: Basic Books, 1976), p. 14.

The New Realities: The Economics of the Reversal

Chapter 14

 ...—◉—...

The Growth Machine

Visualize a figure framed within a triangle. He/she appears to be standing firmly on the base of the triangle with arms pressed against the two sides; it is not clear whether she (let us assume the figure is a woman) is supporting the two sides of the triangle or is being supported by them. As we watch, our first impression is that she is snug and content within the triangle. Together, the geometric and human shapes form a unity. Indeed, it is from this sense of unitary fitness that we deduce the figure's contentment.

But as we watch the scene changes. The body stirs; she appears to be struggling, her face contorted. We see distinctly now that she is cramped by the triangle, virtually its prisoner; we realize that she is exerting a massive effort to push up against its two sides to make more room for herself.

As she presses, gradually the sides begin to yield. They stretch and stretch ever wider until she is no longer tightly confined but can move freely within the triangle. Now the figure relaxes and begins to look around. Tentatively, she steps out of the triangle, stretches, looks around again, startled, a trifle disoriented. Quickly, she scampers back to the triangle, rests awhile, steps out again and walks around.

We watch her as she systematically explores the ground around the triangle—in front of it, in back, to the left and right. Each time the figure steps out her moves are surer, more confident. But then, abruptly, the ground around the triangle becomes soft underfoot. She sinks a few inches into it and can barely extricate herself to return to the triangle. But now she finds no greater security within the triangle. Its sides are misshapen, and the ground on which it stands has grown infirm.

The figure looks around, one foot within the triangle, one foot on the treacherous ground. An expression of bewilderment suffuses her features, followed by irritation and frustration, then again by worry. Resolve returns briefly but is replaced again by anger, confusion. The moods change rapidly, tumbling over one another. Alternately frantic and paralyzed, the figure seems unclear about what to do next.

With apologies to Kafka, this silent scene helps embody the search for self-fulfillment over the past few decades. In the fifties, Americans needed the tight-fitting security of the familial success triangle. In the sixties, many young people, finding the shared meanings of familial success cramped and constricting, started to fight against them. In the seventies and now in the eighties the great majority of Americans of every age and income group have stepped out onto new ground, only to dis-cover that unexpected economic changes have turned terra firma into treacherous mud beneath their feet.

What will happen now? We can hardly go back to the safety of the familial-success triangle, but what will confront us as we move forward into a treacherous economic environment? Our current mood is one of all-encompassing disorientation; a muddled confusion has now become the hallmark of the search for self-fulfillment. If we can overcome it, a good journey to the end of the century and beyond is still possible. But if the confusion persists, a bad trip is inevitable.

If we are to dispel the confusion we cannot confine our attention exclusively to the cultural side of the great reversal that has turned our world upside down. We must make a cold and objective appraisal of its economic side as well, for only when we have a realistic sense of where the economy is headed can a realistic strategy for the self-fulfillment search be projected.

In many ways the shift in the nation's economy is more confusing than the changes in its culture. One reason is the suddenness of the economic change. The economy was transformed more swiftly than the culture. The changes in culture unfolded over a generation—from the early sixties to the early eighties—and is still evolving. The eco-nomic shift came with brutal abruptness.

Before the OPEC oil embargo of 1973, oil sold on the world market at just over $2 a barrel, and the United States paid $4 billion a year for its imported oil. In the decade from 1962 to 1972, the real price of imported oil actually declined by about 1.4 percent each year—contributing to a steady rise in the U.S. standard of living.*

When, in 1973, OPEC quadrupled the price of oil, we chose not to heed the implicit warning that our economy now rested on the vagaries of Mideast politics. On some unnoticed day in the nineteen-sixties, the control of world oil supplies and prices had shifted from the Gulf of Mexico to the Gulf of Aqaba. The Texas Railway Commission—marvelously misnamed considering its key role in the petroleum business—no longer dictated world oil prices. Instead the United States found itself dependent on obscure desert princes and Muslim holy men. Between 1973 and 1980 the real price of oil rose approximately tenfold! Yet, instead of cutting back, we actually increased our imports from the Arab OPEC countries from 2.4 million barrels a day in 1973 to more than twice that amount by the end of the decade—in addition to 3 million barrels a day imported from non-Arab OPEC nations. Instead of paying a modest $4 billion a year for imported oil, our oil bill rose steadily throughout the 1970s, first to $20 billion in 1973, then to $40 billion, then to $60 billion, then in 1980 we paid a staggering $90 billion for it.

Our national policy throughout the 1970s could hardly have been less rational. Having been warned in 1973 that the worst thing we could do to our economy and our security would be to increase our dependence on the Arab OPEC states, we proceeded to do precisely that.

Commenting on the outflow of dollars to OPEC, financier Felix Rohatyn noted that the combined value of all corporations listed on the New York stock exchange equaled approximately one thousand billion dollars. At the rate oil prices were rising he observed that we would ship abroad in a decade or two the accumulated wealth that America had built over more than three hundred years—in exchange for a few more years of carefree driving. Rohatyn may exaggerate—but not much. British historian Paul Johnson has noted that after World War II the world had experienced "a period of 25 to 30 years of American cultural-economic-military dominance, followed by what we are living through at the moment, a period of doubt and questioning which is going on all over the world."†

* Eric R. Zausner, "The U.S. Energy Future: A Time of Impossible Choices," Mitchell Prize Award Paper, Woodlands Conference on Growth Policy (October 1979).

† "Is the American Century Ending? A Conversation with Paul Johnson," *Public Opinion*, Vol. 2, No. 2 (March/May 1979).

So decisive to our economy was the OPEC price increase and our dependence on Mideast oil that the year 1973 should probably be taken as a watershed, sharply dividing the second half of the twentieth century into two elongated quarter-centuries: one twenty-seven-year period extending from the end of World War II to 1973 (the postwar quarter-century), and the other twenty-seven-year period extending from 1973 to the end of the century (the millennial quarter-century).

In the postwar quarter-century economic growth dominated the life of the nation. The millennial quarter-century—we are now in the thick of it—has not yet revealed its essence. But we can be pretty sure it will provide slower and less stable economic growth than in the postwar quarter.

(ii)

The full effect of the economic change since 1973 cannot be grasped unless we keep in mind how discontinuous it is with economic trends in the postwar quarter-century, an epoch that may prove unique in world history. Former British Prime Minister Edward Heath called this period "almost thirty years of the greatest prosperity the world has ever known." Economist Lincoln Gordon characterizes it as a "quarter century of sustained growth at the highest rates in recorded history."*

Between 1948 and 1973 the world's total industrial production expanded three-and-a-half times. The United States did not enjoy the fastest rate of growth: the defeated powers of World War II, Japan and West Germany, did. They were starting from scratch, their prewar economies in shambles, and their growth rate was astonishing. The United States, on the other hand, emerged from the war in a stronger economic condition than when the war began. In the early nineteen-fifties the United States accounted for an incredible 52 percent of the world's total economic output. With 7 percent of the world's population we earned 42 percent of its income. In 1949, per capita income in the United States was the world's highest by a huge margin: $1,450, while no other country exceeded $900, and only five countries were fortunate enough to find themselves in the $700–$900 range (Canada, England, New Zealand, Switzerland and Sweden). The average American consumed 3,186 calories a day, compared with 2,200–2,700 for France, Italy and West Germany and 1,800 for Japan and India.†

* Lincoln Gordon, "Growth Policies in a Global Perspective," Conference paper, Woodlands Conference on Growth Policy (October 1979).
† Potter, *People of Plenty*, p. 82.

On this massive base we continued to expand throughout the postwar years. In 1950, our gross national product rang the national cash register at $534 billion. By 1973, it had swelled to $1,235 billion (in constant 1972 dollars). In the space of a single generation our gross national product had more than doubled.

We should not sentimentalize this period. In many political ways it was a gloomy time, stretching from Joseph McCarthy and the cold war of the fifties, proceeding through the assassinations of the sixties, the riots in our center cities, the Vietnam war and the millions of young Americans disillusioned with our institutions, and Richard Nixon leaving the presidency in disgrace, with the nation desperate to restore the legitimacy of moral leadership in government.

Perhaps the thinker who most clearly sounded the themes from which the students of the sixties fashioned their critique of American society was Paul Goodman. He acknowledged the abundance of our economy but criticized the country for using that abundance badly. "A high standard of living of low average quality," he called it. Most particularly, he judged that we had so distorted the use of our wealth that growing up in America had become absurd.* Goodman contended that with all its material affluence, America did not provide its young people with the most elementary satisfactions of the human spirit: useful and necessary work, sex without guilt and a sense of community.

Throughout the postwar quarter-century there was no shortage of critics to remind us of our failures. But the failures should not blind us to the period's successes. Though it wasn't a golden age, Heath was right to call it one of the great economic success stories in human history. William Batten, Chairman of the New York Stock Exchange, observes that "in 1960 the typical American worker in manufacturing annually produced as much as four Japanese workers or two French or German workers."† From 1948 to 1966 the United States economy sustained on its already highly advanced base an average rate of 3.3 percent annual increase in productivity. Virtually every sector of the economy grew substantially. Between 1950 and 1970 the American labor force grew 32 percent, and most of the growth occurred in the desirable category of white-collar jobs: clerical jobs increased by 80 percent and professional/technical ones by 147 percent. In sharp contrast, less desirable blue-collar jobs grew at a paltry increase of 19 percent—below the 32 percent average growth rate for all jobs. By

* Paul Goodman, *Growing Up Absurd* (New York: Vintage, 1962).
† *The Wall Street Journal*, 12/31/79.

1970, unemployment among black Americans, long a national disgrace, showed signs of improvement as it dipped from double digits to 8.2 percent.

The long-term trend of Americans abandoning the farm continued unabated: in two decades farm jobs declined by 58 percent. The economic miracle of the period is portrayed in the twin phenomena of fewer farm workers needed to feed growing numbers of people, and of the abundance of cheap energy which made our dazzling farm productivity possible (in 1940 each farmer supplied 10.7 people; by the early 1980s, each farmer supplied more than 65 people).

The great economic advances of the postwar quarter were made possible in part because of earlier progress on the agricultural front. Between 1820 and 1930 the supply of energy per capita in the United States multiplied rapidly: "a forty-fold increase in the capacity to convert and utilize resources." Thanks in part to this energy boom, the proportion of the population engaged in the agriculture needed to feed a growing nation fell in the period from 1820 to 1950 from 72 percent to 12 percent, and continued its decline throughout the postwar quarter.* Astonishingly, almost the same number of people are engaged in agriculture today in the United States as in 1840, while the size of the domestic population has increased from 17 million to more than 230 million. In contrast, modern China employs more than 70 percent of its population in agriculture. They are where we were in the early 1830s, nearly locked into agricultural bondage. One Chinese farm worker feeds himself and barely one-half of a non-farm worker. American farm workers feed themselves, the rest of the nation and large numbers of people throughout the world.

The explosion in desirable white-collar jobs was made possible by a combination of growth factors: more education, more businesses, more research and development, more educated women entering the workforce and more savings. In the early part of the postwar quarter only one out of every two Americans had finished high school. But by the end of this period, the high school graduation rate had shot up from 50 percent to 75 percent, with a higher proportion of young people advancing beyond high school. At the beginning of the postwar quarter only one out of every four young Americans had had some college education but by its end almost half (45 percent) were entering college. The

---

* Potter, *People of Plenty*, p. 82.

peak years of the baby boom in the postwar quarter witnessed a triple form of growth: the total number of young Americans grew, the proportion finishing high school grew and the proportion going on to college grew, in combination creating a vast pool of young well-educated Americans.

The male half of this cohort had little difficulty finding jobs. Before World War II there were fewer than 2 million business enterprises. By the 1970s the number of businesses had swelled to 14 million. American exports grew from $4 billion to $180 billion annually. Both the government and private industry invested ever larger sums of money and effort in research and development to maintain leadership for our technology: from the end of World War II to 1970, the compound growth rate for funding university-linked research and development (R&D) averaged 15 percent a year.* In the mid-fifties government spending for R&D averaged $10 billion a year; by the late sixties this form of investment had soared to $30 billion a year (in constant dollars). It is not surprising that in the fifties the United States accounted for 80 percent of all the new products developed in the world.†

All this growth was financed by tax revenues and private savings. In 1950 Americans saved 5.3 percent of their disposable personal incomes; by 1973, on higher incomes, they saved a significantly larger proportion of income—almost 8 percent.

The postwar quarter-century was indeed a period of pulsating growth by nearly every measure. The economy grew, personal incomes grew, the population grew, schools and colleges grew, the labor force grew, the number of businesses grew, science, research and development grew, productivity grew, the government grew and the ownership of products— cars, TV sets, appliances and homes—virtually exploded.

How was all this wealth distributed? As we have seen, egalitarian critics point to the great disparities between rich and poor, and to the fact that as the country grew immensely richer the gap between rich and poor remained constant. Technically, this is true. In 1947, the bottom fifth of the population received 5 percent of all the income, and by the early seventies, they still received 5 percent. Conversely, in 1947 the top fifth got 43 percent of all income, and by the 1970s their share had been reduced by only two points, to 41 percent. This is not exactly

* *A Program for Renewed Partnership: The Report of the Sloan Commission on Government and Higher Education* (Cambridge, Mass.: Ballinger Publishers, 1980), p. 165.
† Theodore J. Gordon, "The Revival of Enterprise," Mitchell Prize Award Paper, Woodlands Conference on Growth Policy (1979).

income redistribution. And it does not take into account the even wider gap between the top and bottom strata of American life in holdings of capital and other property.

But these comparisons should not obscure the fact that the real income of virtually all Americans rose steadily throughout the postwar quarter—in the form of cash earnings for most people, and for those whose earnings fell below minimum levels, in the form of government-sponsored transfers such as Social Security, food stamps, education grants and loans, Medicaid, Medicare, AFDC, housing subsidies and job training programs.

Throughout the postwar quarter our economic institutions delivered economic stability along with growth. Inflation was almost nonexistent. Up to 1966, the annual rate of inflation averaged a paltry 1.6 percent. In 1966, it increased to 3.2 percent, and people got panicky.

In these same years, unemployment moved steadily downward— from 6 percent to 5 percent to 4 percent. As a consequence the government felt little pressure to develop an overall manpower policy either for training or job security. The United Auto Workers negotiated its path-breaking Supplemental Unemployment Benefits contract (S.U.B.), giving auto workers a substantial income floor in the event of a prolonged layoff. The other unions did not even bother to press for similar income security, so far into the past had the 1930s receded from people's minds. Most Americans had come to feel reasonably secure in their jobs.

Government spending fueled the boom. The Highway Trust channeled vast sums into a national highway system, stimulating the automobile market and, along with financial assistance to veterans, helping to create the suburbs and suburban shopping centers. Government loans for education, the GI Bill of Rights and improved scholarships for the needy underwrote the education boom. Schooling was now the principal means for self-advancement. Government also began to broaden its commitments to help those who could not help themselves—a role for the "welfare state" widely supported by the majority of voters. The average citizen felt compassion for those who failed to benefit from the country's growth—the blacks, the elderly, the residual poor. And almost everyone assumed our unending economic expansion would pay for it all.

Chapter 15

····◆◉◆····

The Best of
Both Worlds

The economic boom did wonders for the cohesiveness of American society in many ways—economic, sociological, political and psychological. Economically, what Americans wanted for themselves as individuals also served the society's goal of economic growth, and that growth, in turn, gave Americans the material goods and improved social standing that motivated them to work hard.

The economy in those years also reinforced cultural norms. As long as it "paid off" to work hard and sacrifice for the family, these norms were legitimized, endowing the society with an aura of moral rightness. Sociologists use the term *anomie* to describe the disunity and disarray that ensues when norms collapse and people come to feel there are no rules, or that observing them makes no sense because those who comply with them end up empty-handed, while those who flaunt the rules are rewarded. Anomie is profoundly demoralizing to daily life. It is doubtful that any society suffering extreme anomie could survive for long.

The opposite of anomie is the social cohesion that comes when norms enjoy wide acceptance and authority: rules are clear-cut, people observe them automatically, and are rewarded for doing so. A cohesive society may not be happy, creative or stimulating, but it imparts a stability, for which the majority always yearn. In the fifties and sixties, an expanding economy supported a cohesive culture because it rewarded the people who observed the rules. Americans like to do well by doing good; it makes sense out of the universe.

An expanding economy contributed crucially to our political cohesiveness as well. John Kennedy's metaphor of the rising tide that lifts all boats became the dominant principle of post–World War II politics. Through long experience, Americans have the political wisdom to know that it is easier to satisfy competing economic interests when the economy is expanding than when it is static or contracting.

To help the poor without hurting the rich was the heart of our political philosophy in the postwar quarter—a political consensus shared by both rich *and* poor. We saw this in an earlier chapter when we looked at how Americans regard social mobility. Americans support social legislation to help others when they feel they are improving their own lot. The national psychology is: Since I am getting mine, why shouldn't the other person get his? Only when people feel vulnerable themselves do they resist helping others. These elementary realities of American political life all support the same conclusion: the steady growth of the economy in the postwar quarter provided remarkable political stability.

Even in the psychological domain, which was ultimately to prove the most vulnerable, we achieved cohesiveness. Familial success gave each person a social identity and belonging to a family, a church, a company and a community stimulated confidence that once was part of a larger whole.

Each dimension—economic, sociological, political and psychological—fit snugly with all others, forming a mutually reinforcing structure to which the individual American was connected by links that, though invisible and intangible, could hardly have been sturdier. This is the bond formed by the giving/getting compact that prevailed in the postwar quarter-century.

As the old order now recedes, we catch a fleeting glimpse of what made it work so well. We see that the pattern formed by a restrictive culture and a growing economy contains an inner logic. The rigid rules supporting the self-denial ethic were necessary to the country's economic success while the rewards of economic growth were necessary to reinforce the discipline imposed by self-denial. America in the postwar quarter exemplified Max Weber's grand insight connecting the Protestant ethic (based on self-denial) to capitalism.*

What happens when economy and culture are reversed, as they now

* Max Weber, *The Protestant Ethic and the Spirit of Capitalism*, trans. Talcott Parsons (London: G. Allen & Unwin, 1930).

are? What happens to the society's unity when the self-denial ethic is no longer reinforced by an expanding economy? What happens when the fabled growth machine begins to falter at the very moment that the population's appetites have been whetted and its expectations have reached unprecedented heights?

As long as Americans lived without much economic security in an economy that could not yet meet the needs of its citizens, as in the period prior to the 1960s, the rat race competitiveness and the self-denial of our culture seemed both sensible and tolerable. But once the expectation of affluence replaced the old Depression-bred economic insecurities, the need for so much self-denial suddenly grew problematic, and its moral status grew questionable, as we have seen.

As expectations of affluence took hold, Americans reveled in their new freedom of choice. But just as they turned from the vexing task of how to make a living to the delightful question of how to live the good life, they encountered a most disagreeable surprise.

From a psychological point of view, the shock of the OPEC oil embargo could not have come at a worse time. It had taken a long time, but by the end of the sixties the Depression psychology born in the thirties had finally dissipated. Instead, Americans—particularly younger Americans—no longer expected to meet major obstacles to making a living.

Americans had grown used to the idea that the giant corporations, the government and other economic institutions would simply and eternally be there—to support the aged, build the infrastructure, create jobs, turn out wealth and do the country's work, as much a part of nature as trees and rainfall from heaven. We knew, of course, that our institutions were run by fellow human beings—and we grumbled about government waste and corporate self-seeking. But nonetheless it was assumed that the schools, factories, jetports, old-age homes and TV stations existed for one's convenience and could be counted on to do what they were supposed to do.

The average American gave little thought to the matter. There were better things to think about—self-fulfillment, for example. Indeed, so utterly dependent was the nation on steady growth and stable economic institutions that these seemed a permanent arrangement, requiring no special attention.

By the end of the postwar quarter by no means were all Americans affluent, or even felt they were. But virtually all of us presupposed that our economy would continue to function automatically and successfully, as surely as the sun would rise each morning without effort on our part.

Such faith does not develop in a single day, nor is it underpinned by any one experience. It takes many events and experiences to create and reinforce it. In the postwar quarter the country was surfeited with this type of reinforcing experience, leading some young Americans in the sixties to contrast their own lives with those of parents whose existence they saw as stunted or impoverished because of meager freedom of choice. They knew their parents had disciplined themselves on self-denial, and believed that in so doing had deprived themselves of essential elements of life.

The younger group's rejection of the moral rightness of self-denial never constituted a real generation gap. The lives of the younger generation of Americans exhibit many of the same themes as the lives of their parents raised in the Depression except that the younger people insist that their story have a different ending. The younger Americans tuned into the undertone of regret buried in their parents' accounts of how they had settled for self-denial. Often the parents themselves were aware of the psychic cost of their own self-denial and the massive suppression of desires it required. Their progeny identified with this suppressed element and pledged to fight the battle with the "real world" according to rules which defined self-denial as either unnecessary or at least undesirable.

When I studied the student revolt in the sixties I remember how struck I was by how extensively students identified with the suppressed elements in their parents' lives. Almost universally, they were living their parents' fantasies, dreams the parents had not permitted themselves to act out. This accounted for the awesome intensity of parental interest in the campus revolt of the period, and their ambivalence as they watched with fascinated horror as their children acted out their own rejected impulses.

(ii)

Self-denial is the core of the old giving/getting covenant. If it is deprived of moral legitimacy, the whole transaction is put in jeopardy. The process of questioning self-denial started on the nation's campuses in the sixties but spread to the rest of the population in the seventies. As its moral imperative grew weaker, the search for self-fulfillment grew stronger. But as the shifts in culture spread from campus to mainstream they underwent a transformation little noted at the time but decisive both for the culture *and* the economy of the eighties.

Since the campus rebellion of the sixties fathered the self-fulfillment drive of the seventies, it is often assumed that the same core values are involved, namely the antimaterialism of the counterculture. There are just enough superficial resemblances between the cultural changes of the sixties and the seventies to make this assumption plausible. The language of the two periods has a certain resemblance. In the sixties we were told to "do your own thing," and cautioned that "I'm a human being; do not fold, spindle or mutilate." The language of self-fulfillment in the seventies struck a somewhat similar tone: "I have a duty to myself," "I have my own life to live," "I am a person in my own right," "It is all right as long as it doesn't hurt anybody else."

The campus upheavals of the sixties gave us the first premonitory sign that the plates of American culture, after decades of stability, had begun to shift. Enclaves of upper-middle-class college youth were the first to feel the tremors. Then in the seventies the public as a whole began to experience them and the mass reappraisal of American life values was launched.

Some of the same historic processes that led to campus unrest in the sixties were also responsible for the cultural shifts of the seventies. But what I want to stress here are the differences, not the similarities, between the counterculture of the sixties and the new culture of the seventies and eighties.

It is probably best to regard the counterculture of the sixties and the self-fulfillment search of the seventies and eighties as two distinct forms of cultural expression created by the same historic tide, but each finally assuming a separate shape. The counterculture neither became assimilated into the wider culture nor did it die out. It survived its partial co-optation by the majority and, in certain places, it continues to flourish. Only a tiny minority of Americans, not more than 2 or 3 percent, now belong to it. These are the people who hold that the path to fulfillment is to seek a simpler life: to own fewer possessions, to escape from the tumult of city life, to move closer to nature, to enjoy a few close relationships, to dwell among communities of like-minded people. Most members of this counterculture are young. Many have moved to sparsely populated and gloriously beautiful parts of the continent—Vermont, Colorado, Maine, Wyoming, Oregon, Washington, California, Arizona and New Mexico. They form part of what is called the "voluntary simplicity" movement. It is a movement that exerts a powerful appeal on the same upper-middle-class youth who responded to the counterculture of the sixties. They echo the sentiment Tom Robbins expressed in his novel, *Even Cowgirls Get the Blues*: "There are countless ways to live upon this tremulous sphere in mirth and good health, and probably only one way—the industrialized, urbanized, herding way—to live here stupidly, and man has hit upon that one stupid way."*

Few adult Americans have ever wholeheartedly embraced the counterculture's principled rejection of material comfort. In responding to survey questions, people tend to agree with positively worded statements, especially when these sound moralistic, but in Yankelovich, Skelly and White surveys conducted in the late seventies, a 62 percent majority of Americans consistently rejected the statement: "The way things are today, the fewer possessions you own, the less you have to worry about and the better off you are." A 54 percent majority expressed a desire "to own more things than I have now." The majority of Americans gladly echo the classic retort of Samuel Gompers, founder of American organized labor, who, when asked the objectives of the labor movement, replied with the single word, "More." For the overwhelming majority of all Americans, an important part of living the good life simply means "more."

Most Americans want more material goods *and* more personal freedom. To the comfort we now have, we want to add more leisure. If we enjoy the pleasures of urban living, we want to add closeness to nature —without abandoning our city base. We wish to preserve economic security and also add a dash of adventure, excitement and change. We treasure our political freedom and want to graft onto it new social entitlements. We want to pile more onto what we already have, not subtract from it. We are not nearly as ready as were the privileged youth of the sixties—or their heirs in the voluntary simplicity movement of the seventies—to give up our goods.

This state of mind was expressed well by social commentator Ellen Goodman, who wrote in the mid-seventies: "Many of us want things that we will not accept as contradictory: a clean environment *and* full employment; meaningful work *and* college tuition; social justice *and* a balanced budget."† Goodman's formulation expresses the dominant expectation of most fulfillment seekers that they can have the best of two worlds: the older world created by the economic imperative and the newer world dominated by quality-of-life values. She knows that her demands might appear contradictory, but she says firmly, *"we will not accept [them] as contradictory."* [Emphasis added.] This expression of will was perhaps the defining feature of the public psychology of the

* Tom Robbins, *Even Cowgirls Get the Blues* (New York: Bantam, 1977), p. 192.
† Ellen Goodman, *Close to Home* (New York: Simon and Schuster, 1979), p. 21.

sixties and seventies: the conviction that one set of cherished values need not be sacrificed for the sake of another, that we need not choose among the good things of life but rather can embrace them all.

In the eighties, this point of view has abruptly collided with reality in the form of oil politics, double-digit inflation, shrinking productivity, Ayatollahs, sheiks and a renewed arms race. And so we turn now from the postwar era of the recent past to the turmoil of the present.

Chapter 16

‥━●━‥

Jumpy and Off Balance

The country is just now starting to awaken to its new cultural situation and its troubled economy. Ideally, many Americans would like to have both the excitement of an open and dynamic culture and the material well-being that comes with an expanding economy. Whether this combination, which we experienced fleetingly just before the events of 1973, is possible under the conditions of the millennial quarter-century is a question that remains open before us.

As America advances into the millennial quarter, the significance of events in the early 1970s stands out ever more sharply. The postwar quarter climaxed nearly a century of industrial growth and innovation that future historians may look on in the same way we look back to the great period of Roman power—a glorious if one-sided burst of human enterprise, a peak period in the history of the West.

The OPEC-related shift from cheap to expensive energy did not bring about the economic phase of the great reversal by itself. But it did signal the end of America's economic hegemony in the world, and it launched the millennial quarter-century. Abruptly in some cases and gradually in others, most growth trends that had climbed upward in previous decades now began to falter. Where there had been steady growth, the pace became slower and more fitful. Where stability could once be taken for granted, instability was surfacing. The fabled American economy, still powerful and a dynamic force in the world, began to show signs of strain. Before 1973, it would have been perverse to forecast any direction save upward for the United States economy. Virtually all trends suggested greater growth fueled by cheap energy. Since 1973, however, most trends seem either to have stalled or moved downward.

Even before the events of 1973, there were premonitory signs that trouble lay ahead. A worldwide drought in 1971 caused widespread starvation in Africa and Asia. A larger drought in 1972 underscored the fragility of the ecosystem. Commodity prices rose sharply in 1972, sounding another warning to economists that the Keynesian presumption of "solved" supply problems might be false. Indeed, throughout the seventies, shortages of sugar, coffee, lumber, various metals and other materials challenged the comfortable assumption that we need not worry about the supply side and could henceforth concentrate solely on the "management of aggregate demand" as economists like to phrase it.

Unexpectedly too, our rate of annual productivity increases began to decline. When it fell to the level of Great Britain's, far behind that of other industrialized nations, few ventured to diagnose the illness of American industry as a variant of the so-called "British disease": a state of prolonged economic stagnation. But American scientists worried aloud as our research and development expenditures leveled off and started to decline. The business community worried as the dollar steadily shrank in value, the price of gold zoomed upward and our balance of payments grew bleak. Conservative economists worried as government expenditures steadily mounted. And average citizens worried as taxes rose, the price of gas and home heating oil rose, and the price of hamburger, salad oil, home mortgages and shoes kept climbing with no end in sight.

Inflation had set in seriously in the early seventies. Deficit financing of the Vietnam war coupled with rising deficits in our balance of payments had, along with the problems mentioned above, led to the devaluation of the dollar in 1971 and to the collapse of the postwar Bretton Woods system in which the dollar was deemed equivalent to gold pegged at $35 per ounce. By the start of the new decade, gold was to soar above $800 an ounce as the dollar declined in relation to the mark, the yen and the Swiss franc and as fears of political instability spread throughout the Middle East.

It had been precisely these changes in the international monetary system that had led OPEC nations in 1973 to their fateful decision to boost the price of oil. The devaluation of the dollar in 1971 had created a sharp income decline for oil producers. This drop encouraged some OPEC activists to point out that the decline in United States domestic oil production (due to our dwindling supply) had placed new economic power in OPEC's hands, while at the same time a post-Vietnam psychology made it unlikely that the United States would, or could, respond aggressively to higher producer prices. The activists' estimate proved correct in all respects, and thereafter all OPEC nations felt free to raise the price of oil virtually at will.

Before the events of 1973, the scattered symptoms of economic malaise occurred in the context of a booming United States economy. It would be wrong to say that these were ignored; certainly bankers, economists, business leaders and a handful of political analysts knew that something was amiss in our slowing productivity and mounting balance of payment deficits. But so vast was our economy, so great our wealth, and so accustomed were our people to riding out occasional setbacks that we took the increase in the price of oil in stride, not pausing, after our discomfort, to ponder its significance.

In the initial years of OPEC price rises—roughly from 1973 to the Iranian revolution of 1978 that deposed the Shah and United States influence in Iran—the majority of Americans assumed that the large oil companies were playing games with prices to reap "obscene profits" for themselves. We were convinced that gasoline shortages would disappear as soon as the oil companies won big price increases at the pump. The majority reasoned, erroneously, that there were no real shortages, only collusion between big oil and big government to jack up the price of gas and exploit the consumer. And anyway, nuclear energy would soon come to the rescue. Even if the doomsayers were right about our oil running low, more than 8 out of 10 Americans (81 percent) reasoned that a nation technologically advanced enough to put a man on the moon would surely find a solution to this momentary inconvenience.*

Then, two events occurred which drove home to thoughtful Americans the lessons that had been implicit in the embargo of 1973 but largely ignored by the public once the embargo ended and gas began to flow again—at a higher price. The revolution in Iran disrupted the

---

* Daniel Yankelovich and Bernard Lefkowitz, "The Public Debate on Growth: Preparing for Resolution," Table 9, Woodlands Conference on Growth Policy (October 1979).

supply of oil from the Middle East, and in the spring of 1978 long gas lines appeared, first in California and then in other parts of the country. Suddenly, the embargo of 1973 was no longer a one-time event. The reality of our dependence on Mideast oil began to sink in.

Then in April of 1979 came the drama of Three Mile Island: the threat of a nuclear accident potentially destructive to millions of Americans and their progeny. That the accident never happened did not distract the public's attention from the fact that "the authorities" did not seem to know what they were doing and that safety precautions had been slovenly. Suddenly, the caveats about nuclear safety voiced for years by the Union of Concerned Scientists assumed a new urgency. The "China Syndrome" had jumped from movie screens onto front-page headlines, and abruptly, the "nuclear option" lost a great deal of its appeal and credibility for the general public. Unwillingly and reluctantly, Americans began to grow less complacent about how easy it would be to get a quick technological fix on the energy problem.

But of all the signals arousing the public to the reality of a newly troubled economy, it was inflation that impinged most directly on the lives of Americans. Until the end of the postwar quarter, inflation did not present a difficulty for the average citizen. As we have seen, before 1965 inflation was virtually nonexistent. Even in 1971 an inflation rate of only 4.5 percent, which we would now hail as stability itself, panicked President Nixon into wage and price controls. The decade of the eighties, on the other hand, began with consumer price increases in excess of 18 percent. Throughout the full postwar quarter-century the Consumer Price Index increased less than it did in the few years from 1973 to 1980.

In the fifties and sixties people got tangible rewards from the stable growth of the economy. They acquired the material goods they desired. By 1970, 97 percent of American households owned a TV set, 84 percent at least one car, 72 percent a washing machine and 61 percent a color TV.

Even in the early seventies, people's after-tax real income continued to grow. But it grew more slowly—about 1 percent a year (after inflation) in contrast to more than twice that rate in the preceding decade. Then, from the mid-seventies on, taxes and prices began to grow faster than income. In the first six years of the millennial quarter (1973–1979) family income grew by 52 percent, but the average price of a new single-family home jumped 105 percent (from $30,500 to $62,400); the price of food, medical care and automobiles advanced at a rate that was moderately faster than income, and the cost of a college education forged way ahead of income. Try as they might to keep up, most people could not maintain the standard of living to which they had grown accustomed.

In response, Americans plunged into debt. After 1973, the trend toward increased savings sharply reversed itself. Within a five-year period, the savings rate trend plummeted from its 8 percent high at the end of the postwar quarter, and by 1978 it had fallen back to its 1950 level of 5.3 percent. It has continued to decline thereafter. In 1950, consumer debt had accounted for only 37 percent of after-tax income. By 1978 it had risen to 83 percent! In mid-1980 the stagflation pattern of 1974–75 reoccurred. Unemployment rose, especially in the steel, automotive and construction industries; profits fell; the growth rate fell; but prices remained high.

Inflation kept pushing people into even higher tax brackets: just when they needed more money to pay the higher prices, the government took an ever larger portion of their income. Some groups in the population, particularly the elderly, were "indexed" against inflation, i.e., their incomes were automatically adjusted to increases in the Consumer Price Index. But most Americans were not, and the burden fell most heavily on the young working adults and on those at the lower end of the income scale.

Most of these trend reversals were scarcely noted by the public. By the time we began to pay attention the country was plunged into economic trouble.

(ii)

By the late seventies a mood of pessimism and foreboding had replaced the traditional American optimism. A glance at the survey data of the period reveals the size and nature of the shift.

· Gallup showed that while only one of five Americans in the early 1970s (21 percent) believed "next year will be worse than this year," by the end of the 1970s a 55 percent majority held this pessimistic outlook.

· Survey findings from Yankelovich, Skelly and White show that Americans who believe we are entering an era of enduring shortages (as opposed to temporary ones) increased from 40 percent in the mid-seventies to 62 percent at the decade's end.

- Between 1975 and 1979, the Roper Organization found that Americans who feared high inflation was "here to stay" had grown from 38 percent to 87 percent.

- Perhaps the single most persuasive indicator of a darkened outlook comes from an ingenious scale developed by psychologist Hadley Cantril in the 1950s and used subsequently by various polling organizations. This survey technique shows that from the 1950s to the late 1960s Americans believed the present to be superior to the past and expected the future to improve on the present. By 1978 this pattern had wholly reversed itself—to the majority the past now looked better than the present and the present better than the future, a truly historic shift away from optimism to bleakness.

The pessimism people feel about the economy now pervades their private lives. Traditionally, Americans have distinguished between the economic well-being of the nation and their own personal prospects for a satisfying life: even when they perceived the country to be in economic trouble, they remained optimistic about their own future. In recent years, however, that blithe dissociation has weakened, so that pessimism about the nation's economic future now breeds pessimism about one's personal prospects as well.

This sense of foreboding mirrors actual experience. A survey by Louis Harris shows that 69 percent find it harder to make ends meet than in earlier years, and compared to the recent past, have had to put off buying essentials as well as luxuries. Yankelovich, Skelly and White studies show that between 1974 and 1980, the number of Americans reporting difficulty in paying their bills, saving for the future and paying mortgages or rent more than doubled—from 23 to 48 percent.

The University of Michigan's Survey Research Center conducted a survey of the nation's mental health in the late fifties. They did a second study in the late seventies, asking the same questions of a comparable cross section. In the more recent study they found that Americans were worrying more about their lives in this present period than in the fifties, especially young Americans. In the fifties only a minority of younger Americans (32 percent) held fretful and anxious attitudes about their lives. Now the worriers have swelled to a majority of all younger Americans (52 percent).*

Perhaps today's young Americans find it more socially acceptable to

* *ISR Newsletter*, Vol. 7, No. 1, Institute for Social Research (Ann Arbor: University of Michigan, Winter 1979), p. 4.

admit to worry and anxiety about the future than people did in the earlier period. Maybe today's norms do not oblige people to maintain a stiff upper lip. If so, the research data might not mean that today's younger Americans actually worry more, but merely that they find it easier to admit to doing so. An examination of the data shows, however, that this is not the case: it documents a steep rise in all the behavioral symptoms of increased anxiety—greater frequency of headaches, loss of appetite, trouble in sleeping, upset stomachs and higher levels of feeling nervous, fidgety and tense.

Further confirmation comes from other sources, for example, from the fact that the suicide rate among white adolescents increased an astonishing 171 percent between 1950 and 1975, from 2.8 per 100,000 to 7.6 per 100,000.* A trend study by the Chicago-based National Opinion Research Council (NORC) also documents the growth of feelings of frustration and lack of control over one's destiny. By the late seventies Americans who felt that their lives would turn out pretty much the way they desired were outnumbered almost two to one (61 percent to 37 percent) by those who feared that their hopes and plans would not materialize. A generation earlier, Americans had split almost in half (51 percent to 45 percent) on this question.

In the Michigan studies people were asked why they worried, and what their main sources of apprehension and unhappiness were. More than any other factor people cited a growing concern with what was happening in the country and in their own community. Significantly, the number of Americans who believe their unhappiness and tension is their own fault diminished in the interval between the two studies— from 13 percent in the earlier period to 8 percent in the late seventies. The drop is not large, but its direction is important. It is an unexpected finding in an era dominated by self-assertive psychologies which tell people their destinies are in their own hands. In a culture that has grown more psychology-minded, it is striking to find that today's Americans, though grown more introspective, blame themselves less for their troubles than the last generation did.

Perhaps the sharpest shift in American attitudes has been a steady erosion of trust in government and other institutions, falling from a peak of trust and confidence in the late fifties to a trough of mistrust in the early eighties. Research conducted by the University of Michigan

* Edward A. Wyne, University of Illinois at Chicago Circle, *Phi Delta Kappa Magazine*, Jan 1978.

Election Studies unit show that in the late fifties and early sixties, the majority of Americans believed that:

- "The people running the government in Washington are smart people who know what they are doing." (69 percent)

- "You can trust the government to do what is right most or all of the time." (56 percent)

- "The government is run for the benefit of all, rather than for a few big interests." (72 percent)

- "Public officials care what people like me think." (71 percent)

Only a minority of the public (42 percent) then believed that the federal government "wastes a lot of the money we pay in taxes" and is in general "getting too powerful for the good of the country."

By the start of the millennial quarter-century the majorities expressing confidence in government had disappeared, and the previously small numbers of Americans concerned with waste, government indifference and citizen impotence had grown into large majorities. The changes move only in one direction—from trust to mistrust. They are massive in scale and impressive in their cumulative message. In the course of a single generation Americans have grown disillusioned about the relation of the individual American to his government.

- The level of trust that government will do what is right most of the time has been cut in half, from 56 percent to 29 percent.

- Confidence that those running the government are "smart people who know what they are doing" dropped from a two-thirds majority (69 percent) to less than a one-third minority (29 percent).

- The cynical attitude that the government is run for the benefit of a few big interests rather than for the benefit of all the people jumped from a mere 28 percent in the early nineteen-sixties to an astonishing 65 percent in the late nineteen-seventies.

- The conviction that the government wastes our tax dollars grew steadily from a four out of ten minority (42 percent) in 1958 to virtually an eight out of ten majority (77 percent) twenty years later.

- Studies by the Louis Harris Organization show that the number of people expressing at least a mild form of political alienation—"what

I think doesn't count," "those in power don't care what people like me think," "*They* try to take advantage of people like me"—rose inexorably from one-third minorities in the nineteen-sixties to two-thirds majorities by the start of the nineteen-eighties.

Chapter 17

·····●◉●····

Working Through
to Reality

This portrait of the American public reveals an aspect of American consciousness different from that described in Part II of this book. The handful of Americans whose lives we examined in earlier chapters seemed utterly absorbed in their inner state of being. We saw little discontent with government, and only rare glimpses of pessimism about the country's economic prospects. Thus, we have before us two profiles of American states of consciousness. One shows a shift from economic optimism to gloom, from trust in institutions to mistrust, from confidence in America's future to a jumpy apprehensiveness—as if one were not sure where the next blow was coming from, but quite sure one was coming. The other profile shows a hopeful and inwardly focused America, aware that new opportunities for self-expression and fulfillment exist because so many new choices seem available to each of us. Here we see Americans reaching out—some boldly, others cautiously—to explore tantalizing new paths.

Though they exhibit different moods, one expansive, the other apprehensive, the two current public states of mind do coexist: Americans are hopeful and fearful at the same time. They rejoice in the greater range of personal choices the culture has made possible, and they press forward vigorously on this front, urging new roles for women, new uses for leisure, new sexual freedoms, new careers, greater physical fitness, more intimacy with nature, new modes of being. At the same time, they fret over their eroding economic status, wondering anxiously what the future will bring. And sometimes this worry brings them close to panic. Maintaining these two states of mind simultaneously creates an almost intolerable level of tension and confusion. "In the long run," observes sociologist Amitai Etzioni, "such high ambivalence is too stressful for societies to endure."*

Before the decade of the eighties has run its course, Americans must reduce the dissonance between these opposing perspectives if we expect to reestablish a coherent world view. But we have barely begun to do so. We are just beginning to realize that a contradiction exists between our two states of mind.

The British art historian, Kenneth Clark, has aptly referred to the period in Western civilization of which the postwar quarter was the climax as an age of "heroic materialism." It gave rise to a widespread psychology of affluence whose outstanding features are worth recapitulating here, for it is this outlook that must now be confronted and challenged. As we have seen, its most prominent feature is an "ampersand" mentality: the expectation of a high material standard of living & clean air, water and other environmental protections & affirmative action programs for the disadvantaged & protection against illness, unemployment, old age and other life risks & the full rich life built around leisure, self expression and personalized life styles. This is the familiar "we-expect-more-of-everything" outlook.

A second feature of the psychology of affluence assumes that acquiring more of everything is a matter of personal entitlement rather than a mere hope or desire. Such presumptions of entitlement take on a quasi-judicial status, whereupon they move out of the marketplace into the arena of government, single-issue politics, protests, hearings, and other legal and moral imperatives.

Its third characteristic is to take for granted that the economy will function more or less automatically. The economy is Big Mother, indestructible and bountiful, though sometimes she won't respond unless one screams and yells. Many of the regulations and constraints on the economy were imposed in the sixties and seventies by zealous young lawyers in Washington and state agencies who mistrusted the corporations their agencies regulated. Ironically, however, they fully believed in

---

* Amitai Etzioni, "Choose We Must," Lecture at Georgia State University (February 20, 1979).

corporate omnipotence and indestructability. They assumed the corporations could do virtually anything they wanted. As a result, government regulation grew into a peculiar mishmash of legitimate social goals mandated by the people, and punitive excesses that were the judicial equivalent of screams and shouts at Big Mother. One of the most notorious examples is O.S.H.A.—the Occupational Safety and Health Administration. Its thousands of picayune regulations assume unlimited corporate resources accompanied by a total absence of good faith or even common sense on the part of the regulated industries. It will take decades to eliminate these excesses.

A fourth feature of the psychology of affluence is that it turns the self-denial ethic on its head. Instead of a concern with moral obligations to others pursued at the cost of personal desire, we have the concept of duty to self pursued at the cost of moral obligations to others. Personal desire achieves the status of an ethical norm.

In the seventies, many Americans came to endorse all four tenets of the new psychology of affluence with high fervor; it became part of the cultural climate of the times, an expression of the *Zeitgeist*. In its most extreme and naïve form, this psychology might be expressed as follows: "I am entitled to more; I owe it to myself to get more. To do so, I need to learn who I really am and then to assert myself." The astonishing fact about the final years of the postwar quarter was not that so many held this view, but that it actually worked as often and as well as it did.

One of the few valid conclusions that can be drawn about our new era, the millennial quarter, is that while the demand for more of everything remains widespread, it lacks its former chief attraction: the demand no longer works very well. We may insist on more of everything, but the environment grows ever less responsive, less able or willing to meet the demand. This truth is not yet as self-evident as it is destined to become as the millennial quarter unfolds. To many, in fact, this new reality is not obvious at all, and that tells us a great deal about the instability of the present moment in American life.

The unprepared mind plays tricks on itself. People take note of the changed economic climate but assume that it is transitory and will soon be replaced by a more benign normalcy or that it is the result of some villainy practiced by government and big business and can be corrected once blame is fixed and the villains are punished.

People continue, out of habit—even when they know it no longer makes sense—to behave as if old economic conditions still exist. They are distressed and confused by changes that undermine their expectations, but they expend considerable emotion—and waste motion—avoiding the confrontation with a changed world.

Americans have yet to reconcile themselves to the new, unwelcome conditions. They have yet to find strategies for coping, based on lowered economic expectations. We are just beginning to comprehend our new economic situation and we are not sure what concessions or sacrifices it entails.

Thus, we Americans are still in the early stages of what psychologists call a "working through" process. Think of a person in a state of shock because he has lost a cherished goal or object: for example, a man in his mid-fifties who had been expecting to retire comfortably at age sixty-five, and then learns abruptly and accidentally from people he mistrusts that the pension which he had long been counting on has been taken away from him. At first, he will be angry, anxious, depressed, confused, incredulous, suspicious and thrown off balance. A year or two later, he will have regained his composure. The harsh reality will not have changed: he has indeed lost his pension and his chances for a comfortable retirement; but his state of mind is not what it was immediately following the loss. He is now more reconciled to the new condition. He has changed his retirement plans, scaled down his expectations. He may still be angry, but he has reoriented his thinking about the future and is again in control of himself.

The reaction to loss, in extreme cases what psychiatrists call the "grief reaction," usually follows a clear-cut pattern. There is a definite phase-by-phase process of assimilation that shows up in an outpouring of emotion, inconclusiveness and inconsistency. As the process unfolds one should expect to find in swift alternation expressions of anger, confusion, disbelief, denial, barely suppressed panic, scapegoating, grasping at straws, depression, exaggeration, fatalism, instability of attitudes (saying one thing one day and another the next), lack of realism and Pollyannaish wishful thinking that everything will turn out to be for the best, that nothing really has changed. In early stages of the process, people will overreact or refuse to accept realities they know to be true.

These are not pathological or abnormal symptoms: they are the temporary—and perhaps inevitable—human responses to unanticipated and threatening changes in one's environment. They are signs of the huge effort it takes for people to keep panic at bay when they first feel threatened and before they adapt to new circumstances.

This working-through process also implies movement toward a goal. It is a dynamic process, not a static one, so that when the sound and fury of the struggle have abated, the stricken person will digest the new realities and find appropriate strategies for dealing with them. When the internal work is done, a new program of action will gradually emerge, accompanied by acceptance of the loss and accommodation to new conditions.

The working-through process confronting Americans in the eighties is to accommodate to new economic realities which, in effect, constitute a severe blow to the expectations that dominated our recent past, and probably a death blow to the psychology that one is entitled to more of everything. Those survey data that now show a pessimistic, gloomy, reality-denying and overreacting public should begin to show a more adaptive response within the next several years, assuming, of course, that national populations under stress follow the same adaptive patterns as individuals do and that the economic situation does not become literally catastrophic.

Chapter 18

---◆---

Goodbye to
the Inner Journey

Everyone knows what it is like to be concentrating on a task that requires total attention when suddenly something unexpected occurs that breaks the concentration, leaving one disoriented and unsure of what to do next. The task that preoccupied many Americans in the seventies was rethinking their personal goals: what success meant to them, what they wanted out of marriage, family life, work and leisure, the proper relations between the sexes, and their overall place in the scheme of things.

Such basic rethinking is a rare event. It involves a form of reflection that has not been a notable part of our cultural heritage—introspective thinking. As noted earlier, in the late seventies our surveys showed 72 percent of Americans spending a great deal of time thinking about themselves, which they describe as a marked change from their previous habits of thought. We do not have comparable data from earlier periods, but it seems likely that this is a high point for introspection as a mass phenomenon; it would be surprising if it were otherwise. Large populations do not ordinarily devote much time to reappraising their basic life values. In most cultures and at most times, people absorb prevailing values as part of the "atmosphere," leaving the reassessment of values to deviants, geniuses, artists, intellectuals and other malcontents.

The mass introspective project turns on two questions: "How can I avoid being trapped in forms of family life, work and living patterns that ensnare and engulf me, depriving me of my personal freedom?" And, "If I do succeed in preserving my personal freedom, what do I do with it?" These two raw questions are what the stretching of the familial-success triangle is all about. They can be clothed in fancy psychological jargon—the language of self-actualization and fulfilling one's potentials —but the rawness is what remains after the rhetoric is discounted.

Inevitably, when they try to answer these questions people make mistakes. They go to extremes, become self-preoccupied—so much so that clever observers take note and apply labels like the "me decade" and the "culture of narcissism." By definition introspective thinking *is* oriented toward the self—and the nature of the project makes self-concern inevitable.

In our new economic circumstances this type of thinking is no longer adaptive. The preoccupation with self, with one's inner journey, is not going to answer practical economic questions. Is Margaret Greenson's fear that she may be forced to return to bookkeeping well founded? Is Professor Agnoli correct in his surmise that he really cannot "better himself" economically in the California think-tank world? Will Sam Moscowitz's birdwatching job survive and can the hardware store continue to send him his dividends? The answers to such questions do not lie within the self. They are worldly questions. A reasonable assessment of the economic conditions on which people hang their self-fulfillment hopes requires a different kind of effort from introspective thinking. It calls for what we might term "realistic" thinking. The two modes of thought, introspective and realistic, are utterly different. Interrupted in the introspective project of recasting our life goals, the sudden harshness of economic reality has momentarily disoriented us. We have not yet adjusted to it. We are stumbling around in the dark.

Walter Small had lived in Santa Monica for most of his life. For twenty years he had worked on a suburban newspaper owned by a Midwest-based chain. In the late 1960s he was promoted to assistant editor at $20,000 a year. He was in his early thirties at the time, married, with two young children. To celebrate his promotion he bought a small ranch house for $40,000. In 1979, the newspaper chain asked him to relocate. The wanted him to move to northern California as assistant editor of an ailing paper they owned in Marin County. He accepted the job. At the time he moved north he was earning $35,000 a year, having received a series of small annual pay raises throughout the seventies. To reward his willingness to relocate, the owners increased his pay to $50,000. To his delight, he was able to sell his house in Santa Monica for $95,000. In an expansive mood he bought a new house in Marin County close to his job for $160,000. Shortly after he and his family moved to the new house he began to spend money lavishly on himself and the house, and soon found himself overwhelmed by debt. To keep up the payments on their new possessions his wife went to work, though she did not want to. But even this was not enough. To meet monthly payments he had to spend money he had put aside for his oldest son's college education, thereby provoking a bitter confrontation with his son who felt his father had "sold him out."

Mr. Small, sensitive, well-educated and intelligent, had fallen victim to conflicting signals caused by inflation. Having virtually doubled his income over a ten-year period, he had come to regard the small annual increases in his salary as symbolic confirmation of progress he was making in his career. (In fact, he had barely kept up with inflation.) Selling his house for more than twice what he had paid for it, he came to see himself as a successful entrepreneur, a person who had cunningly managed to beat inflation. And as the owner of a $160,000 home, he thought of himself as a person who had truly made it.

He slept uneasily, however. One part of him knew that his new house and salary did not mean what he thought they did. But he pushed this unwelcome intrusion out of his mind. The increased salary and costly house seemed tangible proof that he had indeed arrived at the pinnacle of success.

In hard economic terms, of course, he had gotten nowhere: from the point of view of the purchasing power of his disposable income and assets he remained, in effect, the same $20,000-a-year assistant editor of a local newspaper he had been for the previous twenty years. Inflation had swamped his sense of reality. It had deluded him with the appearance of swift upward mobility. It had manipulated emotion-laden symbols—salary increases and expensive homes—that no longer meant what they once did.

Swift social and economic change conveys mixed signals to people. One signal told the editor that he was achieving the material success his father had dreamed of and never attained. Another signal, that of communicating economic reality, came across more faintly and did not grow audible until, misled by the first signal, Small had fallen into a trap which distressed and embittered him.

Walter Small is a conventional person. His values and choices are traditional. He is not busy inventing new ways to live. His commitments are stable and fixed—to his job and employers, to his family and to conventional ideas and symbols of familial success. But he got caught up in the new, powerful economic crosscurrents of American life. He responded to signals that contradicted each other and confused him. He is angry with himself for being a fool; but he also harbors a resentment toward the society he cannot quite define. Conditioned to pursue goals enshrined throughout most of this century in the form of the American dream, he rushed toward a door marked SUCCESSFUL PEOPLE ENTER HERE. To him it looked wide open, but it slammed shut in his face.

Walter Small is as much a victim of the confusion of the great reversal as Robert Agnoli or Abby Williams. Indeed, to describe his predicament I find myself using the very metaphor Abby Williams had used to describe herself: her recurring anxiety-laden fantasy that all doors were opening for her and yet were closing at the same time. Over three decades, people like Small were lulled into a sense of economic security. Thanks to it, they began to reshape their life goals, expanding the culture. Now in the midst of the reshaping process, they are suddenly confronted with a new set of questions.

· "Is the career change I'd been planning possible now, or had I better stick with the job I have?"

· "Can I really afford to take early retirement?"

· "Does my refusal to make the move the company wants jeopardize my job?"

· "Will I be able to afford to go back to school as I had hoped?"

· "Should I be making more of a commitment to my job?"

· "Was it smart to pay such a high mortgage rate and burden ourselves with monthly payments we can afford only if both of us keep working?"

· "Since it looks as if we are in for rough times ahead why shouldn't
we spend it all now and enjoy it while we've got it and let the future
take care of itself?"

Finding answers to questions like these calls for making assumptions
about our economic future. Americans are now making such assumptions but without thinking them through carefully. Virtually everyone I
interviewed assumed that the economy in the near future will fall into
one or the other of three patterns.

The first pattern assumes that the economic roof will cave in, that
disastrous economic hard times lie ahead—a real depression as in the
1930s, or perhaps a runaway inflation like those in some South American countries or even the kind of hyperinflation Germany experienced
between the two world wars.

A second pattern expresses a nostalgia for the balmy years of the
postwar quarter, convinced that we will shortly find our way back to
steady economic growth, low inflation and unemployment, and continuing improvement in the standard of living of those who are willing
to work hard and put their economic well-being ahead of other values.

The third pattern reflects the psychology of affluence that developed
in the sixties: "I have a right to more of everything and can get it by
asserting myself." This pattern simply ignores the fact that we have
moved into a new economic environment. We are growing less confident
of the realism of this outlook, but the power of the psychology of affluence persists.

Almost no one who voiced one or the other of these three assumptions had any basis for doing so beyond the chemistry of their own hopes
and fears. These are not studied conclusions or rational assessments of
economic and political conditions. They are psychological projections,
in which the economy serves as a kind of Rorschach test. They are precisely what one might expect from a mind suddenly roused from introspective thinking. The people interrupted have not had time to switch
mental tracks—from introspection to the consideration of external
reality.

I am not asserting that even in their most practical and realistic
frame of mind people can or should think like economists, with the lat-
est figures about the money supply and growth rates at their finger-
tips. My point, rather, is that people like Walter Small, someone of
above-average intelligence, require no formal economic training to
think realistically. Small's confusion did not stem from the lack of

facts: he knew the inflation rate and he knew how to add and multiply. His was not a failure of arithmetic, but a blurring of focus. He did not make the rudimentary calculations demanded by realistic thought because he was off on another mental track. Like most middle-class Americans he assumed that he was sharing in a great economic boom by virtue of his inherent ability, his willingness to abide by the rules and his good fortune. As matters turned out, he had congratulated himself prematurely.

All three projections are, I believe, unfounded. Apart from the general proposition that history does not repeat itself, the weight of evidence suggests neither that utter economic disaster looms ahead, nor that the country will return to the boom-growth of the postwar period, nor that it will satisfy all those who press for more of everything. We will not relive the past, but move toward a future with its own unique properties. No one, not even the most prescient soothsayer, can predict the shape of this future. But at least we can free ourselves from the irrational projections bred by looking within ourselves for answers that lie somewhere else.

In recent years our thinking has grown excessively psychological, too heavily influenced by the so-called human potentials movement in psychology. This offshoot of psychology offers many valuable insights, but also a misleading metaphysics. In a later chapter I will discuss how we can discard the mischievous element: the idea of a private psychological self that stands apart from culture and history and makes choices in a vacuum. But for now I want to concentrate on the "economic" component of introspective thinking that conceives our economy as Big Mother, a Big Mother who sometimes makes you give up more than you'd like before she agrees to satisfy your demands, but who has the power to yield whatever you want. Given this assumption, a strategy for making choices follows automatically: first one calculates what one wants by looking inward, and then negotiates with the world—Big Mother—to provide it.

But this view of the economy turns out to be time-specific. It applies only under the very special conditions of upper-middle-class life in the America of the sixties and early seventies, conditions that no longer obtain. Not only is this approach to the world now obsolete, it is likely to be destructive to those who continue to rely on it.

If the economy is not Big Mother and cannot satisfy all our demands, and if the self is not an entity apart but enmeshed in the realities of the culture and the economy, then an introspective strategy looks silly. Looking inward will tell us nothing about the changing world, and an exclusive focus on self will show only a fragment of our embeddedness in the larger whole. The goal of self-fulfillment may remain valid, but the strategy for achieving it will have to depend more than ever before on realistic thinking. The path taken by the inner journey must now point outward.

Chapter 19

······●◐●──···

The
Three Claims

The first step in turning the inner journey outward is to make a realistic appraisal of our economy. If we were examining England, with a pattern so similar to ours of slipping productivity, nagging inflation and rising unemployment, we might come away dispirited. England's economy is weak, and the resources at its disposal for solving its economic problems are scarce.

The United States economy, on the other hand, may now be problem-ridden, but its strengths and potential vitality remain formidable. Though less competitive than in the postwar quarter, the United States economy still outproduces and outconsumes any other in the world. Although our rate of productivity increase has declined steadily since the millennial quarter-century began, our rate of creating new jobs—three to four million a year—is the envy of the industrial world. Though we are running out of oil, our coal reserves are virtually untapped, and the long-term promise of renewable energy resources is bright. Though some of the economy's core industries are producing less competitive products than heretofore, others still hold a clear lead. Even the troubled auto industry is starting to adapt to the new realities: the average fuel efficiency of the General Motors fleet improved from 12 miles per gallon in the mid-sixties to virtually double that in the early eighties. And, overall, the energy efficiency of the United States in the 1980s is increasing at a more rapid rate than that of Western Europe.*

The actual condition of the United States economy, which is soft in spots but still potentially awesome in its productive power, does not necessarily justify the public pessimism, sometimes bordering on panic, about the "land of plenty" becoming a "land of want." The gloominess derives more from the abruptness of the change—the nasty shock—than from a cool assessment of reality. With its presumption of ever-growing affluence, the country has been ill-prepared to absorb several massive economic claims that are now being made against our standard of living, claims that come as such a disagreeable surprise that we seek ingenious ways to avoid them. But they cannot be avoided with impunity. The threat they represent to our well-being has eroded our optimism. We are thrown off balance.

It is the country's unreadiness to confront these claims that created the present inflationary economy.

(ii)

There are three such claims. Each is different, but together they are so massive that in their combined effects their costs are to be reckoned in hundreds of billions of dollars a year. They draw so hungrily on our resources that they must inevitably lower the American standard of living, at least for a while.

The first we have already discussed. It is the startling increase in the cost of imported oil to the United States from $4 billion a year to $90 billion, plus the indirect costs of the military and political policies required to protect our sources of supply in the Middle East. The overall increase in costs to America clearly exceeds $100 billion a year. Most of this money is shipped abroad, which means less capital to create jobs in the United States and less money for the American consumer.

In the short term, the costs of energy will inevitably rise further. When imported oil reaches a certain price level, say $40 a barrel, alternative forms of energy begin to look more attractive than oil, and at that point the United States may start to lessen its dependence on oil from the Middle East.

By the end of the century the United States will probably have made progress toward exploiting coal reserves, developing synfuels, advancing

---

* Schipper, Lee, Lawrence Berkley Laboratory, quoted in *The New York Times*, 5/14/80.

solar, biomass and other renewable energy sources, evolving a policy on the troublesome question of nuclear power, building still more fuel-efficient cars, transforming the transportation system so that work-related travel is less dependent on the private automobile, incorporating principles of conservation into our architecture and reversing the trend toward automobile-dependent housing in the suburbs and exurbs. But all of these tasks will require years and perhaps decades to accomplish on a sufficiently large scale. Some unforeseen new technology may come to the rescue and make them easier, or even unnecessary. But this is not going to happen with the time perspective most of us live by, namely, the next three to five years of our lives.

The second claim is different in character. It was not imposed on us from the outside; it comes directly from the domestic politics of the United States. In the sixties and seventies Congress passed and various Presidents signed a series of entitlement programs that give qualified recipients a legal claim to certain benefits, mostly cash. These programs are designed to help the aged, the poor, the handicapped, the disadvantaged, the temporarily unemployed and the sick.

Congress did not pass them in a fit of absent-mindedness; all such programs were willed into being over a period of several decades by a population determined to build more security and compassion into the political system. They symbolize deeply felt national values, and even under conditions of economic strain the majority of Americans continue to support them. Most Americans do not want to cut back the vast array of government money programs such as aid to education, Medicaid, Medicare, Social Security, unemployment benefits, veterans' assistance, workmen's compensation and other forms of social insurance and transfers that now make up a large share of the federal budget.

In fact, half the federal budget now serves these purposes, raising the standard of living of tens of millions of Americans significantly beyond the level of their earned incomes. Slowly and laboriously a security net has been built under American life. Liberal critics complain it is not enough; conservatives claim it is too much. But what cannot be disputed is the arithmetic by which entitlement programs consume a rising proportion of the national wealth.

A few stark numbers show an unmistakable trend. In 1965, when Congress passed the Medicare legislation that now provides medical services to approximately 25 million citizens sixty-five and older, legislative research estimated that by the year 1990 its costs would reach

8 billion dollars a year. No more immune from the psychology of affluence than the rest of us, our representatives were willing to take the risk that the nation's wealth would support this level of expenditure in 1990 without undue strain. By 1979, however, the annual costs for Medicare were already running at three times the projected *1990* rate ($24.4 billion a year), and growing rapidly. Furthermore, in the nineteen-eighties the population of Americans over sixty-five will increase by 20 percent. Most people over sixty-five have one or more chronic ailments, the medical treatment of which accounts for about 30 percent of the entire nation's medical expenses. The total cost of the nation's medical services is estimated at 9 to 10 percent of our gross national product, or approximately $323 billion in 1983. Given these facts, by 1990 the cost of this one entitlement program, Medicare, is likely to exceed $80 billion, not the $8 billion originally calculated.

In the total federal 1981 budget, almost half (48 percent) is for entitlement programs. In 1959, entitlement programs accounted for only 15 percent of a much smaller federal budget. Even in 1970, at $62 billion a year, they accounted for less than a third of the budget. By 1981 they came to nearly $300 billion a year, and were moving upward.

Between 1955 and 1978, payments for entitlement programs grew in excess of 8 percent a year, more than twice the growth rate of the economy overall. Economist Alan Greenspan calls this "one of the extraordinary statistics of the post–World War II period." He points out that we may have failed to notice how massive a factor it had become in the national budget because it was partly obscured by the sharp decline in real spending for defense in the 1968–1975 period.*

Sixty-five million Americans (30 percent of the total population) are now recipients of one or another tax-supported income transfer program. In the nineteen-seventies, as more people sixty-two to sixty-five years of age retired and started to draw Social Security payments, the dependent population virtually doubled. In the early postwar years, when the United States economy was a fraction of its present size, comparable government programs for the dependent population consumed 6 percent of working people's personal income. As the economy expanded, the nation decided that it could afford to take better care of the vulnerable and dependent people in our society. It was widely assumed that this could be accomplished painlessly through economic

* Alan Greenspan, "Inflation: The Search for a Permanent Cure," *Public Opinion*, Vol. 3, No. 2 (April/May 1980), p. 7.

growth, that is, without taking a significantly larger proportion of working people's income. But this assumption has now proven incorrect. By the end of the seventies, the proportion of a worker's personal income required to pay for transfer payments had more than doubled, to 13 percent. Furthermore, since 1975 Congress has protected people on Social Security against inflation by tying their benefit payments to increases in the Consumer Price Index: as the cost of living goes up, so does their income. Most Americans feel this is only fair. The rub comes in the fact that the working population is not equally protected: most people's paychecks are not indexed. As working people fall further behind, an even higher proportion of their diminishing personal income goes toward defraying the costs of entitlement programs to others whose stipends are tied to the cost of living.

These programs have grown so expensive that even with the higher rates of taxation automatically imposed by inflation, the government is unable to keep up with their costs. Consequently, it finances these programs partially in the form of budget deficits, borrowed money for which it must pay high interest rates. One of the largest items of uncontrollable expenditure in the federal budget is interest paid on the national debt: $55 billion in fiscal 1981. Thus, to the huge direct costs of the entitlement programs must be added the ever-increasing cost of servicing the national debt, a burden that grows more onerous each year. The decade of the seventies, therefore, added annual costs for entitlement programs calculable in hundreds of billions of dollars, or literally thousands of dollars a year per average wage-earning family.

As if the combined costs of OPEC oil and domestic entitlement programs were not enough, there is a third claim against our economy whose costs are more difficult to measure but which probably also lie in the $100 billion a year category: the decline in the competitiveness of United States industry. This is one of the most perplexing features of the millennial quarter-century. It manifests itself in many forms, including a steady decline in relative rates of labor productivity.

In an earlier chapter I quoted New York Stock Exchange President William Batten's observation that in the nineteen-sixties the typical American worker outproduced the Japanese worker by a factor of four, and French and German workers by a factor of two. But we must contend with his added observation that these other countries have now virtually caught up, and if present trends continue, will by the middle of the millennial quarter-century substantially outproduce us, worker for worker. Over the decade of the seventies we gave up our huge productivity lead.

Throughout most of the postwar period the United States had enjoyed substantial annual increases in its productivity rates. And since American workers kept their wage demands largely within the limits of productivity gains, the American economy presented a model of both stability and improving income. In the late sixties, however, our rate of productivity increases began to falter. By the start of the millennial quarter in 1973, they had fallen to less than one percent a year from three times that rate in earlier years. By the end of the seventies, annual productivity gains had disappeared altogether. In at least this one respect we had joined England at the bottom of the list of all industrialized nations.

This loss of comparative advantage in industrial productivity is not the only sign of growing weakness in United States competitiveness. Other factors are also at work. Futurist Theodore Gordon sums up: "Things have changed, the level of enterprise has diminished. In terms of innovation, productivity, competitive position or even a qualitative feeling of vitality, the trend [of decline] is apparent everywhere . . . There are no indicators to the contrary."*

Gordon blames this faltering on our failure to maintain our large investments in research and development (R&D) and other forms of enterprising risk. He notes that while the United States was lowering its rate of investment in R&D, the Germans, Japanese and others were increasing theirs. Not surprisingly, the rate at which new products were developed in other nations increased sharply. In the late 1970s patents issued to foreign citizens more than tripled, just as American equipment was growing older and less competitive. With accelerating inflation, profit margins slipped and it became more difficult to accumulate investment capital. United States decision makers grew nervous about launching long-term ventures.

If one combines the higher costs of energy, the growth of government deficits to finance social welfare and defense programs, the decline of the dollar and the consequent rise in the cost of imports due to diminished United States competitiveness, these factors together impose huge claims against our standard of living. For each American family they cancel approximately half of the income gains accumulated in the past twenty-five years.

* Theodore J. Gordon, "The Revival of Enterprise," p. 18.

Federal Reserve Board Chairman Paul Volcker had these claims in mind when he said:

> "I would point out that productivity growth in this country is actually negative . . . and of course we import fifty percent of our oil so that the higher revenues going abroad do not go to the American citizens. Under these conditions *the standard of living of the average American has got to decline.* I don't think we can escape that when we are producing less with the same amount of effort." [Emphasis added]*

The average American may not know all the economic facts, how they fit together and why his standard of living is under siege. But the surveys cited earlier show plainly that Americans are aware that something has gone wrong in the nation's economic life. They fear for their own and the nation's economic future. And their fear is not unfounded.

* *The New York Times,* 1/4/80.

Chapter 20

···◄●►···

The New Realities: The Peculiar Connection

Had we not been lost in our introspective reveries, we might have noticed what was happening to us. If we had known how vulnerable we were we might have looked at ourselves and the world differently. The three huge claims made against our standard of living in the seventies would have been difficult to cope with under any circumstances, but if not for our psychology of affluence our response might have been more adaptive.

Without a psychology of affluence we would have conserved energy after 1973 instead of doubling our oil imports from the Arab nations. Without a psychology of affluence we would have built smaller cars and developed alternate sources of energy at the same time—in fact, we did neither. Without such a psychology, once we realized that our entitlement programs were going to outstrip costs estimates five- or tenfold, we would have modified them and made our wasteful medical programs, for example, more efficient. We would have obliged citizens to choose between these programs and other expenditures. The issue was never to scrap the entitlement programs because they are too costly. A minority of Americans may feel this way, but surveys show clearly that the majority does not. Rather, the issue was and is to face the costs and take responsibility for them. But our psychology of affluence prevented us from doing so. To the extent that self-fulfillment was on our minds we were looking inward when we should have been paying attention to the external world.

These three claims and our inadequate response to them led to the inflationary conditions that now plague the country and will continue to do so throughout the eighties. Inflation is a new economic condition and we should assume, therefore, that this decade will not, when it ends, have recreated the thirties, the fifties or the sixties, but will have its own character, largely shaped by the inflationary consequences of the encounter between the psychology of affluence and a harsher economic environment than existed in the postwar quarter-century.

Ordinarily we think of inflation as a technical economic problem. But the current inflation is different. At its heart is a cultural, not an economic dilemma. As economist Irving Friedman states:

> Existing methods of attacking inflation are simply wrong because they are based on a misunderstanding of the nature of modern inflation. The basic causes of modern inflation differ greatly from those of classic inflation. They are not confined to the economic field . . . but are now deeply rooted in society and in its political, social and psychological structures. I call them societal causes.*

Friedman attributes modern inflation to a gap between the escalating demands of an expanding world population and the limits of world resources. The moral claim to a higher standard of living is not confined to the United States. In a world of finite resources, governments all over the world are finding they cannot keep up with the demands people make on them in growing numbers and with growing impatience.

Other nations than the United States are now making their bid for a greater share of the world's resources—the OPEC nations in their way, Germany, Japan and the other industrialized nations in theirs. At home we try to ignore these claimants and continue to live as if nothing has changed. Our psychology of affluence persists, but we no longer have the resources to support it and to work our will on the world. So we are gradually drawn into the fantasyland that got Walter Small, the California newspaper editor, into so much trouble. We are living wildly beyond our means.

Economist Henry Kaufman has done the grim arithmetic to quantify the extent to which we are doing so. He has developed an ingenious

---

* Irving S. Friedman, "We Can End Inflation," *Industry Week*, Vol. 207, No. 3 (Nov. 10, 1980), p. 63.

measure that might be called a borrowing-from-the-future index. First he adds up the market value of all shares of all American corporations. Then he subtracts the total national indebtedness—the combined unpaid amount owed by government, corporations and individuals. In 1964, this calculation yielded a $366 billion gap: our indebtedness exceeded our holdings by this amount. Between 1964 and 1980, the market value of our shares doubled, but the amount of our debt quadrupled, resulting in a staggering $3 trillion gap—an awesome measure of the extent to which we have been willing to dissipate our capital and borrow against the future. We have, as a farmer succinctly phrased it, been "eating our seed corn." This is the gap in which inflation flourishes as an economic phenomenon with psychocultural roots.*

(ii)

The current inflation in the United States began with our failure to raise taxes to pay for the war in Vietnam. Had the costs of the war been distributed at the time they were incurred, every citizen and business would have received a bill for a proportionate share of the war's costs in the form of higher taxes or reduced income. Had the war bill been paid, the public would have had less to spend or invest. With less to spend, demand for goods and services would have declined, and with reduced demand, prices would also have fallen. The "normal" economic response to a large added cost is recession, not inflation. It is normal, that is, if two conditions prevail: if the bill is paid out of current income, and if the market system works unimpeded.

Inflation occurs when a society is confronted with a claim against its standard of living and instead of paying it, decides to avoid it altogether. Modern economies have many ways of finessing costs, but the simplest, though ultimately the most destructive, is one that governments sometimes resort to when backed into a corner: they dilute their currency.

The Romans diluted their currency by clipping their coins, producing, literally, short change. The French in 1720 and then again in the assignat inflation of the 1790s expanded their money supply by flooding the market with paper currency. During World War I, the Germans increased their money supply by 340 percent, setting the stage for one of the most disastrous inflations of all times, the hyperinflation of 1920–

---

* Jason Epstein, "Is the Party Over?" *The New York Review of Books,* Vol. XXVII, No. 16 (October 23, 1980), p. 10.

1923 when the purchasing power of money fell nearly to zero; a loaf of bread cost several million marks.

One definition of inflation, therefore, is that it is a device used to avoid paying one's bills in full by diluting the value of the currency with which the bill is paid. This definition is partly a matter of semantics and partly of substance. The semantic aspect is important, for much confusion arises out of the failure to define what the term inflation means. Some analysts define inflation broadly as meaning a general rise in the price level, while others define it narrowly as a form of "bad money, that is, money that does not hold its value."*

Often the broad and narrow definitions are used interchangeably, making an already murky subject still more impenetrable. I prefer the narrow definition of inflation as "bad money" for several reasons. First, the broad definition is too broad to be useful—at a minimum, we should know whether inflation is beneficial, harmful or neutral; and second, any definition that covers so much territory that sometimes it refers to a normal economic process and sometimes to a pathological political one, is mischievous at worst and useless at best.

It is possible and even reasonable to have an increase in price levels without bad money as its cause. Higher prices may simply reflect the normal operation of supply and demand: as a commodity grows more rare, its price will tend to increase; as it becomes more plentiful, its price will decline. In the great silver speculation of 1980, a few Texas billionaires and Saudi princes almost lost their fortunes playing the silver market. As they bought vast quantities of silver, the price increased. But when the high prices encouraged miners to reactivate old silver mines, the production of silver shot up and silver prices plunged. By including under the single heading "inflation" price increases stimulated by the normal workings of supply and demand and also increases that come from diluting the money supply, it becomes difficult to discern the grave damage done to a society by inflation in the narrow sense of bad-money inflation.

A lucid explanation of inflation in the narrow sense of avoiding one's bills, cheating, sleight of hand and subterfuge is to be found in a short book by the former editor of *The Times* of London, William Rees-Mogg. Rees-Mogg is explicit on the moral content of inflation: "All inflations, except for those which have begun in an increase in the gold supply, have fraud at the heart of them."†

* William Rees-Mogg, *The Reigning Error* (London: Hamish Hamilton, 1973), p. 31.
† Ibid., p. 33.

The fraudulent aspect of inflation, as Rees-Mogg sees it, always arises from the same source: government dilution of currency. As the supply of money increases faster than the supply of goods and services, prices rise and the money buys less, for the simple reason that it has been clipped just as surely as the Romans clipped their coins.

For Rees-Mogg, as for Irving Friedman and increasing numbers of analysts, the causes of modern inflation lie outside the economic system. The key question for Rees-Mogg is not the economic question of how to control the money supply through technical monetary policies, but the political question of *why* governments engage in the fraud of inflating the money supply when they know that in the long run it will be destructive. He concludes that governments inflate because they believe they have no practical alternative. They are responding to pressures they feel they cannot resist.

If American political leadership had been able to persuade the nation to face directly the huge claims against the economy that Americans incurred in the 1970s, we might have had some reduction in the national standard of living, but we would have avoided inflation. But few political leaders could fight the psychology of affluence; instead, they took the easy way, resorting to the monetary dilution that led to the inflation. Not knowing how to respond to the "uncontrollable" costs represented by the three claims, and politically limited in the number of tax increases that could be levied on an already burdened United States taxpayer, our government resorted to subterfuges such as huge off-budget credit extensions which, in effect, ballooned budget deficits beyond the official figures and expanded the money supply in an inflationary fashion.

As measured by the Consumer Price Index, the inflation rate at the start of 1980 was 18 percent and for all of 1980 it was 12.4 percent; the year before it had been 13.3 percent. At an 18 percent annual rate of inflation the value of a 1980 dollar in 1990 would be 19 cents. At a 13 percent rate it would be 29 cents in 1990, at 10 percent, 38 cents, and even at a 6 percent rate, the value of the dollar would be virtually cut in half to 56 cents. That is bad money,* and we have only begun to suffer from its bad effects.

---

* *Key Elements in Fighting Inflation* (Draft of unpublished CED report, May 15, 1980).

(iii)

What prevents our political leaders from levying the charges for these claims or drafting policies to make their costs smaller? Why have they taken refuge in that ultimately most costly of forms of avoidance, mortgaging the future by inflating the dollar to pay for the present?

Examined close-up, the American polity in the eighties is organized into an immense variety of interest groups, each with its own lobbying power: businesses, trade unions, physicians, developers, teachers, environmentalists, farmers, older Americans, the handicapped, veterans, truckers, unwed mothers, alcoholics, druggists, etc. To protect themselves and their interests, virtually all have grown proficient in wielding political pressure at the state, local and federal levels of government. They are implacably determined to avoid being the victims and losers of an economic downturn, and they exert all the political pressure they can muster to be winners. Single-minded in pursuing their interests, they identify the national interest with their own concerns.

This process is not new. But the sheer number of such groups has proliferated uncontrollably in recent years. John Gardner, founder of Common Cause, compares the results to a vast checker game with many players, in which each player places his thumb firmly on his own checker and says: "You may play with all the others as long as you don't touch mine."

Unfortunately, the sum of all their vetoes and pressures practically immobilizes government, especially in a nation mesmerized by the psychology of affluence. Nor is the United States the only nation so beguiled: "The notion of lowering expectations is an extremely hard thing to accept. It's a terrible thing. We're very, very rich people here [in Sweden] and everyone has grown up with the idea that you can always expect more. Now we've got to go back a few steps. But the mental change required is very painful."* In such a state of mind, any call for discipline or restraint is brushed aside as a ploy. Politicians hesitant to meet the demand for "more" are accused of bad faith or even viciousness; they are marked for political extinction.

Given the determination of Americans to hold on to their gains whether productivity goes up or down, it is not surprising that people insist their paychecks stay ahead of inflation. If they cannot force economic institutions to respond to their desires, they turn for redress to

* Olaf Ljunggren, Swedish Employers' Association, *The New York Times*, 5/14/80.

the political process. Political leaders then try to honor as many competing claims as they can, and when the sum of these claims exceeds the available resources, they engage in sleight of hand. To postpone the moment of painful truth, they resort to inflationary subterfuges.

In the early stages of an inflation, few people are aware of what is happening and how dangerous it may eventually be for them and the country. Many belong to an organized interest group that has devised its own special protective angle that leads members to believe they have personally beaten the inflation game. In the short term, they may be correct. A business passes cost increases along in the form of higher prices. A strong union protects its members through cost-of-living adjustments in their contracts. Lobbyists for older citizens threaten Congress that their clients, having time on their hands, will wreak vengeance at election time on all who rebuff the claims of the elderly to tie their medical and pension benefits firmly to increases in the Consumer Price Index.

It is only in the middle and late stages of an inflation that these protective devices fail, and then even "protected" groups realize that they, too, are falling behind. Of course, even in the early stages of the inflation, the unprotected—the weaker unions, the businesses unable to pass along costs, the nonunionized workers, the faculties of colleges with shrinking enrollments, the welfare recipients, the unemployed— fail to keep pace with inflation. Inevitably, their fear of the future grows stronger, and resentment against scapegoats begins to crop up. Political life grows tense, violence prone, unstable.

Like alcoholism, inflation is addictive. It gives brief relief from worrisome problems and then assumes a dreadful life of its own. Like alcoholism, it soon creates secondary effects that may be more crippling than the problem which led to the habit in the first place. The original problem was how to meet claims that might for a few years modestly reduce our standard of living: import less oil, raise the retirement age, cut medical costs, manage better. This was merely expensive and bothersome to deal with. In other periods of our national history we might easily have taken these claims in stride, and dealt with them without assuming we had done something wonderful, or even unusual.

But the secondary effects of a galloping inflation, like those of progressive alcoholism, are not merely bothersome, they are devastating. They distort every aspect of life: they undermine people's economic security, and our surveys show that they spread suspicion, fear and resentment throughout the society. The majority of Americans (81 percent) have come to suspect that those who follow the rules inevitably get cheated while those who know the angles and ignore the rules do well.

Nothing feeds social resentment as much as this conviction that obeying the rules no longer makes sense. The history of several inflations shows that such resentment loosens the social bond. That is why inflation so alarms the thoughtful citizen. A society's inner cohesiveness is a precious and fragile thing; much of our national energy should be devoted to nourishing it, strengthening it, reinforcing it, not mindlessly subverting it. If a society is asked to give the individual more breathing space—more latitude, more freedom, more opportunity for self-fulfillment—that society has to be strong enough internally to support these demands.

(iv)

The psychology of affluence insists: "We do not have to choose, we have a right to more." But confronted with the economic realities of the eighties, eventually we will be forced to say: "Hard choice is inevitable." The discord arising from these opposing themes sets the tone of the decade. As long as these themes remain unreconciled, inflation will continue. As long as inflation continues we will know we are avoiding the pain of hard choice by resorting to the subterfuge of creating bad money.

Sooner or later the psychology of affluence will be forced to yield to a social ethic better suited to the new economic realities. But before it does we can expect a period of tense and bitter political conflict:

· There will be an unavoidable short-term reduction in the American standard of living. This is now happening and the inherent logic of the situation makes it inevitable that it will continue for several years or longer. The only question is what form the reduction will take, whether as a direct one involving a deliberate political decision on how to distribute the costs of the claims, or more likely, as an indirect one through the inflationary redistribution of income.

· Inflation is now built into our system through many indexing devices, and feeds on itself. Conflict is sure to grow more intense between those who are indexed and those who are not. The strong unions will grow stronger, the weak ones weaker; big business, able to pass its costs along, will prosper; small business, caught in the squeeze, will suffer. Home owners will be protected; renters are less likely to be. Some pension plans will permit its members to retire; others will force them to remain in the labor force. The scramble for indexation will distort both the economy and people's private lives, and make inflation still more difficult to combat.

· Sharp conflicts divide those who work from those who do not. This is partly an age conflict, and we can expect to see ever more bitter battles between young and old. It is also the familiar conflict between haves and have nots, exacerbated by inflation. The traditional victims—the racial minorities and the poor—are whacked yet again by an inflation that has undermined the modest gains they won in the sixties and seventies. This inevitably means more racial strife, more unemployment, more suffering, more divisiveness. Inflation is a virtual machine for generating this kind of divisiveness.

· The poor and disadvantaged feel that their source of security—big government—is being taken away from them by people acting in bad faith. The near-poor, hard-working, salaried Americans also believe their security—the fruits of their own work, their savings and their loyalty to society's rules—is being undermined by inflation, taxes and chicanery. Millions of middle-income Americans—home-owning, dual-earner families—feel they are on a treadmill or adrift in a dangerous world with inadequate leadership. In such circumstances, the majority of the American people can be expected to react angrily, cynically and suspiciously to political initiatives not directly responsive to their economic concerns.

· There is even a novel resurgence of regional conflict in the United States caused by the energy problem. The West has many energy resources and is worried about safeguarding its environment; the rest of the nation wants these resources and may be less concerned about the ecosystems of other regions. The Northeast wants cheaper oil, but does not want to build refineries. The South is willing to build refineries, but does not want New England to benefit thereby at their expense. The Sunbelt is thriving; the cities of the Northeast continue to deteriorate.

Lurching and halting through the 1980s, the country will seek to rebuild some of its former economic clout. It needs to do so to overcome its growing political/military weakness in the world arena, a weakness that flows partly from economic flabbiness. If such flabbiness persists it will soon become clear what our losses will be: not only the loss of in-

fluence and leadership in the world, but the risk of chaos, a blow to the
American standard of living from which it may not recover, grave military dangers and the abandonment of our democratic institutions to
unendurable strains they may not be able to withstand.

It is in this tense political-economic climate that the next phase of
the search for self-fulfillment will unfold. If those of us who are engaged
in it persevere in a self-defeating strategy based on a psychology of
affluence and a me-first theory of self, then it will prove impossible
either to find individual fulfillment or to tackle the nation's problems
in a fundamental way. But if the self-fulfillment search responds to new
realities in an adaptive fashion, the culture may come to the aid of our
political-economic troubles and provide the impetus for new vitality in
American life.

For this to happen the psychology of affluence must give way to
a new realism of expectation and a renewed emphasis on the social
virtues of sharing, giving, committing, sacrificing, participating and even
denying one's own pleasure of the moment. And above all, there has
to be renewed interest in the future: in thinking about it, planning for
it, saving for it and taking responsibility for it.

Is this likely to happen? Is it possible? Such questions bring us to
the final part of this inquiry: the matter of where the self-fulfillment
search is heading.

Part IV

An Ethic of
Commitment

Chapter 21

······━━◉━━······

America's First Cultural Revolution

In Part I of this book we examined the search for self-fulfillment as a grass-roots phenomenon, a spontaneous outburst of millions of new experiments in how to live the good life.

In Part II we looked at certain characteristics of the self-fulfillment motif: how diverse it is; how it presses against the structure of traditional familial goals but without seeking to destroy or abandon them; how it affects middle-aged and older people as well as youth, middle- and lower-income Americans as well as the upper middle class, and how it strains against the giving/getting compact.

Then in Part III we reviewed some of the new economic realities we will confront in the coming years, among them inflation as a symptom of a national unwillingness, due to a psychology of affluence, to settle the large claims that have accumulated against us.

Now, in Part IV, we reach the more general and philosophic questions raised in this inquiry. I take my argument a bit beyond the data presented in Parts I, II and III. In the search for new ways to find self-fulfillment amid the peculiar blessings of an advanced industrial society, now inflation-prone, I want to discuss three broad questions:

· In what respects is the search for self-fulfillment the leading edge of a genuine cultural revolution?

· Why is this happening now at this stage of our history?

· How can we channel its energies so that they serve an adaptive purpose for society and individual, rather than a destructive one?

From a practical standpoint the third question is the most important. Will we prove able to divest the search for self-fulfillment of its fallacies, contradictions and moral ambiguities? If not, the cultural revolution will tear our civilization apart, leaving us with the worst of both worlds —the wounds of industrialism and also the disabilities of slow growth. Or can we do what no other society has yet done: create a civilization that is economically viable, politically stable, sociologically integrated, and also open to the full promise of individual life; in other words, what seekers of self-fulfillment want? Our future, as individuals and as a society, hinges on the answer to this question.

We have used the term culture to refer specifically to shared meanings. What is meant then by a "revolution" in shared meanings? Hannah Arendt has written insightfully about the meaning of revolution in the twentieth century, and we turn to her for a definition of what a cultural revolution is.

In Arendt's work two principles define all revolutions. One is that a true revolution always starts a "new story" in human affairs: "The course of human history suddenly begins anew, an entirely new story, a story never known or told before, is about to unfold."* A true revolution always involves a new beginning, one that introduces genuine novelty into the human adventure.

Arendt does not use the word "story" carelessly or casually. The word implies that as it unfolds the revolution will have an inner coherence: a beginning, middle and end; a plot line and a meaning. Arendt was a critic of careless language in others, and a scholar who delighted in tracing words to their Greek and Latin origins and then following their evolution throughout the centuries. Her insistence that revolutions are to be regarded as stories must be taken seriously. She dismisses the idea of revolution as mere change; change comes in the ordinary course

* Hannah Arendt, *On Revolution* (New York: Viking, 1963), p. 28.

of events and is the daily business of "normal" history. The events that highlight American history in the sixties and seventies—the assassinations of John and Robert Kennedy, Martin Luther King and Malcolm X, the civil-rights movement, the campus rebellion, the Vietnam war, Watergate, the Arab oil embargo—these are the stuff from which ordinary historical change is made. Such events may move within a larger pattern but they do not interrupt or redirect the course of history as revolutions do.

In writing of revolution, Arendt returns again and again to the theme of founding and foundation. The importance of making a new beginning in human affairs impressed her with its gravity and momentousness. When some special event distinguishes itself from run-of-the-mill change by launching a society in a new direction, it may grow into a revolutionary shift if and only if the novelty it creates so deeply disturbs the status quo that all of the old beliefs, values, meanings, traditions and structures are disturbed and profoundly modified.

Arendt's second principle is that a genuine revolution will always advance the cause of human freedom ("The aim of revolution was and always has been freedom"). The theme of freedom surfaces often in Arendt's books, and she repeatedly describes it with a metaphor. She speaks of freedom as a "lost treasure," a heritage that may disappear for centuries at a time only to reappear suddenly and unexpectedly—and then vanish once again, leaving those who have known it bereft.

The essence of what Arendt means by freedom is suggested in her distinction between "liberation" and "freedom." Liberation is concerned with restoring rights that have been lost or abused. Political revolutions mostly concern liberation, she says, not freedom. If people have been physically constrained, if they cannot assemble and air their grievances, if they are intimidated and cannot speak without fear, they may rebel and press for liberation. Liberation is a necessary precondition for freedom, but Arendt insists that it should not be mistaken for freedom itself. It is what people do with their liberation once they have it that determines whether or not they will be free.

Liberation, then, is essentially negative; it is liberation *from*. Freedom is a positive state; it is freedom *to*. But freedom to do what? With this question we reach the core of Arendt's thought and of our own immediate dilemma as America faces an uncertain decade. In Arendt's view, true freedom, unlike liberation, can flourish only when the "treasure" is not wholly spent on private satisfactions. Freedom always involves the larger community, what the Romans called the *res publica*, what thinkers of the eighteenth century called the "public happiness" and what we would today call society or culture.

If Arendt is correct, freedom occurs when in some profound sense citizens participate in shaping the course their society will take. If the great choices that determine our destiny are made for us by others— by elites, by technicians, by elected officials—then we are not free, though we may be wholly liberated. If by distortions and tricks the public is manipulated into seeming to make its own choices without actually doing so, it is not free. As long as parents make the critical choices, the child is not free; a subject in a dictatorship is not free; an employee in a hierarchical organization is not free within the workplace. If, in searching for self-fulfillment the citizens of a "free country" like America pay attention only to the private self, they are not free in Arendt's sense, though they may be liberated.

Arendt insists that freedom is not a right. Liberation is the right. While liberation can be demanded, legislated or granted by political processes, freedom is more elusive. Societies, even modern societies such as ours that cherish freedom in the abstract, do not necessarily understand the conditions under which it can flourish. All Arendt will tell us is that when those who have lost the treasure of freedom regain it, they recognize it and rejoice.

For her there is no question about the meaning of human fulfillment: it is to find and safeguard the lost heritage of freedom, as the ancient Greeks knew it briefly and as others throughout the centuries have found it, only to lose it again.

Arendt provides us with an apt example of a cultural revolution that exemplifies these two principles. Comparing the influence of the American and French revolutions, she writes: "The French Revolution, which ended in disaster, made world history, while the American Revolution, so triumphantly successful, has remained an event of little more than local importance." But she points out that long before 1776, America launched a series of events that proved genuinely revolutionary: it was the experience of founding a new kind of society. This *cultural* revolution took place many years before the political events of liberation from British rule.

What captured the attention of Europeans about colonial America was the demonstration it offered that it was possible to build a society in which the mass of the population was not condemned to live in abject poverty. Throughout history, poverty for the majority had been accepted as part of the nature of things. Poverty was eternal; poverty was destiny.

The emergence of colonial America as a society virtually without poverty (as poverty was understood in Europe) exhilarated the thinkers of eighteenth-century Europe and provided the philosophes of the Enlightenment with a new model of what is humanly possible. "The social question [of mass poverty] began to play a revolutionary role only when, in the modern age and not before, men began to doubt that poverty is inherent in the human condition. . . . The conviction that life on earth might be blessed with abundance instead of being cursed by scarcity was pre-revolutionary and American in origin; it grew directly out of the colonial experience. . . . The stage was set for revolutions in the modern sense of a complete change of society."*

The colonial experience came, of course, long before the industrial revolution. As Arendt observes, "America had become the symbol of a society without poverty long before the modern age in its unique technological development had actually discovered the means to abolish that abject misery of sheer want which had always been held to be eternal." Arendt also distinguishes between being poor, as many American farmers and laborers were, and the grinding, degrading poverty of the European masses. She acknowledges that the Europeans who drew this lesson overlooked totally the four hundred thousand black slaves, 20 percent of the prerevolutionary American population, whose poverty, often worse than the Europeans, was invisible to virtually all observers.

The founding of American society meets Arendt's two criteria of genuine revolution: it started a new story in human affairs, with novelty involved in almost every aspect of the early American experience, from the Puritans' covenant of equality before God in the early seventeenth century to the efforts of enlightened eighteenth-century Americans like Franklin and Jefferson to translate abstract rights of man into a secular society based on political freedom. And a new chapter of human freedom unfolded as the shared meanings of America set themselves against the received traditions of the European heritage. This revolution was cultural, not political, precisely because it revolved around shared meanings, not toppled institutions. And it was revolutionary because its new story concerned human freedom. The new shared meaning—mass poverty can be overcome by a free people—combined with others to shape the themes of political freedom and material well-being that have formed the American dream in subsequent centuries.

These twin themes of the quest for freedom and the conquest of poverty run like a symphonic leitmotif throughout the history of the

* Arendt, op. cit., p. 22.

United States. At the end of the nineteenth century, the locale of the dream of freedom-with-plenty shifted from the small town, the countryside and the frontier to the factory and the city. With characteristic energy, in less than a century—roughly in the fourscore years from 1893, a year of panic and depression, to 1973, the year of the fateful Arab oil embargo—the United States transformed itself from a second-rate, provincial-agricultural country to the peak of its industrial-military might.

In this compressed time span we traveled further and faster along the troubled road of modernization and industrialization than Western Europe had traversed in three hundred years. Because our national experience was rapid and intense, and our resources and determination great, we reaped many benefits. But we also suffered many scars, the consequences of which we are now confronting.

Chapter 22

⋯━◉━⋯

Rewriting the Giving/Getting Compact

We must now ask how the search for self-fulfillment is launching a new cultural revolution. What novel meaning does it introduce into American life? What new story does it begin? In what ways does it promise to advance human freedom beyond the political freedom won in the earlier revolution? Why is this happening now?

Some tentative answers were offered in Part I. The search for self-fulfillment begins a new story because it introduces important new meanings into our culture, revolving around the struggle to lessen the influence of the instrumental forces in our lives and to heighten the sacred/expressive elements. The freedom that seekers of self-fulfillment pursue—the treasure so easily lost—is not only political but cultural as well: it is the freedom to choose one's life according to one's own design. And this novel meaning of freedom has suddenly grown urgent because simultaneously tens of millions of Americans have concluded that the old giving/getting compact that served our society so well for so long must now be revised because it fails to accommodate the sacred/ expressive yearnings that lie at the heart of people's experiments in self-fulfillment.

* * *

The great triumph of the old giving/getting compact was how well it succeeded in aligning private goals with public ones. A growing America gave people something to work for: a conviction that a way of life built around growth "paid off" for the individual and for the country. The growth, in turn, was made possible by a stable, well-educated, hard-working, highly motivated, product-hungry population.

In psychological jargon, to be "socialized" means to want what the society wants you to want. In this sense, the post–World War II generation was extraordinarily well socialized. It wanted the fruits of growth and it helped to produce them. Each American could, by pursuing his private ambitions, satisfy his sense of moral rightness as well as his purse, pride and comfort. To work hard and consume well was a patriotic duty. When private goals resonate with public ones, the tones of moral harmony grow strong.

Though it came under criticism for its flaws, the epochal experience of the "old era" worked remarkably well. The high value placed on acquisition and material well-being fueled the forward march of the fabled American economy. The organization of daily life around a clear-cut division of labor within the family, the workplace and school supported the economy, spread the wealth, advanced moderate and even generous politics, reinforced social justice, strengthened institutional legitimacy and shaped the kind of consensus in values that holds a society together.

Small wonder, then, that during our most rapid period of growth and power after World War II, the mass of Americans chose to ignore the many criticisms of industrial society coming from both the right and the left of the political spectrum. From the time of the French Revolution to the present, conservative critics on the right have faulted industrial society on the grounds that it fatally weakens the bonds of community, belongingness and emotional security that characterize traditional life styles at their best. Philosophical conservatives like sociologist Robert Nisbet* argue that in industrial society human relationships grow impersonal, commercialized. Giant institutions (big government, big business, the communications media) destroy what Edmund Burke called "the inns and resting places of the human spirit"—the smaller, more human-sized institutions of the society: the local church, the old neighborhoods, the small schools, the local shops and family relationships. In modern industrial society we often purchase our material well-

---

* Robert Nisbet. See *The Sociological Tradition, Tradition and Revolt, The Quest for Community* and *Social Change and History*.

being at a high human cost, the chief symptom of which is the destruction of *community*.

The idea of community is precious to people, although they often do not know how precious until it is lost; it must come from social arrangements that have endured long enough to enjoy some stability. Although difficult to define abstractly, the idea of community evokes in the individual the feeling that: "Here is where I belong, these are my people, I care for them, they care for me, I am part of them, I know what they expect from me and I from them, they share my concerns, I know this place, I am on familiar ground, I am at home."

This is a powerful emotion, and its absence is experienced as an aching loss, a void, a sense of homelessness. The symptoms of its absence are feelings of isolation, falseness, instability and impoverishment of spirit.

From the left of the political spectrum the radical critique of industrialism stresses other defects. The young Marx focused particularly on alienation in the workplace: the separation of the person from his work and the depersonalizing effects of having one's work converted into the impersonal commodity of "labor" to be bought and sold in the marketplace. For Marx this was converting people into objects.

Since Marx, this theme of the depersonalizing, "objectifying" and alienating tendencies of modern industrial life was to reappear again and again not only in radical critiques, but also in the work of existentialist and literary writers who feared that modern industrial life reduced everything and everyone to the status of objects to be manipulated for their instrumental use.

The modern world of instrumentalism was vividly foreseen by Max Weber early in the century. He conceived it as an "iron cage" in which reality grows "dreary, flat and utilitarian,"* leaving a void filled by meaningless activity. Life in the iron cage is regulated by a law Weber called "rationalization," which is instrumentalism practiced systematically. It is what a modern plant manager does when he "rationalizes" his production line; i.e., organizes it so that it can produce the most products at the greatest speed for the least effort at the minimum cost— with all the standardization and controls that this process implies.

Weber recognized the impulse behind rationalization as the thrust toward mastery of the environment. He foresaw that the attainment of such mastery would create a peculiarly modern form of hubris. Observ-

---

* Arthur Mitzman, *The Iron Cage* (New York: Knopf, 1970), and Julian Freund, *The Sociology of Max Weber* (New York: Random House, 1968).

ing the high price in human satisfaction exacted by such instrumentalism, Weber wondered whether so much activity might not cover up an underlying despair. He noted that ultimately rationalization demystifies life—stripping it of all mystery and charm. In a fully rationalized society even death—a break in efficiency—is robbed of its fully human significance.

Cultural historian William Irwin Thompson, has updated Weber's diagnosis. "The major drift of advanced industrial society," Thompson says, "is towards an authoritarian system in which large labor unions join with large multinational corporations to create a system in which the citizen becomes the subject, and all that is worked out and administered by an intelligentsia coming from the universities who helped bring behavioral modification into the grammar schools and Skinnerian psychology into the graduate schools." Thompson sees "the whole culture spinning downward to darkness in a tightening spiral."*

These various strands of critical thought—conservative, aristocratic, radical, existential, literary, cultural—merge, crisscross, combine and conflict with each other in complex patterns. But all share one conclusion: all condemn modern industrial society for tendencies that purportedly make it impossible for people to achieve a full measure of humanity.

Until the 1970s, however, the majority of Americans emphatically rejected all of these criticisms out of hand. Some thought the critiques were signs of a sniveling, unmanly weakness. Others felt that it was simply the nostalgia of the well-to-do who resented having to share the benefits of growth with newcomers, especially the general public. Others rejected it for the opposite reason: it smacked of radicalism and a Marxist-inspired denunciation of our free-enterprise society. In all events, the majority agreed that the benefits of political freedom with material progress—the fruits of the cultural revolution forged in colonial America—far outweighed whatever "inconveniences" our industrial society might create.

Americans are practical people; they know there are costs associated with progress. One may not like TV commercials, but it's better than having to pay to watch the entertainment. One's job may not be as interesting as one would like, but it provides a living. Superhighways create problems, but make it easier and faster to go where you want

* *Bill Moyers' Journal*, op. cit.

to go—in your own car. Thompson states ruefully, "The great majority [of Americans] would rather have a new car than clean air." This is close to the mark, but not quite correct. The great majority, until recently, assumed they could have both a new car *and* reasonably clean air, that is, clean enough so that the soot and the smog would not kill them.

Certainly, the Depression generation of the 1930s, for whom dirty air in places like Pittsburgh meant jobs and meat on the table while clean air meant unemployment and despair, and also the war-scarred generation that came of age in the 1950s and 1960s shrugged at the suggestion that our material success might at the same time rob us of essential elements of livability.

Suddenly, in the seventies, Americans began to heed the criticisms of industrial society and to take them seriously. Particularly those Americans involved in social movements—students, ethnic and racial minorities, consumerists, environmentalists—made and gave their assent to statements that echoed the various critiques. Though they differed in where they placed the blame, these movements shared a common diagnosis that something is wrong with American life that urgently needs correcting. The "something wrong" is that the rights of a group or part of the environment are being violated, exploited or otherwise used *instrumentally* in ways that fail to respect inherent value.

The majority of Americans remain less concerned with social movements than with their private lives. Most of the life experiments—involving divorces, remarriages, moving from one part of the country to another, seeking new careers, going back to school, cultivating new life styles—have few ideological overtones. But once Americans decided to combat the restrictiveness of the familial-success triangle in their own lives, the "something wrong" made itself felt.

Sorting out the reasons that the American majority suddenly desired to change the giving/getting compact will occupy social historians for decades, for the change is a fateful one and its causes are not self-evident. There are various explanations.

In later editions of *The Lonely Crowd*, originally published in the fifties, David Riesman reconsidered what he regarded as his own earlier mistake of judgment. In 1969 he wrote: "*The Lonely Crowd* made the assumption, somewhat novel at the time, that the economic problem of abundance had been fully solved on the side of production if not on the side of distribution," a conclusion he describes as the significantly "mistaken notion that economic work is no longer important and that we can afford the post-industrial attitudes now so widely prevalent." He concludes, "Contrary to what I once thought, the economy is not self-propelling. . . . Problems arise when a society becomes psychologically post-industrial long before the economic infrastructure is sound enough to bear the weight of steadily rising expectations."* Along with himself he blames Paul Goodman, John Kenneth Galbraith and other critics for "having spoken prematurely in the same vein."

Daniel Bell offers a different explanation. The title of the book, *The Cultural Contradictions of Capitalism*, refers to the contradictory tendency of our economy to seek as workers people who are ideal "producers" and at the same time to seek as customers people who are ideal "consumers," though the two types conflict with each other. Producers are people who work hard, save, postpone their pleasure, develop discipline, concern themselves with efficiency, know how to husband their time and subordinate personal considerations to getting the job done. Ideal customers, however, do not postpone their satisfaction—they spend their time and energies consuming, not producing.

"The Protestant ethic was undermined," writes Bell, "by capitalism itself. The single greatest engine in the destruction of the Protestant ethic was the invention of the installment plan, or instant credit. Previously one had to save in order to buy. But with credit cards one could indulge in instant gratification."† Bell's conclusion is that superimposed on the normal tensions of an economy dedicated to rationalization while its culture dedicates itself to fulfillment of the self, we have now added a new set of tensions that decisively tip the balance away from the values of the Protestant ethic. These come from the efforts of our economy to stimulate the "cultural wants of a hedonistic world."‡

So great are these tensions, states Bell, that they lead us to "a watershed in Western society: we are witnessing the end of the bourgeois idea —that view of human action and social relations, particularly of economic exchange—which has molded the modern era for the last 200 years."§

Riesman is surely correct that we stimulated postindustrial attitudes prematurely, and these gave rise to the illusion that the problem of production was solved "automatically," so why not pause for fun? And,

---

   * David Riesman et. al., *The Lonely Crowd: A Study of the Changing American Character* (New Haven: Yale University Press, 21st Printing, 1969), pp. xvi and xviii.
   † Bell, *Capitalism*, op. cit., p. 21.
   ‡ Daniel Bell, *The Winding Passage: Essays and Sociological Journeys 1960–1980* (Cambridge: Abt Books, 1980), p. 330.
   § Bell, *Capitalism*, op. cit., p. 7.

Bell is correct that serious tensions exist between the discipline, work orientation and efficiency demanded by the workplace on the one hand, and the values of a consumer society on the other. No explanation of our current plight would be complete without these insights.

But there is another explanation that cannot be overlooked, one that assigns greater credit for intelligence and judgment to the American public. For many decades the flaws that critics perceived in industrial society did not strike the average American as unacceptable when weighed against its gains. But people do revise their thinking as circumstances change. By the start of the millennial quarter-century, we had grown accustomed to the gains of industrial society and had come to take them for granted; simultaneously, the costs, both private and social, began to loom ever larger. There was less privacy and personal safety—one could no longer walk the streets safely or leave one's door unlocked. There was more cheating. The demands on one's energies piled up faster than the rewards. Everyone's rights except one's own seemed important. The TV blared constant bad news of environmental degradation, slovenly safety precautions at nuclear plants, acid rain, fires and cancers caused by careless disposal of chemical wastes. The profits of oil companies seemed to rise in direct proportion to public inconvenience, and the automobile industry refused to make fuel-efficient cars years after the need for them was evident. Government developed a vested interest in inflation as graduated income taxes pushed people into ever higher tax brackets, swelling the federal budget irrespective of the squeeze on the average citizen.

Throughout most of this century, Americans believed that self-denial made sense, sacrifice made sense, obeying the rules made sense, subordinating the self to the institution made sense. But doubts have now set in, and Americans now believe that the old giving/getting compact needlessly restricts the individual while advancing the power of large institutions—government and business particularly—who use the power to enhance their own interests at the expense of the public.

This judgment, in one form or another, has now been made by the overwhelming majority of the American people—ranging between 70 and 80 percent. They are not saying: "Forget the family; to hell with my obligations to others; I couldn't care less about money, status and respectability." As we have seen throughout this book, people want to retain some elements of familial success—marriage and family, material well-being, respectability—but they are also struggling mightily to make room for greater personal choice against institutional encroachments.

The old compact demanded a lot, but it also gave a lot in return. Americans now suspect it demands too much and gives too little in return. Each person's life experiment is designed to change the giving/getting compact of private life, but the sum of tens of millions of life experiments transform public life as well.

These experiments have the makings of a true cultural revolution because the new shared meaning they introduce—the assumption that it is wrong to subordinate the sacred/expressive side—has an awesome power to change our lives. By wrong, people mean three things: it is no longer necessary; it is not worth it; and it is destructive. Not everyone intends all three meanings; people generally stress one or another. But the overall judgment holds so that by the mid-seventies a majority of the American people had reached a conclusion comparable to that reached by intellectual critics of industrial civilization in earlier years, namely, that our civilization is unbalanced, with excessive emphasis on the instrumental, and insufficient concern with the values of community, expressiveness, caring and with the domain of the sacred. Characteristically, with an outpouring of energy and enthusiasm that matches the drive for material advancement, Americans are now striving to achieve a new balance in the only domain over which they have real influence: the giving/getting compact in their own lives.

This recasting of the social bond introduces a new story in human experience as fundamentally different as the story begun in colonial America. The shared meaning that launched that innovative story maintained that a free people can, with sufficient will and energy, improve their material lot by the exercise of their political freedom. This commitment still sustains us, and it remains our message to the world. It is a story still unfolding on the world scene; the original cultural revolution born in America retains its vitality.

But now we have simultaneously launched a new cultural revolution, and inevitably the new story is having its effect on the old one. The new story is far different. It may not be as successful as the old story; after all, most revolutions fail. It may not unfold according to expectation. And it may not even reach its fullest expression in the United States, although it is starting here. But it is exploring new ground.

The new shared meaning bears a resemblance to the old one. The old one said, poverty is not destiny. The new one says, instrumentalism is not destiny. The old meaning insisted that political freedom can coexist with material well-being and indeed enhance it. The new meaning insists that the personal freedom to shape one's life can coexist with the instrumentalism of modern technological society and can civilize it.

It took several hundred years and boundless energy to bring the old meaning to fruition; the new meaning is just at the start of its long journey.

Following Whitehead's dictum that great ideas enter our reality in strange guises, the new meaning has entered the American reality of the millennial quarter in the strange guise of the search for self-fulfillment with all of its fallacies, contradictions and ambiguities. The success of this new cultural revolution hinges on how skillfully the seekers of self-fulfillment can, in the new economic conditions of our era, now discard the most harmful and obsolete features of their life experiments and simultaneously encourage the healthy and adaptive features to come to the fore.

Chapter 23

---◆◉◆---

Stepping Off
Maslow's Escalator

We have briefly encountered the two most maladaptive features of people's self-fulfillment strategies. The first—the psychology of affluence—is clearly inappropriate to survival in the millennial quarter-century. Even if our economy had not taken a turn for the worse, the assumption that we are entitled to more of everything would eventually have run into trouble. All calculations show that in a world of finite resources with world population due to grow to 6.5 billion people by the end of the millennial quarter, and with other nations fiercely competing for scarce resources, even a booming United States economy could never hope to satisfy the rising claims that Americans make upon it. Such claims exceed available resources by a huge margin even under the best economic conditions. In the present economy, the disparity between entitlement claims and resources looms so large that a self-fulfillment strategy based on a more-of-everything premise is simply futile.

The other candidate for the junkheap is the "me-first" outlook on life. As a grass-roots phenomenon, the quest for self-fulfillment is, inevitably, a creature of its times, borrowing its forms of expression from whatever sources are most convenient. Unfortunately, the materials closest to hand have been the odd combination of a psychology of affluence and an outlook whose tenets are live for the moment, regard the self as a sacred object, be more self-assertive, express all feelings, hold nothing back.

Where did these attitudes come from?

Early in the postwar quarter-century, the psychology of affluence and the primacy of self merged in a school of thought called "humanist psychology," or "third force" psychology (to distinguish it from psychoanalysis and behaviorism) or the "human potentials movement" or simply "self-psychology." Self-psychology received its most influential expression in the work of A. A. Maslow, Carl Rogers, Erich Fromm, Charlotte Bühler and others. These psychologists popularized certain seminal ideas proposed earlier in this century and in the last. Heavily influenced by existential philosophy, post-Freudian revisionism, a faith in the infinite flexibility of the human person and inspired by the traditional American values of self-improvement and individualism, they, in turn, influenced an entire literature of pop psychology. Their thinking permeated the culture through such self-help and inspirational books and movements as EST, Gail Sheehy's *Passages,* books on self-assertiveness and other works with titles such as *Looking Out for #1, Self Creation, Pulling Your Own Strings* and *How to Be Your Own Best Friend.*

In particular the theories of A. A. Maslow ingeniously combined a psychology of affluence with a vision of inner self-development, and so are especially germane to our discussion here. In the nineteen-fifties, Maslow posited a hierarchy of human needs that has become part of the conventional wisdom of our time. According to the hierarchy, people who are preoccupied with meeting "lower-order needs" for food, shelter and economic security have little energy left for pursuing the higher-order needs of the spirit. Vital energies are released to the search for "self-actualization" only when these lower-order needs are met. We move up the hierarchy of needs in an orderly fashion, on an escalator of increasing affluence.

I have always felt uncomfortable with Maslow's notion of self-actualization as the pinnacle of a hierarchy of inner needs. Its appeal is falsely seductive, especially for students in elite colleges who thrill to the idea that because they are privileged students they exist on a higher level of being than those less privileged who, having to scramble for a living, miss the delights of self-actualization—though the fate of these unfortunates is not their fault, of course.

For his followers' abuse of his theory, Maslow himself is not to blame. Obviously, human priorities do function according to a hierarchy. When we are sick all that counts is getting well, and when our survival, physical or economic, is threatened, it powerfully concentrates the mind (as Samuel Johnson observed about the prospects of one's hanging). But the idea that the high achievement of genuine self-actualization presupposes our ascension through various stages of economic well-being is a peculiarly self-congratulatory philosophy for a materialistic age.

In Maslowism, the self-actualized person who steps off at the top of the escalator is visualized as a particular personality type: he or she is assumed to be a creative, autonomous self, virtually independent of culture. This theme of the autonomous individual who exists outside of culture is to be repeated over and over again in the literature of self-psychology and its pop psychology progeny. It is an American replay of Jean-Paul Sartre's existentialist belief that man makes himself, that in some profound sense, we are our own creators. Wayne Dyer's *Your Erroneous Zones* speaks glowingly of the theory that "you are the sum total of your choices."

In the writings of Erich Fromm we find the religious concept of the sacred superimposed on the Maslowian self. As psychologist Paul Vitz observes, Fromm argues "that the concept of God has evolved to the point where today man is God and if the sacred exists its center is in the self and the selves of others."* In Fromm's theory, therefore, what is sacred lies squarely within the self. Each of us has become his or her own potential object of worship.

Psychologist Carl Rogers adds the quintessentially American idea that the truly creative, autonomous and actualized person gradually evolves from one whose feelings and potentials have been "unblocked" and is therefore able to express himself openly. This is a major source of the ethical principle that we have a duty to ourselves. If our inner feelings are the most authentic part of the self, if they are blocked and denied full expression, and further, if they are sacred, it follows that we have a moral duty to unblock them and let them find their way out.

Existential psychotherapist Rollo May, drawing on the European literature, elaborates further on the idea that we create ourselves. May stresses the yearning for transcendence, but his definition of transcendence, as Vitz points out, is an unusual one. May's version of transcend-

* Paul Vitz, "The Religion of Psychology: The Cult of Self Worship" (N.Y.U., unpublished paper).

ence does not mean reaching *beyond* the self or outside the self. Quite the contrary, transcendence is moving from one level of internal development to a higher level *within* the self; that is, moving up Maslow's escalator of self-actualization. The penalty for failing to do so, says May, is guilt—moral guilt caused by the failure to develop one's own true potentials. Here again we encounter the notion of a moral duty to oneself.

The pervasive influence of self-psychology in its various forms has led to a conception of the human self that underlies the most misleading premises of the search for self-fulfillment. The root fallacy is the assumption that the human self can be wholly autonomous, solitary, contained and "self-created." In everyday conversation people do not use this language; indeed, rarely does anyone even ask what a "self" is. But in the search for self-fulfillment this particular concept of self is presupposed. As we have seen, seekers of self-fulfillment such as Sara Lou Wellford, Lyndon Hendries, Abby Williams and Robert Agnoli are forever fussing over their "potentials" which, if left undeveloped or suppressed, leave them with feelings of guilt and failure. Selves are assumed to be capable of "growth," which is assumed to consist of realizing as many potentials as possible. Selves have "needs," and relationships with others involve complex negotiations aimed at recognizing, acknowledging and satisfying them. Aspects of the self are categorized as either "real" or "artificial." People express their "artificial" selves when performing social roles that conform to the expectations of others or when expressing feelings that are not genuine, that is, not "in touch" with their true selves. "Being in touch" is a particularly vivid image, conjuring up the presence of some inner being imprisoned beneath layers of blocked feelings.

Selves can thus be blocked, rigid, unfeeling, inauthentic, conformist, unintegrated and uncreative—all "unreal" states of being and hence, failures. But these states, in Carl Rogers' theory, can be overcome through the warmth of the proper type of encounter with another person (often a therapist) who will receive and accept one on one's own terms. The self's potentials will then be unlocked and one becomes free to discover the "real self." Then wonderful things happen. One becomes spontaneous, autonomous, natural and creative. A fulfilled person gradually emerges from behind the blockage.

The aggregate of these theories of self-psychology comprise the make-your-own-self kit of today's pop psychology—the root fallacy of the search for self-fulfillment. No one person I interviewed demonstrated this root fallacy in pure form. But virtually all strong formers embrace one or another aspect of it. Abby Williams, for example, ardently endorsed one of the more extreme versions: the self as an assemblage of needs. I found Abby Williams an appealing, sympathetic and poignant person; when I interviewed her I liked her at once. She was struggling with real issues of independence in a man's corporate environment and with her own self-fulfillment in a queasy marriage with her husband, Mark. Abby's interview was replete with the language of needs: it will be recalled that she assumed automatically that all must be filled, as if they were sections of an ice-cube tray, and fulfillment were the act of filling the tray to the brim.

Here is an intelligent, attractive, well-educated woman with a career she values, married to someone she loves (however troubled the marriage is) and fretful about whether she is being too "greedy" and narcissistic. By temperament she is eager to be flexible and to compromise. Yet she is haunted by anxiety attacks, and fearful that she will end like the shopping-bag women who sleep in New York's Central Park.

Admittedly, even if Abby were to divest herself of her self-image as a collection of needs, she would not solve all her predicaments. But it would not be a bad place to start, for this image distorts her thinking, and leads her unwittingly to strategies that frustrate her.

I am thinking of frustration in an elementary sense. If you believe it is imperative to fill all your needs and these needs are contradictory, or in conflict with those of others or simply unfillable, then frustration must follow. To Abby, and to Mark as well, self-fulfillment means having a career *and* marriage *and* children *and* sexual freedom *and* autonomy *and* being liberal *and* having money *and* choosing nonconformity *and* insisting on social justice *and* enjoying city life *and* country living *and* simplicity *and* graciousness *and* reading *and* good friends *and* travel, and on and on. All are seen as needs they are morally obliged to fill.

By "needs" Abby obviously does not mean biologically rooted, organic deficits; she means desires. And desires are infinite. Anyone trapped in the fallacy that the self is a failure to the extent that all one's desires are not satisfied has set herself or himself up for frustration.

The root fallacy does not encompass the entire philosophy of self associated with such terms as "need," "growth," "potential," "self-actualization," and so on. Indeed, it would be a serious loss if these terms disappeared from our psychological vocabulary. Properly defined, they belong in any adequate theory of psychological development. But the assumption that they are properties of a culture-free self seriously distorts their meaning.

This assumption is deeply rooted in our culture, but it should be identified and extirpated, for the longer it persists the more harm it does. It is destructive both to the individual and to the society. The individual is not truly fulfilled by becoming a free-standing machine for filling "needs." Indeed, to move too far in this direction is to risk psychosis—the ultimate form of culture-free "independence."

Even moderate forms of the assumption that selves are culture-free and wholly autonomous run the risk of alienation, loneliness, meaninglessness and futility. We are not our own work of art. We do not create ourselves as an artist paints a picture or writes a novel. Constant changes in commitments and outlook are not the route to real self-fulfillment. Suppression of needs is not always bad; in fact, some suppression is required if one is to avoid becoming a blob of contradictions. The Christian injunction that to find one's self one must first lose oneself contains an essential truth any seeker of self-fulfillment needs to grasp.

We know that each of us dies alone, and therefore lives alone as an essentially private and solitary being. But this is not the whole truth. There is another sense, and it is perhaps more important, in which the self is not totally private and solitary.

It sometimes happens that one has a friend who is dying and knows he is dying, yet that person glows with an incandescence that intensifies his sense of selfhood. Later, cherishing the memory, you think of your friend as having never before been so alive and vital, so much of a self as in these last days of his life. You recall his concern about others: a spouse, a parent, mutual friends, yourself and your family. You marvel that your friend, on the verge of dying, could care so much. It is the caring that makes you think your friend has risen to new peaks of selfhood.

The care your friend expressed was not confined to the present moment or to the pain and suffering of his own body. It was a quality of connectedness to others and to a world that still mattered, a concern about a future your friend would never see but still invested with caring. It was this reaching beyond the dying self that made your friend's selfhood so real.

There is also the opposite experience. Someone else you cherish is dying. You see him in his final days. Later you say, "He was not really himself. I prefer to remember him as he really was—caring about other people, about the future, about us. He suffered so much in his final days that he ceased caring." It is almost as if the real self had died before the moment of technical death had arrived.

Intuitively, we equate selfhood with caring. When one ceases to care—about the world, the future, friends and family—and when the meaningfulness of experience vanishes, so does an essential part of self. The dimension of time is particularly important to selfhood. We live not merely in the here-and-now, but also in the past and future. Take away the past, as sometimes happens with very old people who cannot remember what they said or did five minutes ago, and some essential part of self is gone. Curiously, long-term memory sometimes remains, and the events of sixty or seventy years before may continue to flourish vividly: to that extent, the person remains very much a self. In my father's last years, when he was in his late eighties, he used to lie on his bed singing Russian songs. The songs of the village in which he grew up had become more real to him then than all of the experiences of the intervening decades. The distant place in the distant time formed an intimate part of an old man's selfhood.

In this simple human way, we acknowledge a truth we all know: a mere body is not a self. A person cut off in time from past and future and cut off in space and spirit from other people, from ideas, from things and from community, is diminished as a self precisely to the extent that he or she is cut off.

It turns out, therefore, that we all "know" two truths about the self: one is that the self is private and alone and wholly encased within one's body. The other is that one is a real self only to the extent that caring and reaching beyond the self continue. We "know" these two truths about the self, but do we know how to reconcile them? They are, in important respects, contradictory; indeed, each leads to different strategies of self-fulfillment.

The tension between these two truths has virtually obsessed philosophical thinking about human experience for the past few centuries. The attempt to reconcile them has in this century culminated in a series of difficult works written by such seminal thinkers as Edmund Husserl, A. N. Whitehead, Ludwig Wittgenstein and Martin Heidegger. My one-time co-author, William Barrett, professor of Philosophy at N.Y.U., has devoted much of his career, in a series of insightful studies extending over several decades, to understanding the significance of this crucial issue.

Along with other contemporary philosophers, Barrett believes that a major breakthrough of twentieth-century philosophy has been to resolve the puzzle of the subject-object split handed down by Descartes from origins that go back to Plato and Aristotle. The gist of the solution is to demonstrate the primacy of the second truth about the self—that it is not an isolated "object," a ghost locked in a machine or a mere private consciousness located within a body.

Whitehead provided a crucial bridge of logic to lead us out of the subject-object impasse by identifying what he called the "fallacy of misplaced concreteness" and the "fallacy of simple location." When I was a graduate student studying mathematical logic at Harvard in the early postwar years, Whitehead's analysis burst upon me like an epiphany. Suddenly I realized that what I had heretofore regarded as clear facts, concrete and real, actually were abstract ideas. Whitehead demonstrated brilliantly that many "objects" in space and time were complex abstractions. He argued that because something occupies a particular region of space/time, as a rock or body does, this does not make it any more "real" than entities that lack the property of simple location, entities such as a thought, mathematics, the notion of time, consciousness itself. One should not arbitrarily award the status of reality to objects or events that have simple location (i.e., physical things) and deprive the status of reality to those that do not.

After absorbing that subtle but fundamental lesson, I was ready some years later for the insights of Wittgenstein and Heidegger who move boldly beyond where Whitehead and Husserl leave off. The effect of their thought is, in Barrett's language, to turn us away from "the fictitious conception of an inner cabinet of the mind into the open and public world . . . to pass . . . beyond the privacy of consciousness which would mentally divide us between two worlds."*

The insights of these seminal thinkers tell us that our conception of the self as a private consciousness independent of culture is utterly misleading. It takes an abstraction, the idea of the autonomous self, too literally.

The self is not miraculously created by acts of individual will as Sartre presupposed ("first we exist and then we create ourselves," he

---

* William Barrett, *The Illusion of Technique* (New York: Anchor Press/ Doubleday, 1978), p. 78.

said). You do not "find yourself" solely by looking inward, because the search for self must, if one is truly attentive, immediately direct you outside again. You do not literally "transcend" the self when you attend to the reality of the outside world; you are, as it were, already "outside" in the world. You are not only what you eat; you are also what you see and believe and feel and "mean" in common with others. You are inextricably enmeshed in the web of meanings shaped by the psychoculture that you help to form and that, in turn, helps to form you.

This conception of self is not simple, and I regret its abstractness. But it must be grasped in the abstract before it can be discussed concretely. The abstraction is essentially this: the self is not confined to private consciousness in the sense of feelings and potentials unique to you and somehow imprisoned within your skull or skin. That is one aspect of the self. But the self is also part and parcel of the world: to isolate it artificially—the fallacy of simple location—is not to be self-fulfilled but merely abstract and one-sided.

The concrete implication of this philosophical insight is far-reaching: you do not get in touch with the essence of self solely by looking inward. There is no "real" me—a tiny homunculus hidden beneath layers of frozen feelings. You are not the sum of your desires. You do not consist of an aggregate of needs, and your inner growth is not a matter of fulfilling all your potentials. By concentrating day and night on your feelings, potentials, needs, wants and desires, and by learning to assert them more freely, you do not become a freer, more spontaneous, more creative self; you become a narrower, more self-centered, more isolated one. You do not grow, you shrink.

The search for self-fulfillment cannot succeed unless its seekers discard the assumption of the self as private consciousness, the more private the more real. Only when one understands that the self must be fulfilled within the shared meanings of psychoculture is one pursuing self-fulfillment realistically.

Admittedly, it is not easy to conceive of the self in these terms. For example, many people believe they can achieve self-fulfillment by dropping out permanently from the larger society. From the perspective offered here, this is a high-risk strategy, almost certain of failure. To be sure, some people may cut themselves off momentarily from the larger culture as a form of relaxation, renewal or therapy. Others may bring their culture with them, as exiles often do. But dropping out permanently is an act of alienation, not fulfillment. It severs the bonds of caring and of history, and hence diminishes the self.

If we are going to face the real problems of the next decades we will have to grow accustomed, in our language and images, to a simpler, more primitive, less abstract sense of self; a self that can "move away" from the larger culture only to the extent that it first exists as an inherent part of that culture.

Chapter 24

————◉————

Toward an Ethic
of Commitment

I feel some remorse about making Abe Maslow, who was a generous and sympathetic person, the symbol of the most flawed aspect of the search for self-fulfillment. But his thought does betray a blind spot peculiar to our age. It was his unfortunate genius to have combined in a single theory the two massive defects of the self-fulfillment strategy: the idea of a self as an aggregate of inner needs, and the concept of a hierarchy of being that makes economic security a precondition to satisfying the human spirit. Thousands of years of human experience testify against this conclusion.

The most damaging effect of these fallacies is an indirect one. Faulty thinking about the self has led to faulty thinking about social rules, keeping us from developing a sound social ethic to replace the eroding ethic of self-denial. When millions of Americans began to forsake self-denial, they did so because our culture had encouraged them. They were participating in new shared meanings—perhaps not universally shared, but sufficiently widespread to give conformist souls like Sara Lou Wellford the social support she needed to leave her husband, attend law school and move to San Francisco with her children.

What is different about our culture today is not that Americans have new *desires*. The same desires persist from one generation to the next.

But now the culture endorses as morally acceptable many desires that were not acceptable in the past. Again and again in my interviews middle-aged people would say, "Oh, when I was growing up, divorce was unthinkable," or, "When I was married, not having children was unthinkable." Today few such actions are unthinkable, or unthought, or unacted upon.

Seekers of self-fulfillment abandoned self-denial when it failed to do justice to the sacred/expressive aspects of life. They then began to develop alternative strategies. For a while, self-psychology, with its message of duty to self, seemed like the perfect alternative. Fromm, Rogers, May and Maslow had all effectively criticized the stifling and restrictive effects of self-denial; all had reserved their highest moral approval for those aspects of the self that are "authentic"—unblocked, spontaneous, well-nourished. It thus became a moral obligation to liberate these authentic aspects of the self. The rhetoric of self-psychology, with its implication that the seat of sacredness lies within the self, misled many Americans into thinking that the inner journey was the most direct path to the sacred/expressive life as well as to "more of everything."

They soon discovered, however, that authentic feelings also include merely selfish or hedonistic ones, and after a while the distinction was obliterated. I interviewed a number of people who were too exhausted or embarrassed or ashamed to indulge all of their pleasure-seeking impulses all of the time, and yet, prodded by the duty-to-self ethic, felt moral guilt for failing to do so! One man even felt guilty about missing an evening of "swinging" with another couple because of fatigue from a business trip. He feared that he and his wife had lost an opportunity for a "meaningful experience," and he felt diminished as a person.

When people rebel, their first impulse is to reject traditional rules outright. Think, for example, of rebellious adolescents. It is only after wholesale rejection of parental beliefs that the adolescent gradually frees himself enough to discriminate. In the end, he may even reincorporate into his system of values most of what he initially rejected. But if his rebellion has been successful, there will remain a decisive difference between the pre- and postrebellion person: his values are now his own, not those of others; he has become his own person.

Any rebellion against traditional rules will typically pass through two phases: a reject-everything phase, and a discriminating/consolidating phase. It is only in the second phase that the true nature and significance of the rebellion reveals itself. American culture, our surveys show, is now entering this more subtle and advanced phase of its rebellion against the self-denial ethic. People are just now beginning to discriminate, to learn from their life experiments what they really want and what they believe to be a morally sound strategy for achieving it.

By now millions of Americans have garnered extensive—and painful—experience with the duty-to-self alternative to self-denial. In chapter after chapter of this book we have seen people transform their lives as they shifted from a sacrifice-for-others mode to a me-first approach to life. By and large, the me-first strategy has disappointed them. Indeed, in the light of their experience it is surprising that the duty-to-self ideal has lasted so long and enjoyed so much credibility.

It has, to be sure, some benefits to offer, but its core idea is a moral and social absurdity. It gives moral sanction to desires that do not contribute to either the individual's or the society's well-being. It contains no principle for synchronizing the objective requirements of the society with the goals of individuals. It either does not discriminate between socially valuable and destructive desires, or it works perversely against the real goals of both individuals and society. And it provides no principle other than hedonism for interpreting the meaning of the changes and sacrifices we must make to adapt to new economic/political conditions in the world.

The error of replacing self-denial with a duty-to-self ethic has proven nearly fatal, for nothing has subverted self-fulfillment more thoroughly than self-indulgence. Fortunately, Americans are just now starting to formulate new rules as a basis for a social ethic that will substitute for both self-denial and duty to self. In this final chapter I want to explain why this replacement is indispensable to the success of a self-fulfillment strategy, and how it promises to strip the search for self-fulfillment of its strange guises and to permit its healthy adaptive core to emerge.

(ii)

Any viable social ethic has real work to do: it binds the individual to the society; it synchronizes society's goals with those of each person; it holds society together and keeps it from degenerating into a chaos of competing interests. Its sole purpose can never be to provide moral justification for individual desires. Far from justifying them, a well functioning social ethic will *curb* certain desires.

Freud held an extreme version of this idea. In *Civilization and Its Discontents*, he speculated that the essence of civilization is repression of libidinal desire. Freud was elevating the special case of his own culture into a general principle, thereby overgeneralizing his conclusions.

But in a more moderate form, it is surely correct that for civilizations to prosper, some desires must be channeled, harnessed, tamed.

Repression is an extreme method of channeling, and perhaps its least successful one. A civilization that relies primarily on repression will be poor in spirit. But a civilization that indiscriminately approves whatever people desire cannot long survive.

A social ethic does not constitute the whole domain of morality and ethics, nor even its most important part. It does not speak to universal moral truths. It is merely an aspect of psychoculture, hence it is always relative to one's times. A social ethic changes with history, and therefore will even reverse itself when conditions change.

The Protestant ethic, for example, gives moral sanction to profit making through hard work, organization and rational calculation. But for many centuries before the rise of capitalism, Christian social ethics had condemned profit making. People had always made profits from moneylending or trading, but such activity was regarded as unethical (just as moneylending for profit is regarded as unethical in Iran under the mullahs). When Calvinism conjoined hard work, profit making and ethical rightness, the Protestant ethic began to take shape as a determining force in Western history. Rational profit making involved hard work and self-denial in the present for the sake of later gratification. Self-denial thus received the dual blessing of ethical rightness and practical payoff, an unbeatable combination.

This shift in the shared meaning of profit making—from immoral to ethically worthy—took several centuries to complete. But the shift from self-denial to duty to self has taken place within our lifetime, as have the great changes in sexual morality, attitudes toward credit and indebtedness, and toward women working outside the home, divorce, abortion, and so on.

In traditional society, the moral authority of shared meanings was usually conveyed by religion. In our modern industrial democracies, the opinions of the majority or influential minorities carry considerable moral weight. The decade of the nineteen-fifties demonstrated the awesome moral power of social consensus. Since then we have been engaged in a cultural tug-of-war between the part of the American public that continues to adhere to the old rules, and the part that embraces its free-to-be-me opposite, with the majority in the middle, picking and choosing from both sides.

The battle has just begun. Essentially it rages around the ethical status of desire and the question of what moral meaning to assign to needs and wants. For example, a woman finds herself pregnant and wants to abort, or a man feels bogged down by commitments to job, spouse and children, and wants out. A person's aging parents are inter- fering with his pleasures, and he wants someone to take them off his hands. A man wants to sleep with his secretary, or is tired of making a living and desires relief from his commitments. How we, as a society and as individuals, view the decisions made about fulfilling these desires is the crux of the problem.

Desire is always a powerful force, even when the dominant social ethic opposes it. But a functioning social ethic is also a powerful force, even when opposed by desire. It is when the two are aligned in mutual reinforcement that civilizations glow with vitality. The genius of a great social ethic is neither to suppress desires indiscriminately nor to endorse them indiscriminately. It is to make certain desires and social goals compatible with each other—to make the goals of society responsive to fundamental human yearnings and at the same time to socialize the individual so that he wants to achieve society's goals and thereby create the best forms of human existence that economic and historic conditions permit. This means that a social ethic may assume a variety of forms, changing when objective conditions change, but always responsive to the requirement that individuals fulfill themselves through advancing goals that are good for the society.

When a social ethic is in force, people will interpret their experience in its light, thereby transforming the meaning of pleasure and pain. Men and women will accept the frustrations of their jobs, child care and housework only when the dominant social ethic tells them that these frustrations give their lives moral significance. Bernard Lefkowitz's father defined a *mench* as someone who did what he had to do to make a living without sniveling about the work or the boss. If he had rejected the social ethic of being a *mench* and instead sought fulfillment through an ethic of duty to self, interpreting his job in that light, his life would have been intolerable and meaningless to him.

People will put themselves through agonies of jogging, dieting and exercising when they think it is good for them to do so. If an external authority had forced them to take the same actions against their will, they might complain—justifiably—of cruel punishment. Some Marine Corps recruits and medical interns recount how their reaction against "the system" eventually turned to positive endorsement once the mean- ing of their experience was transformed in their minds from gratuitous cruelty to an initiation with a moral and professional significance.

Between now and the year 2000 Americans will be called upon to make many changes, some painful, to accommodate new economic realities. If we see these all as setbacks, thwarting our aspirations for fulfillment, American society will move in one direction. If we see them as having a positive ethical meaning we will move in another. If the changes are interpreted as national failures caused by a weakened economy, most Americans will see them as a step backward for themselves as well as for the nation. It will confirm their worst fears that this land of plenty is indeed becoming a land of want. Some will be only mildly disgruntled, accepting sacrifice as unpleasant but necessary. Others will grow angry, resentful and resistant. The shared meaning of the change will be wholly negative: a net loss in our standard of living and self-esteem. Americans will see in the new realities only failure, loss and meaningless sacrifice.

If, however, along with some belt-tightening, Americans also find that a new range of positive life choices has opened for them, and if, further, these promise greater fulfillment than some of the choices they have lost, then change will assume a different meaning. It will imply mastery and the positive expression of will. It will signify gain in quality of life, not merely adjustment to loss. It will bolster self-respect and self-esteem.

The key is not merely what happens in reality, but how it is perceived through the lens of a social ethic. We can no longer count on the old stand-by of self-denial to make belt-tightening and sacrifice for its own sake morally acceptable. It is too late for that. We can rely even less on its duty-to-self replacement which makes Americans impatient with any change that does not immediately add to the sum of their private satisfactions.

So we now need a new social ethic. Without one we are disoriented, lacking a firm basis for choice. We need new rules to define the epochal tasks that must be accomplished in our era to bring about that minimal harmony between individual and society that is the mark of a successful civilization. We need new rules to bolster respectability—the opportunity to seek honor and esteem in the eyes of others. People feel good about themselves when they believe what they are doing is good for others as well as for themselves—when they believe it is morally right. Finally, and not least important, life is too complicated to rely wholly on rational calculation. For the fundamental decisions of life, we inevitably fall back on ethical judgments about what is right and wrong. Confidence in the right social ethic is indispensable for doing this.

(iii)

We come then to the critical questions: How does all this relate to you and me, individual Americans caught in the maelstrom of the millennial quarter-century, clinging to whatever shreds of autonomy we can salvage? What does a new social ethic mean to us? Where do we fit in the cultural revolution? What part in the "new story" shall we play? What are our chances of finding fulfillment? What can we do to nudge those chances along? In short, what should our personal self-fulfillment strategy be in this upside down world?

The answers depend critically on whether we can develop a social ethic better equipped to achieve the goals of self-fulfillment than either self-denial *or* duty to self. If American psychoculture develops such an ethic, each individual can then adapt his or her personal ethic to it. In this way the individual participates in the larger story of our times, and the society begins once again to function as it should.

The raw materials of a successful new social ethic can be mined out of the painful lessons self-fulfillment seekers have learned from their life experiments. Our research findings suggest that out of these experiments people *are* developing fresh approaches to balancing the sacred/expressive aspects of life with its material aspects. While it is true that these efforts do not yet constitute a full-blown social ethic, they appear to have the potential for evolving into one. In the interest of furthering this development I gave these tentative approaches a name, referring to them as the first expressions of an *ethic of commitment*. The word "commitment" shifts the axis away from the self (either *self*-denial or *self*-fulfillment) toward connectedness with the world. The commitment may be to people, institutions, objects, beliefs, ideas, places, nature, projects, experiences, adventures and callings. It discards the Maslowian checklist of inner needs and potentials of the self, and seeks instead the elusive freedom Arendt describes as the treasure people sometimes discover when they are free to join with others in shaping the tasks and shared meanings of their times.

This embryonic ethic is now gathering force around two kinds of commitments: closer and deeper personal relationships, and the switch from certain instrumental values for sacred/expressive ones. The two types are closely related, but it is useful to illustrate them separately for they are the materials out of which both society and individual will weave the new rules of conduct. I shall attempt to describe the present stage of development of this ethic of commitment in American society.

                              *   *   *

One of this ethic's two chief forms of expression—a hunger for deeper
personal relationships—shows up in our research findings as a growing
conviction that a me-first, satisfy-all-my-desires attitude leads to relationships that are superficial, transitory and ultimately unsatisfying. This
conclusion then leads people to seek deeper, more sustained relationships—to other people, and also to things, ideas and places.
Yankelovich, Skelly and White surveys show that 70 percent of Americans now recognize that while they have many acquaintances they have
few close friends—and they experience this as a serious void in their
lives. Moreover, two out of five (41 percent) state they have fewer close
friends than they did in the recent past.

Feeling this void causes people to grow less preoccupied with themselves and to look for closer ties with others. In 1973, the "Search for
Community" social trend, whose status my firm measures each year,
stood at 32 percent, meaning that roughly one third of Americans felt an
intense need to compensate for the impersonal and threatening aspects
of modern life by seeking mutual identification with others based on
close ethnic ties or ties of shared interests, needs, backgrounds, age or
values. By the beginning of the nineteen-eighties the number of Americans deeply involved in the Search for Community has increased to 47
percent—to almost half of the population—a large and significant jump
in a few short years.

Statistics such as these indicate the start of a countertrend away from
duty to self. Signs of a shift also show up in the lessons people have
learned from their life experiments. Sara Lou Wellford came to reject
the casual sexual encounters she had initiated to meet her sexual
"needs." Jane Coates, who gave up the Cadillac and country club life
with her wealthy husband because it was too superficial, found more
depth in a life that replaced conspicuous consumption with simple,
direct relationships, unencumbered by the pursuit of money and status.
Cynthia Muller, the wife of the photographer/lobsterman, has come
to see that her marriage is degenerating into a business partnership. She
feels she and her husband have built a sound, practical relationship:
they are helping each other build equity in a house, care for their child
and make a living. Instrumentally, things are working well. But
Cynthia feels an emotional void she cannot quite define. She doesn't yet
know what to do about it, but she knows she is distressed by it—a necessary first step toward a remedy.

The national cross section of men interviewed by Louis Harris in a poll for *Playboy* magazine seem to have arrived at similar conclusions from their life experiments. They were asked what qualities they now seek in an "ideal lover." *Playboy* was surprised that the vast majority of American males did not define an ideal lover as "someone who is sexually exciting." This definition ranked far down the list, selected by only one out of four men (23 percent). The ideal lover chosen by the majority (53 percent) was "someone to be totally open and honest with."* Sexual titillation, physical pleasure and virtuoso performance at body orifices played a subordinate role; the men hunger for sexual relationships that are direct and free of role playing where they can express their feelings openly.

In the past several years, advertising aimed at the growing singles market has boomed. One TV commercial shows a woman with long billowy hair dressed in a shimmering hiphugging dress driving a sports car. She drives to the beach at night to contemplate the ocean and to revel in the sheer delight of being foot-loose, independent and free to do what she wants when she wants. The commercial caters openly to the idea that being single, unencumbered and self-involved expresses a widespread yearning among Americans in their twenties and thirties.

But there is an interesting survey statistic that raises doubts about this appeal. In 1970, 96 percent of all Americans declared themselves dedicated to the ideal of two people sharing a life and a home together. A decade later, this number was precisely the same—a virtually universal 96 percent. Yet in this same decade, from 1970 to 1980, the number of single households expanded so dramatically that some observers began to wonder whether the conventional couple was doomed to extinction.

But the ideal of the couple who share bed, roof and life together has persisted undiminished in its appeal. The stable 96 percent statistic suggests that when people's experiments with variations on marriage and family slow down, as they will, we can expect the idea of the family to revive, at least in the residual form of the mated couple. If this interpretation is correct, we will see fewer casual divorces and serial marriages in the future and a return to more enduring and stable relationships between couples. Couples may or may not marry legally, but they are likely to grow less casual about separating, less self-focused and more serious about the give-and-take needed to deepen the twosome commitment and make it last.

* *The New York Times*, 1/23/79.

Nor is the hunger for deeper personal relationships confined to the bonding of couples. The greatest source of stability in the life of Lyndon Hendries, the successful but dissatisfied public relations executive, is his relationship with his children ("an incredible overriding affection and a communality of experience and love"). Jane Coates, Sara Lou Wellford and Robert Agnoli, though preoccupied with their own projects, are making greater sacrifices to protect their relationships with their children than in any other domain of their life. The young, ambitious Tom Wheeler, the only one of six sons to rebel against factory work, acknowledged that despite his differences with his mother and brothers, "it is important to be close to one another." He has restricted his rebellion so as not to threaten that closeness. Many of the women I interviewed said they had discovered an unexpected side benefit in their struggle to shake loose from stereotyped sex roles: they had learned they could develop friendships with other women that have come to mean a great deal to them.

A seventy-three-year-old woman said:

> "Part of the reason I got involved in organizing the block association was for safety, tenants' rights and so on. But when you get right down to it, what it really was was that I was craving more real, human contact with my neighbors. For years and years, I let myself get accustomed to the no-eye-contact, live-in-your-own-world ways we'd come to regard each other. I decided that even at my age, it was worth struggling out of that to something better, something more like community."

I interviewed a couple in their mid-forties who were on the verge of abandoning their highly successful professional careers. "Sheila and I don't have time to talk to each other," the man, a successful executive, said. "We are going to move to the West Coast and look for reasonable jobs with reasonable incomes where we can enjoy the work, and above all enjoy each other. I've been successful; I don't have to prove anything."

I could cite innumerable other examples and statistics that all have in common this reaching out for involvements that go deeper than the surface to satisfy a yearning at odds with mere self-absorption.

In its other current form of expression, the new ethic of commitment pursues the goal of striking a better balance between the instrumental and the sacred/expressive aspects of life. It does so through a willingness to sacrifice those material/instrumental values that inhibit the sacred/expressive ones. The sacrifice generally involves money or status, and countless examples can be found. I heard a home-maintenance expert warn his radio listeners about the pitfalls of rehabbing old houses. "It is not always true," he said, "that rehabbing can be done profitably by the amateur." He cited the experience of a professor in Beverly, Mass., who bought an old Victorian house for $15,000. For an additional $50,000 he renovated and restored it, and he is not yet finished. The real estate agent finally admitted to him that its market price is $15,000 less than his expenditures. But the professor answered, "That's okay. Restoring that house has become my life's work. In that way, I not only draw from the past but I am also giving to the future."

In my interviews I often encountered this theme of reaching out symbolically to both the past and the future, even when money or position had to be traded off. It is almost as if people are aware that excessive instrumentalism flattens their perception of time, leaving them with the same superficial relationship to time they have to people.

People also speak of abandoning instrumental values in favor of a closer relationship to land, plants, mountains, oceans and nature in general. One man whose wife and he both have high-pressure urban jobs spoke of their decision to move from the city to a far northern suburb of Chicago where they get some of the tranquillity of rural living. The man says:

> "We grow our own vegetables, or most of them. Not just to save money or to avoid chemicals or pesticides and such. In fact, it probably ends up costing us more to tend the vegetable garden the way we do. . . . We express ourselves in the care and attention we give to our vegetables. We give away or barter with the produce we don't consume or preserve ourselves. It's a very human activity for us; good for our psyches, good for our bellies, and maybe if we're lucky, good for our community too."

I also interviewed a number of professionals who have changed their careers, sacrificing financial and status values for expressive ones—a law professor who, drastically reducing his income, now channels his energies into arts and crafts; an accountant who gave up his lucrative practice to open an engine repair "studio" because fixing engines gave him greater self-expression than fixing balance sheets; an engineer who quit his corporate post to work in an observatory because he loved both the stars and the telescopes.

All over the country, Americans are weighing the rewards of conven-

tional success against less lucrative but more satisfying personal achievements, and are choosing, or seriously considering, the latter—if they
can afford to do so.

These activities highlight the expressive rather than the sacred aspect of
the self-fulfillment goal. The two cohere in an ambiguous relationship.
Sometimes they are separate; sometimes not. Consider, for example, the
rise of fundamentalism—Christian, Jewish, Moslem—in American society. On the one hand, this phenomenon is a backlash against the
excesses of the duty-to-self ethic. But, it is also a revolt against the
older giving/getting compact with its stress on material rewards, and a
revolt against instrumentalism in general with its devotion to technique
rather than purpose.

Theologian Colin Williams explains:

> Behind the fundamentalist resurgence . . . is the concern that the
> modernising [sic] process . . . has left us floundering and direction-
> less. It is not just that as the result of the loss of faith we are rich in
> things, but poor in soul. It is also that being poor in soul, we are
> now endangering the things as well since the inner decay in our
> culture has left us with no clear sense of purpose.*

In the extreme practicality of the American mind Williams sees the
paradox that instrumentalism, in elevating the efficient and the rationalized to the highest value, ends not only by creating an iron cage for
the spirit, but also by subverting even the material side of life. Lacking a
context of ultimate religious values to contain it, instrumentalism leads
inexorably to utilitarianism, to the pleasure principle, to hedonism and
to duty to self, which in the end undermines the disciplined effort required to sustain a modern industrial society.

Fundamentalism is only one possible response to the suspicion that
in instrumentalism we have lost our way and must now rediscover the
transcendent. Others who share the same suspicion may be opposed to
fundamentalism and continue to cherish their secular humanism, but
they too are developing a deepened sense of the limits of instrumental
reason, and are searching for values of ultimate concern in which to
anchor our technology and rationalism. One version of this secular
humanist yearning for the sacred is defined by philosopher Henryk

---

* Colin Williams, "Ethics, Religion and Governance" (Unpublished Wye
paper, 1980).

Skolimowski* as "reverential thinking," which he describes as a rever-
ence for all living things: plants, animals, wilderness, people. Reverential thinking pays homage to the interdependence of all forms of
life. It seeks a life in harmony with nature. It stimulates a concern for
maintenance and preservation, for working with rather than against
nature.

Reverential thinking also expresses itself in the ideal of community,
as for example in the hospice movement which opposes the instrumental
bureaucratic efficiency of the modern hospital with the simplicity and
dignity of a hospice, where the terminally ill may die in a community
that accepts death as a part of life and not as a failure of technology. In
the years to come we should expect the quest for the sacred to intensify
in a variety of forms—from deeper religious beliefs and increased
church-going to a resurgence of patriotism.

I have friends in California, a couple in their forties with a severely
handicapped child. The husband has a degree in economics and has held
several conventional jobs that he has acquitted with competence and
success. Several years ago, he and his wife sold their house in the city
and moved to a small community on rural farmland, sharing it with
other parents of handicapped children. Together they form an informal
mutual-help society. They explained that a lively subculture exists
among parents of handicapped children. The husband said his decision
to give up his career and to move into the new community had been influenced by several factors: the drying up of economic opportunities,
the added responsibility of having a handicapped child in need of the
extra support others can give, and his and his wife's own deeply felt
desires for "sharing community with others" rather than living an
isolated professional existence.

(iv)

There are two distinct steps required to develop an ethic of commitment. One of them lies wholly within each person's control, for it
involves nothing more—or less—than a change in the strategy of self-
fulfillment. The change involves abandoning the calculus of inner needs
and its assumptions that needs are synonymous with desires, that the
more desires filled the better and that this pursuit is a morally worthy
one. Instead, the new strategy builds on these premises: that the self is

* Henryk Skolimowski, "Reverential Thinking" in *Through the '80s* (Washington, D.C.: World Future Society, 1980).

not synonymous with the sum of one's desires; that self-fulfillment requires commitments that endure over long periods of time and that the expressive and sacred can only be realized through a web of shared meanings that transcend the self conceived as an isolated physical object.

In practice, this shift in strategy need not create drastic changes in action, and indeed, is unlikely to do so because it incorporates many existing elements of self-denial and duty to self. Changes in consciousness—in self-conception and attitude—will be greater than changes in behavior. How might the lives of the people we have glimpsed in this book—the Agnolis, the Greensons, the Mullers, the Youngstowns, Tom Wheeler, Miguel Feliciano and the others—be modified were they to take a first step toward adopting an ethic of commitment?

Miguel Feliciano would probably try to maintain his commitment to both his bicycle racing and his growing family. Though the pressures on him to be "realistic" and give up racing are likely to be intense, it is probably important for him—and his family—that he keep both commitments. Together they bring him the belongingness, honor and self-esteem he seeks. To give up his bike racing might plunge him into the despair of the person who is always forced to surrender what he wants most in life. Then his family life would suffer, as would he. But juggling the two commitments will require some compromises on his part—for example, being more helpful around the house than his machismo background would ordinarily permit.

Were Lyndon Hendries to take this first step toward an ethic of commitment, he would stop treating himself as his own work of art and instead refocus his creative energies on the world—onto commitments to his children, or his work, or his marriage, or doing something for others, commitments he might actually find more satisfying than his present stance of detachment.

For Abby Williams, taking this first step would surely cause her to question her assumption that no potential or need, however tiny, should go neglected. As the cultural climate shifts away from duty to self it should not be difficult for her to drop her compulsive Maslowism and to realize that she is not morally obliged to have everything she wants. Her life experiment, already under way, can bring her to the threshold of fresh insight into what to junk and what to preserve, and perhaps her nightmare of closing doors will fade.

Sara Lou Wellford already has a commitment to a new life in San Francisco and to a law career. The danger for her is that her newly won love of adventure may tempt her to make yet another change in her life —at the expense of her children and also of the chance to build the stable adult relationships she craves. An ethic of commitment would require her to consolidate her existing involvements, especially her commitment to her children which she fulfilled when she was in law school but has now begun to neglect under the influence of her strong duty-to-self orientation.

In adhering to the values of the husband as sole provider and wife as homemaker and mother, the Youngstowns now have a firm commitment to tradition. In our present-day pluralistic America, this commitment does not enjoy the social support it had when it was the majority viewpoint, but it remains powerful among a minority of Americans. In our cultural pluralism, the Youngstowns' older ethic of self-denial can readily coexist with the newer social ethic. The main problem the Youngstowns have is not cultural; it is the practical question of whether and when the steel company will rehire Mr. Youngstown. If it does not, the dilemma the Youngstowns will face is whether to seek work for their "provider" in another city or type of job, or to accept a solution neither of them want: that Mrs. Youngstown find a job outside the home. From a practical standpoint, the latter course may seem prudent. But from the standpoint of an ethic of commitment, keeping faith with the old values, regardless of inconvenience and hardships, may be exactly the right thing to do.

Practical concerns also trouble the Greensons. Mrs. Greenson shrinks from returning to part-time bookkeeping to pay for her education. But if she is truly committed to a new career in archaeology, she may have no choice. My impression from the interview with her is that if she had to pick up bookkeeping again she would grumble for a time and then accept it with good grace, as she has already accepted so many demands and sacrifices under the ethic of self-denial. To meet her new commitment, she might need more support from her husband than she has received in the past. But from what she says about him, he would probably give this support.

Tom Wheeler's predicament is similar to Feliciano's: the resistance of people close to him to what he wants to do. He wants to make a commitment to McDonald's management training program, thereby straining his relation to his parents and five brothers, and also to his wife-to-be. Under the self-denial ethic, he might be persuaded to give up his dream. Under the duty-to-self ethic, he would try to hold onto everything—his parents and brothers, his fiancée *and* his training program, making no concessions to the needs and concerns of others. Under an ethic of commitment, he—and his fiancée—have to face the difficult task of making the mutual sacrifices needed to maintain several commitments simultaneously.

Under an ethic of commitment, hard choice will often be necessary. Economics may force Sam Moscowitz to give up his birdwatching job in Florida, but not necessarily to return to Chicago and an environment he loathes. Economics may also force Dan Turner to leave rural Vermont, to which he is not truly committed, although he enjoys it. Coaching and teaching are where his commitments lie, and perhaps the next time he can win a few battles with the bureaucracy.

To take his first step, Professor Agnoli, now so envious of others and so resentful that a professorship doesn't bring the status or money he had hoped for, must pour energy into rebuilding his life around a few stable commitments, setting aside his concern that some undiscovered inner gift may wither.

The Mullers—with whom this book started—may have to confront the fact that their marriage will be undermined unless they find time away from jobs and mortgage payments to give more to their own relationship, even if it means a smaller house, or that Mrs. Muller give up a job that she values less than she thought she would.

Among those I interviewed there were no creative geniuses, no master builders, no people endowed with unusual religious or moral sensibilities. But their life experiments are leading them neither toward a return to the automatic stifling of self as in the past, nor to its dialectic opposite, cultivating one's own garden oblivious to the world and to others. They lead to a new path.

(v)

Survey data showing that Americans are growing less self-absorbed and better prepared to take this first step toward an ethic of commitment, though sparse, is fairly clear. One would, however, hesitate to conclude on such scanty empirical evidence that something as momentous as a new social ethic was taking shape. A social ethic requires that a further large step be taken. The first step was described as if people make their commitments in a social vacuum, whereas for a successful social ethic to take hold, people must form commitments that advance the well-being of the society as well as themselves.

For this to occur people must receive clear and distinct signals from the larger society—from political leadership, the mass media, institutional leadership (business, religion, education, labor, artists and scientists, the intellectual community) and from informal interchange of views with friends and neighbors. These signals should convey the terms of the new giving/getting compact, communicating to Americans that we have now entered a new age, offering new opportunities, tradeoffs, choices and constraints. The signals must permit people to understand how they can link their personal aspirations to the new realities.

This process of developing new social signals, transmitting them and then assimilating them will take at least several decades, so that the new giving/getting compact is unlikely to reveal all of its ramifications much before the end of the millennial quarter-century. Prognostications about it should be made with this time dimension in mind.

Americans have a history of responding well to signals about society's changing rewards and constraints. The self-denial ethic was itself a response to signals that to gain the "getting" part of the giving/getting compact, Americans needed to surrender important aspects of self. For generations, life experience reinforced this response: self-denial did pay off. Once the signals shifted, the self-denial ethic began to lose its appeal.

Initially, the duty-to-self ethic also arose as a response to clear social signals, except we now realize that these were misleading. It responded to false economic signals that said affluence comes automatically, entitlements are guaranteed by government, more of everything is a realistic goal and the problems of supply are solved forever. It also responded to misleading psychological signals that inner feelings are sacred objects and that undivided dedication to them will satisfy one's cravings for transcendence. People's life experiments, abetted by new economic realities, now drive home the lesson that these signals conveyed false information.

The response to social signals is not passive. People do not merely absorb information. There is constant screening, interpretation and selective perception. People respond mainly to their own hopes and fears. Given what these are, we should expect the public to react to signals about a new giving/getting compact with considerable skepticism, but also with a profound yearning for the values embodied in an ethic of commitment. Actually, the new economic realities seem less onerous for an ethic of commitment than for the duty-to-self ethic or even for self-denial—because they do not insist upon a pot of gold at the end of the rainbow. An ethic of commitment does not require ever-increasing affluence or prodigal expenditure of resources. Developing deeper relations with people and things does not demand great amounts of money, nor does reverential thinking, or the creation of community, or a deepened concern with past and future.

Nonetheless, it would be unrealistic to expect a new giving/getting compact to be born without travail. At least until the latter half of the nineteen-eighties we should anticipate intense social conflict, economic stress and confusion in signals. As we have seen, Americans face large economic claims against our standard of living that we are not psychologically prepared to assimilate. The public is still mired in unrealistic expectations and still entranced by the seductions of duty to self. The voices that interpret to us the meaning of changes in the world—our political leadership, the mass media—come across muffled and confused.

The eighties are proving a rough decade. We are forced to live more practical lives and to pay more attention to gritty economic realities—jobs, homes, food bills, personal safety. The struggle between the haves and have-nots is bound to intensify because of the raw injustice of one part of society being protected against inflation while another part is not.

We should also expect new types of conflict. Younger Americans who work for a living are being pitted against retired older people who feel entitled to all the benefits they receive, and more, but whose demands place an intolerable tax burden on those who work. Out of the cultural counterrevolution that has already begun will come more divisive battles on abortion, prayer in the schools, sex education, criminal justice, the death penalty and the censorship of school books and television shows. Outbursts of racism and bigotry may also grow in intensity and ugliness.

Eventually we will have to face the fact of rot in our institutions and infrastructure—the inability of our schools to teach; slovenliness in standards of efficiency and precision; the decay of our railroads, bridges, harbors and roads; the aging of our industrial plant; the litigiousness of an overlawyered society; the decline of our political parties; the bland arrogance of the news media; the living-in-the-past of our labor unions; the irrelevance of our colleges; the short-term myopia of our industrial leaders; and the seeming inability of government to do anything efficiently and well. These and other symptoms of a troubled society nag at us like a neurotic boss who is aware of his own power and prerogatives but has forgotten how to do his job.

I recall an interview with a postman who was furious with departmental regulations that forbade him, on the grounds of safety, from wearing sunglasses even during the glaring light of midsummer. Several

years ago blind students at Harvard University protested because new
government regulations designed to help those confined to wheelchairs
had required that a number of curbs and steps be replaced with ramps
and slopes, thereby removing a vital safety protection for the blind. It
grows ever more difficult to know where to draw the bureaucratic line.
Anyone who has worked for a large institution—corporation, government agency, university—can produce a bottomless supply of examples
of how these institutions inexorably subordinate the individual to their
own rules. We live and breathe in the interstices left to us by our institutions; and they grow more constricting all the time.

Fault or blame is not at issue. Institutions are not villains. They are
simply—institutions. A high level of bureaucratic organization is ende-
mic to advanced industrial society, and the cross pressures created by
its wild and uncontrollable growth crowd out the general interest and
the individual's lifespace indifferently.

We move toward an anarchy of institutions. Anarchy is ordinarily
linked with individual rulelessness. But the threat to our civilization
comes less from individual anarchy—the individual is too hemmed in by
institutions to be effectively anarchic—than from institutions that act as
laws unto themselves.

In this new arthritic and hard-pressed America it is easy to fall into
gloom and despair. But Americans have too much of a stake in their
lives, and have carried their venturesome life experiments too far to let
despair set in. Nor do objective realities warrant it. For all our troubles
America remains wealthy, powerful, blessed by nature—and essentially
united. I suspect that what is required of Americans in the eighties is
not constant belt-tightening, nor punishing our institutions (we need to
improve them, not cripple them), nor the defeatism that "accepts
reality" and settles for less, and certainly not abandoning the high goal
associated with the search for self-fulfillment. What is required is to
accomplish the one great task that has eluded Western civilization since
the age of science and technology began—breaking through the iron
cage of rationalization and instrumentalism in order to make industrial
society a fit place for human life. Indeed, the millennial quarter-century
may be an excellent time to advance this goal, since we are obliged
anyway to find qualitative substitutes for the mindless pursuit of more
of everything.

My surmise is that the social signals we receive in the next few
years will communicate confusion, faltering leadership and disarray, but
that beneath the surface many of the elements of health and strength

needed to take the crucial second step in building a new social ethic of commitment will be at work. By the latter part of the eighties, the signs of healthy adaptation should begin to outweigh the signals of distress.

Of course, no one can know whether and how a new social ethic will unfold, but one can express one's hopes for the path it will take.

In launching their life experiments, those engaged in the search for self-fulfillment broke many rules. I hope they do not now lose their courage and initiative, and in a time of economic duress feel obliged to return passively to the old rules. I hope the postman wears his sunglasses, despite departmental regulations, that auto workers continue to fight the class lines that separate work on the assembly line from office work, that voters rebel against political leaders who use inflation to increase government revenues, that the public rebels against the power that big institutions—corporations, unions, media—have arrogated to themselves at public expense and that people bring a lively skepticism toward institutions in general.

A new ethic of commitment should help to preserve certain older values Americans cherish, and at the same time safeguard important new ones won in the rebellion against self-denial. The older values Americans wish to preserve include political freedom; the use of that freedom to secure material well-being through one's own efforts; the comforts and consolations of family life; a place of respectability in the community; and pride in America's unique role in history. The new values embrace greater autonomy for both men and women; more freedom to choose one's own life style; life as an adventure as well as an economic chore; leisure; self-expression and creativity; a greater concern for past and future; a more caring attitude; and a larger place for the awe, mystery and sacredness of life.

A new ethic of commitment will also accentuate real self-help: doing more for ourselves to lessen our dependence on doctors, lawyers, government and assorted institutions. We can no longer afford our expert-ridden systems of medical care, social welfare or even education. There is more we must do by ourselves to care for our older people, our own health, our training of the young, and our citizens who find it difficult to cope. We need new self-help methods of child care, bartering for services, apprentice training, mutual assistance and self-governance.

We need new rules to break up the rigid segmentation of American life. Why should people who are still healthy and vigorous at sixty-five retire totally from work and their involvement in everyday life? We need them to pull their own weight. Why should postsecondary education be confined to adolescents who, fatigued with school, are *least* well equipped to benefit from it? Why shouldn't people "retire" for a few years or go back to school in their productive middle years?

We need new rules to encourage people to channel their creativity away from themselves and back onto the concrete tasks that need doing in the new era—creating new forms of energy, taming technology, inventing new industries, creating new jobs, competing more effectively with the Japanese and Germans and Koreans, rebuilding the American infrastructure, reaccumulating capital, launching new enterprises, conquering inflation, advancing science, telling stories, inventing new modes of self-help, making quality of life compatible with productivity, creating community through caring for others.

These are not everyone's hopes. In many ways they differ from the hopes expressed by the people I interviewed. But they share with them at least one belief in common: Sara Lou Wellford, Miguel Feliciano, Sam Moscowitz, Tom Wheeler and many unnamed others now struggle to live life as an adventure and not just as a chore. A genuine revolution does open a new human story, a story that seeks in each age to find again the treasure of a truly human freedom and autonomy. We are not passive TV viewers watching this story unfold. We are living it. And we have a fair chance to bring the story to successful resolution.

Index

repression, Freud's views on, 246–47
research and development (R & D),
        U.S. economy affected by, 168,
        169, 179, 204
respectability, 112, 113–23, 146, 147,
        155
    badges, 116, 117, 120, 121–22, 123
    belongingness as deep meaning of,
        120–23
    as concern for appearances, 122
    growing elusiveness of, 122
    social mobility distinguished from,
        117–20
responsibility, personal vs. societal,
        21
retirement, xv, 21, 106, 202
    early, 149
    economic constraints on, xix, 22,
        214
    extending age for, 22, 214
retreaters, xvi, 151–52
reverential thinking, defined, 256
revolution
    American, 222–23, 228
    freedom advanced by, 221–22, 223
    French, 222, 226
    Iranian, 42, 180–81, 247
    modern use of, 223
    "new story" as principle of, 220–21,
        223
    see also cultural revolution
Riesman, David, 153, 154, 229–30
Robbins, Tom, 175–76
Rogers, Carl, 235, 236, 237, 245
Rohatyn, Felix, 165
Romans, ancient
    currency diluted by, 208, 210
    res publica of, 221
Roper Organization, on inflation, 183
Rothman, Sheila M., 98

sacred
    Maslowian self combined with
        concept of, 236
    as sociological concept, 7
sacred/expressive side of life, 10, 13,
        22, 225, 232, 245
    defined, 7–8
    ethic of commitment and, 250, 253–
        56
    industrialism as attack on, 226–28
    symbols of respectability as, 123
sacrifice, 8, 43, 59, 113, 231
    devaluation of, xviii, 10, 30, 50,
        104
    post–World War II views on, 9, 12
    self-denial ethic and, see self-denial
        ethic
Sartre, Jean-Paul, 236, 241–42

savings
    economic growth fostered by, 168,
        169
    effects of inflation on, 21, 22, 182,
        183, 214
Schipper, Lee, 200n
Schrank, Robert, 43n
scientific management, see Taylorism
Search for Community, 251
secular humanism
    religious fundamentalism as
        critique of, 6
    yearning for sacred in, 255–56
security, 127
    job, 28–29, 50–51, 170
    money as, 76, 111–12, 150, 151
    national, 165, 214–15
self
    as culture-free, 236, 237, 239, 241
    death and, 239–40
    existential views on, 68, 236–37,
        241–42
    as hierarchy of inner needs, 10,
        235–36, 237, 244
    two truths about, 240–42
self-actualization, in hierarchy of
        inner needs, 235–36, 237
self-assertiveness, in self-fulfillment
        strategies, 10, 235
self-denial ethic, 12, 68, 231
    economic meaning of, 172, 173,
        247, 260
    effect of psychology of affluence
        and, 189
    organization ethic and, 153
    rejection of, xviii, 50, 66, 78, 147,
        174, 244–46, 260
    respectability and, 119, 120, 122–
        23
    success and, 85, 146
    weak-form group's belief in, 89
    working-class belief in, 108–9, 110,
        111
self-fulfillment, search for
    comic elements in, 36
    conformity vs. rebellion in, 63–71,
        244
    counterculture compared to, 174–
        77
    cultural revolution as likely out-
        come of, xix–xx, 8, 11, 36–38,
        219–64
    defects in strategies used in, xviii–
        xix, xx, 10–11, 19–32, 59, 159,
        161–215, 234–43, 244
    demands of others in conflict with,
        73–74
    discriminating/consolidating phase
        in, 245–46

About the Author

DANIEL YANKELOVICH is the founder and president of Yankelovich, Skelly & White, Inc., one of America's most respected analysts of social trends and public attitudes. He also serves as president of the Public Agenda Foundation, a nonprofit, nonpartisan organization, that he founded in 1975 with Cyrus Vance. Mr. Yankelovich was educated in philosophy and psychology at Harvard and the Sorbonne, and is the author, with William Barrett, of *Ego and Instinct: Psychoanalysis and the Science of Man*, as well as two previous books on changing values in America. He and his wife and daughter live in New York City.

DATE		
SEP 2 4 1984	APR 2 7 1988	
DEC 1 1 1985	JAN 1 4 2002	
JAN 3 1 1987		
FEB 1 7 1987		
MAR 1 9 1987		
MAR 2 5 1987		
NOV 2 5 1987		